HOME OFFICE

Prison statistics

England and Wales

1997

Presented to Parliament
by the Secretary of State for the Home Department
by Command of Her Majesty
July 1998

Cm 4017

£18.30

PREVIOUS REPORTS

INTRODUCTION

In this volume we present data on the population of, receptions into and discharges from, Prison Service establishments in 1997, with series in many tables covering the previous decade. Last year we reviewed this annual publication in the course of which we interviewed a set of key people from our main customer groups and conducted a wider postal survey. We have changed the content and format in the light of the review. Chapter 1 now incorporates information previously included in separate chapters on fine defaulters and non-criminal prisoners which we have dropped. Chapter 4 now covers both male and female sentenced adult prisoners. A new section on various aspects of prison regimes forms chapter 7. Chapter 8 contains summary information on disciplinary offences and punishments in prison. The separate Command Paper on this subject will no longer be published, but detailed tables formerly contained in that publication are available on request. Chapter 9 shows data on reconviction rates for prisoners discharged in 1994 and chapter 10 is a summary of relevant recent research papers.

Offenders and Corrections Unit,
Research and Statistics Directorate,
Home Office.

Prison statistics
England and Wales
1997

CONTENTS

LIST OF TABLES (tables cover 1987–1997 unless otherwise shown)

PRISON STATISTICS ENGLAND AND WALES 1997

LOCATION OF CONTENTS

CHAPTER 1

THE PRISON POPULATION IN 1997

Key points

- The average population in custody during 1997 was 61,114, which was greater than in any previous year.

- The population in 1997 was 11 per cent more than the average in 1996 (55,281) and as a proportion the year on year rise was greater than in any year since 1970.

- Recent growth in the prison prison population is a continuation of the rise which started at the beginning of 1993, following a steep fall during 1992. It reflects the increased use of custodial sentences by magistrates' and Crown Courts and an increasing average sentence length at the Crown Court.

- The average remand population for 1997 was 12,130, 4 per cent more than in 1996 but fewer than the average for 1994 when 12,360 prisoners were held on remand.

- The sentenced population rose by 12 per cent between 1996 and 1997 from an average 43,040 to 48,410.

- Also between 1996 and 1997, female prisoners increased in number by 19 per cent from an average 2,260 in 1996 to 2,680 in 1997. Male prisoners increased by an average 10 per cent, from 53,020 to 58,440.

- Between 1996 and 1997 the greatest increases in the number of sentenced prisoners were amongst those sentenced for burglary and drugs offences. Over the last ten years, the number of prisoners held for drugs offences has doubled while the numbers held for rape and other sexual offences have increased by 75 per cent. (Over the same period the population of all sentenced prisoners increased by only 24 per cent.)

- In the ten year period since 1987 longer sentence prisoners (over 4 years) have tended to increase as a proportion of all sentenced prisoners, moving from 25 per cent of all prisoners in 1987 to more than one in three in 1997.

- In England and Wales there were 120 prisoners for every 100,000 members of the general population in 1997. This was more than most other European countries, such as Germany and France with 87 and 90 per 100,000 respectively, but fewer than the USA, with 645 prisoners per 100,000 population, and Russia with 687 prisoners per 100,000.

Figure 1.1

AVERAGE POPULATION IN CUSTODY

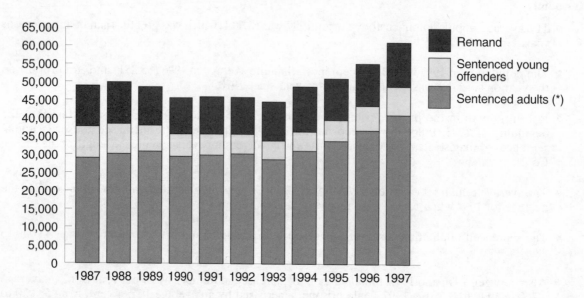

(*) Including non-criminal prisoners

The population in custody (Tables 1.1–1.8)

Changes in the total prison population

1.1 The average population in custody during 1997 was 61,114 which was greater than in any previous year. The average prison population in 1997 was 5,830 above that for 1996. This was an increase of 11 per cent and the largest year on year rise since 1969/70, when the prison population rose by 13 per cent (from 34,670 to 39,030). During the year the prison population rose steadily, from 57,560 at the end of January to 62,320 by the end of July. After a decline to 61,940 in August the population continued to grow to reach 63,720 in November. Between November and December the prison population reduced to 62,040, which is the usual seasonal pattern. Seasonally adjusted figures (not shown) which can be a better guide to the underlying trend, put the greatest month end prison population during 1997 at 64,700, at the end of December.

1.2 Since the beginning of the century, the average population of male prisoners has increased, from 15,870 in 1901 to 58,440 in 1997. As table 1(a) and the Figure 1.2a show, the male prison population started the century at 16-18,000 but had reduced to less than 10,000 by 1916 and did not increase substantially beyond that figure until 1946. Apart from reductions between 1951 and 1956, and between 1986 and 1991, the male population has increased steadily since then. Between 1946 and 1988 the average total prison population rose from 15,800 to 49,900, an average rate of increase of 800 per annum. Policy interventions between 1989 and 1992, illustrated in Figure 1.3, below, led to reductions in the prison population to an average of 44,600 during 1993, although the prison population had already begun to increase again during that year.

1.3 Figure 1.2b shows that the pattern of increase when expressed as the rate of prisoners per 100,000 male population is similar, except that the total increase between 1901 and 1997 is less. Between 1901 and 1997 the male prison population increased in absolute terms by nearly four times, but expressed as a rate per 100,000 male population, the rate of increase was around two and a half times.

1.4 For female prisoners, the pattern is different. The average female prison population in 1997, at 2,675, was lower than in 1901 when the average number of female prisoners was 3,112, or in 1906 when the average was 2,972. In the Commissioners of Prisons report on the last peacetime year before the first world war (year ending in March 1914)[1], it was reported that nearly half (15,000 of 33,300 in total) of

---

[1] 'Report of the Commissioners of Prisons and the Directors of Convict Prisons, with Appendices. (For the year ending 31st March 1914 Part I.' Cd 7601 HMSO 1914.

women received on conviction into local prisons had been convicted of drunkeness. Another 8,000 had been received after being convicted of prostitution. During 1997 only 11 females were received into prison having been sentenced to immediate imprisonment for drunkeness offences (plus seven who had been received in default of payment of a fine, see table 4.5 in chapter 4) while only less than 10 women (of all ages) were received under immediate sentence for prostitution offences (not shown in the table) out of a total of 5,200. The difference between the early years of this century and 1997 in terms of the type of offences for which women were being received into prison is clear. Men were also much more likely in 1913/14 than in 1997 to have been sentenced for drunkeness offences, however. Such offences accounted for 38 per cent of males received in 1913/14 but less than 0.5 per cent in 1997. Whether or not expressed as an absolute figure or as a rate per 100,000 population, the long term pattern is for a steady reduction in women prisoners between 1901 and 1936, with only modest increases through to 1971 despite a surge in the number of female prisoners held between 1941 and 1951. From 1976, however, the number of female prisoners has increased steadily, apart from a temporary reduction between 1986 and 1991. (See table 1(a) and Figures 1.2(c) and 1.2(d).)

Table 1(a)   The prison population 1901–1997, by year and sex of prisoner

England and Wales

Year	Males	Females	Total	Females as a proportion (%)
1901	15,868	3,112	18,980	16.40
1906	18,102	2,972	21,074	14.10
1911	17,325	2,472	19,797	12.49
1916	8,210	1,848	10,058	18.37
1921	10,791	1,388	12,179	11.40
1926	9,972	888	10,860	8.18
1931	10,884	792	11,676	6.78
1936	9,939	674	10,613	6.35
1941	9,667	968	10,635	9.10
1946	14,556	1,233	15,789	7.81
1951	20,687	1,093	21,780	5.02
1956	19,941	866	20,807	4.16
1961	28,094	931	29,025	3.21
1966	32,127	959	33,086	2.90
1971	38,673	1,035	39,708	2.61
1976	40,161	1,282	41,443	3.09
1981	41,904	1,407	43,311	3.25
1986	45,163	1,607	46,770	3.44
1991	43,250	1,559	44,809	3.48
1997	58,439	2,675	61,114	4.38

1.5   Policy changes and events which may have affected the size of prison population in the last 10 years are listed below with some estimates of their likely impact. The changes and events are summarised in Figure 1.3 which also shows how the prison population varied over this period. Further details of the legislation are given in the notes at the end of this volume.

● The introduction of half remission for prisoners sentenced to 12 months or less in August 1987 reduced the prison population by 3,000.

● The Criminal Justice Act 1988 changed the mode of trial for certain offences from October 1988. The effect on the prison population is estimated as a reduction of about 700 in the sentenced population and as a small reduction in the remand population.

● The new sentencing structure for young offenders in the Criminal Justice Act 1988 is estimated to have reduced the population of short and medium sentenced prisoners by several hundred.

● Government measures toughening up punishment in the community, including probation service action plans targeted at young adult offenders, followed the publication of the Green Paper "Punishment, Custody and the Community". Together with the expansion of bail information schemes and bail hostel places, and schemes to deal with mentally disordered offenders in the community, these measures are estimated to have reduced the prison population by about 350 in 1989/90, 1,000 in 1990/91, 1,500 in 1991/2 and 3,100 in 1992/3.

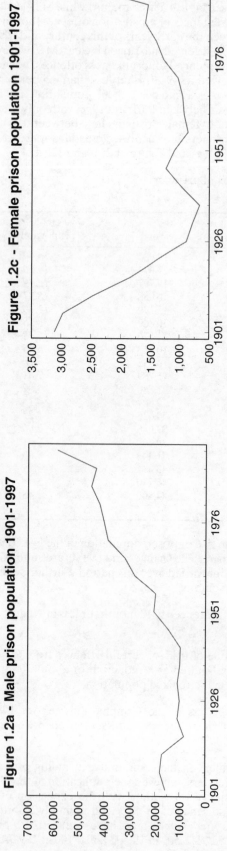

Figure 1.2a - Male prison population 1901-1997

Figure 1.2c - Female prison population 1901-1997

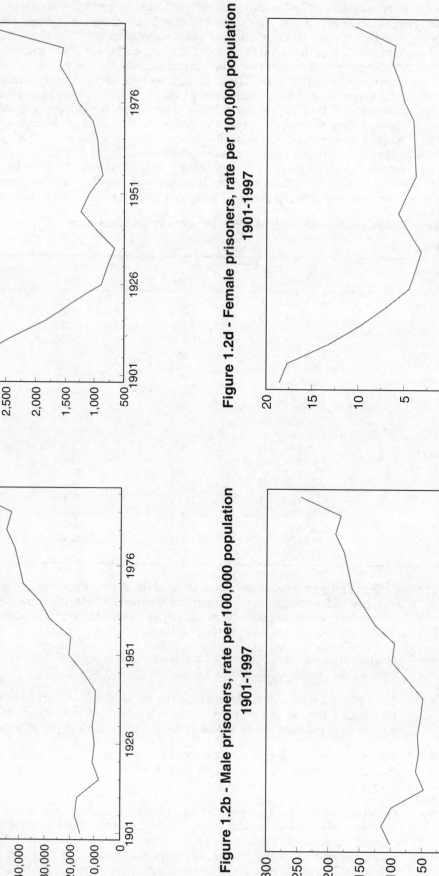

Figure 1.2b - Male prisoners, rate per 100,000 population 1901-1997

Figure 1.2d - Female prisoners, rate per 100,000 population 1901-1997

4

- The Criminal Justice Act 1991, implemented in October 1992, affected the numbers sentenced to custody and the sentence lengths given, and also introduced new early release arrangements, with a liability for recall, replacing the previous remission, release and parole schemes.

- Provisions of the Criminal Justice Act 1993, implemented in August 1993 restored to courts their power to take into account previous convictions and sentences (the Criminal Justice Act 1991 only allowed this in restricted circumstances). Offending on bail was made a mandatory statutory aggravating factor in sentencing.

- Provisions of the Criminal Justice and Public Order Act 1994 increased the maximum sentence length for juveniles from 1 to 2 years for offences committed from February 1995 onwards; longer sentences for serious offences can still be given under section 53 of the C&YP Act 1933. The Act also relaxed the requirement for pre-sentence reports for those aged 18 and over.

- The Criminal Procedure and Investigations Act 1996 was enacted during the year. The Act introduced numerous changes to court procedure which were to be implemented during 1996 and 1997. These included arrangements for 'plea before venue' by which defendants are required to enter a plea before the venue for trial is decided, although this was not enacted until October 1997.

- In July 1996 the Offensive Weapons Act was implemented introducing increased maximum penalties for carrying offensive weapons or having an article with a blade or point in a public place. Further provisions to control knives were implemented in September. Increases were seen during 1996 in the numbers receiving community sentences and immediate custody for these offences.

- The White paper 'Protecting the Public' published in March 1996 may also have had an effect on the use of custody. The White paper proposed, among other things:

    — Automatic life sentences for offenders convicted a second time of serious violent or sex offences

    — Mandatory minimum sentences of seven years for class A drug trafficking offences for those with two or more previous convictions for similar offences.

    These policies were taken forward in the Crime (Sentences) Act, which received Royal Assent in March 1997.

- Events such as prison camp openings (1988), the prison disturbances in 1990 and the murder of James Bulger (in 1993) are sometimes thought to have an influence (however temporary) on public opinion and the use of custody by the courts.

Figure 1.3

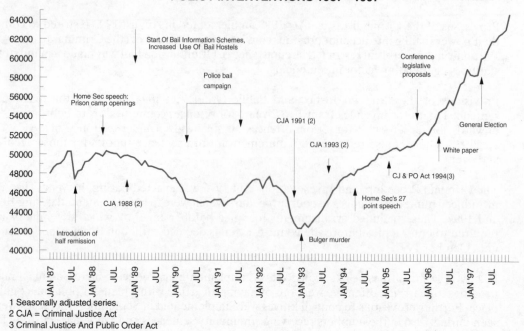

PRISON POPULATION (1)
POLICY INTERVENTIONS 1987 - 1997

1 Seasonally adjusted series.
2 CJA = Criminal Justice Act
3 Criminal Justice And Public Order Act

1.6 As Figure 1.3 shows, growth in the prison population has been particularly rapid since 1992. The number of persons sentenced for indictable offences at all courts during 1997 was 1 per cent fewer than in 1992 but the custody rate, the proportion of those sentenced given immediate custody, had increased from 44 per cent to 60 per cent at the Crown Court and from 5 per cent to 10 per cent at the magistrates' courts, as is shown in Table 1(b) below. It is the changes in the custody rate and in sentence length, rather than the numbers proceeded against or sentenced, which appear to have had the greatest impact on the prison population. The average length of sentence given at each type of court for persons aged 21 and over is as follows:

Average sentence length for indictable offences (months)

Year	Crown Court	Magistrates' courts
1992	21.0	2.7
1993	21.6	3.2
1994	21.4	3.1
1995	21.8	2.8
1996	23.4	2.7
1997	23.9	2.6

Source is Criminal Statistics England and Wales, 1996. 1997 data is provisional.

Table 1(b) Proportion of persons sentenced for indictable offences by type of sentence or order, and type of court

England and Wales   Percentages

| | Type of sentence or order | | | | | |
Year	Discharge	Fine	Community sentence[1]	Fully suspended sentence	Immediate custody[2]	Total number sentenced[3] (Thousands) (= 100%)
Type of court						
Magistrates' courts						
1992	26	42	21	2	5	241.4
1993	26	41	24	—	6	238.2
1994	26	40	28	—	7	243.6
1995	24	37	28	—	9	228.9
1996	23	35	29	—	10	229.2
1997(ᴾ)	23	35	29	—	10	241.7
Crown Court						
1992	6	6	28	14	44	81.1
1993	6	5	34	3	49	67.0
1994	5	5	33	2	52	68.5
1995	5	5	30	3	56	71.5
1996	3	4	27	3	60	70.7
1997(ᴾ)	3	3	28	3	60	76.4

Source: Criminal Statistics England and Wales 1996

[1] Probation orders, supervision orders, community service orders, attendance centre orders and combination orders (from 1 October 1992) or curfew order.

[2] Detention in a young offender institution, unsuspended imprisonment and partly suspended imprisonment (before 1 October 1992).

[3] Includes offenders otherwise dealt with.

(ᴾ) Provisional.

Components of the prison population

1.7   Among the prison population in 1997 were an average 48,410 prisoners under sentence (79 per cent of the total). These included 38,800 sentenced adult males, 7,560 sentenced male young offenders (generally aged under 21) and 2,050 sentenced females. The population held on remand consisted on average of 11,530 males and 600 females. The prison population also included 570 non-criminal prisoners, who were mainly persons held under the Immigration Act 1971 but also included prisoners held for civil offences such as contempt of court. Overall 2,680 females were included in the total prison population, making up 4.4 per cent of the total.

Figure 1.4

**MAIN COMPONENTS OF THE PRISON POPULATION
AVERAGE DURING 1997**

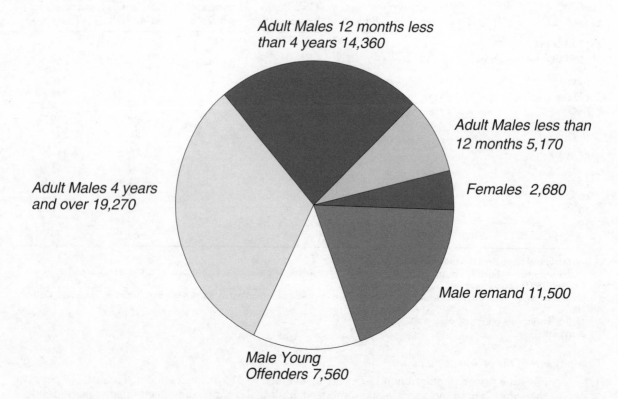

Adult Males 12 months less
than 4 years 14,360

Adult Males less than
12 months 5,170

Females 2,680

Adult Males 4 years
and over 19,270

Male remand 11,500

Male Young
Offenders 7,560

1.8   The recent growth in the prison population has mainly been among sentenced prisoners. The average remand population during 1997 of 12,130 (males and females) was only 4 per cent more than the 11,610 average during 1996 and fewer than the average for 1994 when 12,360 prisoners were held on remand. Sentenced prisoners, by contrast, averaged 48,410 during 1997, compared with 43,040 during 1996, a rise of 12 per cent. Sentenced male young offenders increased by 16 per cent, from an average of 6,490 during 1996 to 7,560 during 1997. The sentenced female population increased by 21 per cent, from an average 1,700 in 1996 to 2,050 in 1997. Adult males under sentence increased by 11 per cent, from an average 34,860 in 1996 to 38,810 in 1997.

1.9   Female prisoners (whether sentenced prisoners, held on remand or non-criminal) increased by 19 per cent from an average 2,260 in 1996 to 2,680 in 1997. Male prisoners increased by an average 10 per cent, from 53,020 to 58,440. Females accounted for a greater proportion of the total prison population in 1997 than in 1996, at 4.4 per cent compared with 4.1 per cent during the previous year. This appears to be part of an ongoing trend, with the proportion of female prisoners having been 3.5 per cent in 1993, 3.7 per cent in 1994 and 3.9 per cent in 1995.

1.10   Among the adult male sentenced prisoners larger than average increases were seen for adult males sentenced to 12 months or more. While adult males sentenced to less than 12 months increased only by 4 per cent, from 4,970 to 5,170, those sentenced to 12 months but less than 4 years rose from 12,800 to 14,360, an increase of 12 per cent and those sentenced to 4 years and over (including life) rose by 13 per cent, from 17,090 to 19,270.

1.11   The male prison population in 1997 consisted of an average 4,025, or 7 per cent, prisoners held in remand centres, 21,849 (37 per cent) held in local prisons, 26,161 (45 per cent) held in training prisons (including 3,853 or 7 per cent in open prisons) and 6,402 (11 per cent) in young offender institutions. Nearly two in five of the male prisoners held in remand centres were either sentenced prisoners or non-criminal prisoners, including an average of 312 held under the 1971 Immigration Act.

1.12 Sentenced young offenders and remand prisoners aged 15 to 20 accounted for 18 per cent of the male prison population in 1997, with an average prison population of 10,435, of whom 61 per cent (6,401) were held in young offender institutions. 3,691 (35 per cent) were held in remand centres and 338 (3 per cent) were held in local prisons during 1997; the proportion of young prisoners held in local prisons was substantially down on 1996 (9 per cent). All female prisoners were held in female prisons during 1997 and there was no use of police cells to allay overcrowding during the year.

1.13 A summary of the sentenced prison population by offence group is given in Table 1(c), below. Between 1996 and 1997 (taking June 30 as a reference date) the greatest increases in the number of sentenced prisoners, by offence group, were among prisoners sentenced for burglary and drugs offences. The increase of more than 1,600 in prisoners held for burglary offences was an increase of 26 per cent in the population sentenced for this offence. The increase, of 1,400, in drug offenders held as sentenced prisoners was a rate of growth of 25 per cent between the two years. The greatest number in prison by offence, however, were those sentenced for violence against the person offences, who formed 21 per cent of the sentenced prison population. Substantial changes in the make up of the sentenced prison population by offence have occurred over the 10 year period shown in Table 1.6. There was a reduction from 23 to 15 per cent in the proportion of sentenced prisoners who were convicted of burglary offences between 1987 and 1996 although the figures for 1997 suggest a recovery in the numbers held for burglary, which now make up 17 per cent of the sentenced population. Between 1987 and 1997 there was a reduction from 18 to 11 per cent in the proportion convicted of theft and handling or fraud and forgery. There have been increases from 9 to 15 per cent in the proportion of prisoners convicted of drugs offences, from 10 to 13 per cent in the proportion convicted of robbery and from 6 to 8 per cent in the proportion convicted of rape and other sexual offences. The numbers serving sentences for drugs offences doubled over the 10 year period and the numbers held for rape and other sexual offences increased by 75 per cent, while the population of all sentenced prisoners increased by only 24 per cent.

Table 1(c) **Population in Prison Service establishments under sentence on 30 June 1996 and 30 June 1997 by offence group**

England and Wales   Number of persons

Offence Group	30 June 1996	30 June 1997	Change	% change
Violence against the person	9,585	10,424	+ 839	+ 8.8
Sexual offences	3,951	4,077	+ 126	+ 3.2
Burglary	6,422	8,077	+1,655	+25.8
Robbery	5,715	6,438	+ 723	+12.7
Theft and handling	3,905	4,263	+ 358	+ 9.2
Fraud and forgery	1,218	1,225	+ 7	+ 0.6
Drug offences	5,755	7,174	+1,419	+24.7
Motoring offences	1,734	1,915	+ 181	+10.4
Other offences	2,102	3,321	+ 219	+ 7.1

1.14 Since 1994 the numbers of prisoners sentenced for drugs offences has increased. The numbers of prisoners held for unlawful supply and for possession with intent to supply have more than doubled. Less than 10 per cent of prisoners held for drugs offences had been convicted of possession without intent to supply. Details are given in Table 1(d).

Table 1(d) **Population in Prison Service establishments under sentence on 30 June: by principal drugs offence, 1994 to 1997([1])**

England and Wales   Estimated number of persons([2])

Principal drugs offence([3])	1994	1995	1996	1997
All drug offences	**3,500**	**4,300**	**5,800**	**7,200**
Unlawful supply	800	1,150	1,600	2,200
Possession with intent to supply	1,100	1,300	1,700	2,400
Possession	300	400	500	600
Unlawful import/export	1,200	1,450	1,900	1,850
Other drugs offences	50	100	100	150

([1]) Excluding persons committed in default of a payment of a fine.

([2]) Figures rounded to the nearest 50.

([3]) A person sentenced to custody for more than one drugs offence is recorded in this table against the offence which attracted the longest sentence.

1.15   Figure 1.5 and table 1.7 show that since 1987 longer sentence prisoners (over 4 years sentence in this chart) have tended to increase as a proportion of all sentenced prisoners. By 1997 more than one in three sentenced prisoners were serving over 4 years compared with one in four in 1987.

Figure 1.5

SENTENCED POPULATION BY LENGTH OF SENTENCE
1987–1997

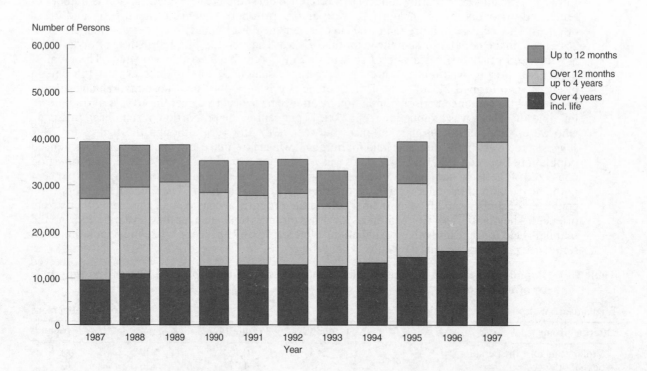

1.16   Table 1.8 shows that the number of the sentenced prisoners aged under 21 on 30 June 1997 was 6,930, an increase of more than 1,000 prisoners or 19 per cent on the number held on the same date in 1996 (5,800). This compares with an increase in prisoners aged 21 and over of 12 per cent, from 37,252 to 41,875. Between 1993 and 1997 the number of sentenced prisoners aged 15-17 more than doubled while the number of prisoners aged 21 and over increased by 48 per cent. Sentenced prisoners aged 18-20 increased by 33 per cent over the same period. Male sentenced prisoners aged under 21 made up 14.3 per cent of the male prison population in June 1997. There had been a reduction in the proportion of prisoners aged under 21 from 23 per cent in 1987 to just over 13 per cent in 1992, but until 1996 the proportions of under 21s in the population was more stable. For females, the proportion aged under 21 fell from 15 per cent in 1987 to 10 per cent in 1991. In 1997 the proportion was 11 per cent, having reached 13 per cent during 1996. These changes may reflect demographic changes to some extent.

1.17   Chapters 2, 3, and 4 in this report contain more details about the characteristics of remand prisoners, young offenders and adult prisoners under sentence.

Receptions (Tables 1.1, 1.9 & 1.10)

1.18   In 1997 around 125,400 persons were initially received into Prison Service establishments, 4,800 more than the 120,600 in 1996. A person received into a Prison Service establishment to serve a sentence may previously have been received on remand after conviction prior to sentence, and before that as a remand prisoner awaiting trial. Table 1(e) gives the number of initial receptions in each category excluding subsequent receptions in a different category. 40,200 persons were initially received under an immediate custodial sentence in 1997; this compares with 80,800 receptions under sentence (excluding fine defaulters) when, as in Table 1.1, those previously received on remand are included. The number of initial receptions as a sentenced prisoner increased from 38,300 in 1996 to 40,200 in 1997, and the number of initial receptions on remand increased from 70,600 to 75,700, but the number of receptions of fine defaulters decreased by 27 per cent, down from 8,600 to 6,300.

Table 1(e)   Initial receptions during 1997 into Prison Service establishments by sex and type of custody

England and Wales   Estimated number of receptions

Persons initially received as:	Males	Females	All males and females
All initial receptions	**116,800**	**8,600**	**125,400**
All remand receptions	70,500	5,100	75,700
Untried	58,100	4,000	62,100
Convicted unsentenced	12,400	1,100	13,500
Sentenced	37,200	3,000	40,200
Fine defaulter	6,000	400	6,300
Non-criminal	3,100	100	3,200

1.19   The number of prisoners received from magistrates' courts under an immediate custodial sentence (i.e. excluding fine defaulters) reduced between 1987, when there were over 23,000 receptions, down to around 16,000 in 1990. The number has since then increased to reach 38,200 in 1997. Receptions from the Crown Court have also increased since the low point of 29,000 in 1992 to exceed 42,300 in 1997.

1.20   The Crown Court accounted for 89 per cent of the sentenced population, which reflects the longer sentences generally given at the Crown Court. The magistrates' courts proportion has fallen from 13 per cent in 1987 to 10 per cent in 1997.

1.21   The following table, 1(f), shows that between 1996 and 1997 the numbers of prisoners received increased for all sentence lengths.

Table 1(f)   All prisoners received into custody under sentence by sentence length([1])

England and Wales   Thousands

	All sentence lengths	Less than 6 months	6 months to less than 12 months	12 mths to less than 4 years	4 years and over (inc life)
Year					
1994	61.2	32.0	6.7	18.1	4.4
1995	69.0	37.2	7.2	19.7	4.9
1996	74.3	38.9	7.2	22.1	6.1
1997	80.8	43.0	7.5	23.5	6.8
% change over one year earlier					
1995	*13*	*16*	*7*	*9*	*11*
1996	*8*	*5*	*0*	*12*	*24*
1997	*9*	*11*	*4*	*6*	*11*

([1]) Excludes fine defaulters.

Fine defaulters and civil prisoners (Tables 1.11–1.14)

1.22   There were 131 fine defaulters in prison on 30 June 1997. This was about a quarter of the level of two years earlier and well below the level at any time in the previous decade. Two major developments which affected fine enforcement practice account for the fall. In November 1995 a Queen's Bench Judgement in Cawley and Others[2] clarified the legislative position whereby all enforcement measures have to be actively considered or tried before imprisonment can be imposed by the courts. A number of initiatives under the Government's Working Group on the Enforcement of Financial Penalties were taken forward in 1996 and will also have contributed to the fall in the use of imprisonment for fine defaulters. These included issuing good practice guidance for the courts in July 1996 and the extension of the power to impose an attachment of earnings order in the Criminal Procedure and Investigations Act 1996.

([2]) R v Oldham Justices and another, ex parte Cawley and other applications. Queen's Bench Division. 30, 31 October, 28 November 1995.

1.23 Most fine defaulters serve only very short periods of detention or imprisonment and there was a general downward trend in the average time served between 1987 to 1990. In 1997 the average time served in prisons was 7 days for males and 5 days for females. This has changed little since 1990 but compares with 11 and 8 days in 1987. As a result of the comparatively short time served, fine defaulters form a much smaller proportion of the total sentenced prison population (0.3 per cent in 1997) than they do of receptions (7 per cent).

1.24 Receptions of fine defaulters were also much reduced on earlier years being, at 6,340 during 1997, less than one third the level of two years previously (over 20,000 in 1995). The great majority of these receptions were males, 94 per cent in 1997. The total number of females received into prison as fine defaulters was 370 during 1997 and as a result of the relatively short times served, the average population of female fine defaulters during 1997 was 3 prisoners.

1.25 Table 1.12 gives receptions of fine defaulters into prison by age, offence group and sex. Fine defaulters were most likely (37 per cent of receptions) to be received into prison after defaulting on a fine imposed for motoring offences.

1.26 Statistics on the population of non-criminal prisoners at 30 June 1997 are presented in tables 1.13 and 1.14. The 557 non-criminal prisoners were 12 per cent fewer than the 633 held on the same date in 1996. All but 19 were male. The majority of these prisoners (476 or 85 per cent) were held under the 1971 Immigration Act, although this does not include persons held in detention centres controlled by the Immigration Service. Forty nine non-criminal prisoners were held for contempt of court (9 per cent of all non-criminal prisoners) and 18 (3 per cent) were held for non payment of local government taxes such as the community charge. Between 1996 and 1997 there were reductions in the numbers of non-criminal prisoners held for most types of committal, including a reduction of 8 per cent in the numbers held under the 1971 Immigration Act.

1.27 Receptions of non-criminal prisoners increased by 2 per cent between 1996 and 1997, from 3,130 to 3,200. Within this increase was an increase of 14 per cent in receptions of prisoners held under the 1971 Immigration Act, from 1,860 to 2,120.

Accommodation (Table 1.15)

1.28 In-use Certified Normal Accommodation (CNA) recorded on 30 June 1997 was 56,300, over 3,100 more than a year earlier. By the end of the year CNA had reached 58,900. The average population during 1997 was 4,800 more than the CNA on 30 June.

Figure 1.6

POPULATION IN CUSTODY &
CERTIFIED NORMAL ACCOMMODATION

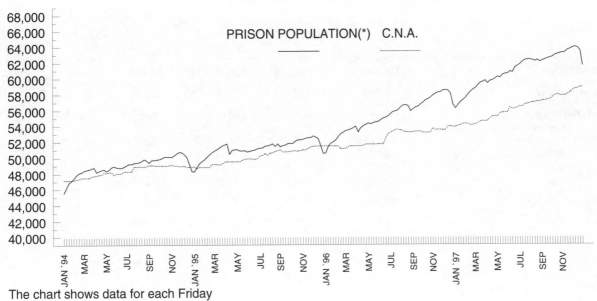

The chart shows data for each Friday
(*) Including those in police cells up to June 1995

International comparisons (table 1.16)

1.29   Table 1.16 gives information on the total number of prisoners (including pre-trial detainees), the rate of imprisonment in relation to the general population and the rate of occupancy of prison establishments in a number of countries. When making comparisons of prison population statistics across different jurisdictions it should be borne in mind that there are differences in both the definitions and the recording methods used.

1.30   The prison population rose by 12% in England and Wales for the period used in these comparisons, i.e. 1 September 1996 to 1 September 1997 (for England and Wales 31 August). There were rises in other countries too with the highest being in Ireland (13%), Belgium (7%), Greece (6%) and the USA (6%). Falls were reported in Sweden (10%), Finland (8%), Russia and Northern Ireland (both 4%).

1.31   The figures show that England and Wales with 120 prisoners per 100,000 people in the general population in 1997 had the second highest rate of imprisonment in western Europe; only Portugal (with 142) had a higher rate. The rate in England and Wales was higher than the rates in Scotland (119), Northern Ireland (95), France (90), Germany (87) and Italy (87). Outside western Europe, however, much higher rates per 100,000 population have been reported, notably Russia (687) and the USA (645).

1.32   The occupancy rate in England and Wales was 109 prisoners for every 100 places available. This was less than the occupancy rate in Portugal (132), Greece (129), Hungary (123) and the Czech Republic (114), and similar to that in France (also 109) but higher than in most other western European countries.

Table 1.1   Receptions into prison and average population in custody: by sex and type of custody

England and Wales 1997
Males and females

Number of persons(¹)

	Receptions into Prison Service establishments			Average population		
	Males	Females	All males and females	Males	Females	All males and females
All persons in custody	**116,800**(²)	**8,642**(²)	**125,442**(²)	**58,439**	**2,675**	**61,114**
Prisoners on remand	**70,540**	**5,124**	**75,664**	**11,532**	**599**	**12,130**
Untried criminal prisoners	58,092	3,974	62,066	8,057	396	8,453
Convicted unsentenced prisoners awaiting sentence or enquiry	33,988	2,436	36,424	3,475	203	3,678
Received under Section 37 Mental Health Act 1983	179	17	196	228	11	239
Others	33,809	2,419	36,228	3,247	192	3,439
Prisoners under sentence	**81,949**	**5,219**	**87,168**	**46,360**	**2,052**	**48,413**
Young offenders	18,427	871	19,298	7,556	278	7,834
Detention in a young offender institution	17,325	830	18,155	7,439	268	7,707
Section 53(2) C&YP Act 1933 (excluding life)	499	18	517			
Life (including HMP and custody for life)	66	5	71	105	9	114
In default of payment of a fine	537	18	555	12	1	13
Adults	**63,522**	**4,348**	**67,870**	**38,805**	**1,774**	**40,579**
Immediate imprisonment (excluding life)	57,798	3,978	61,776	35,194	1,644	36,838
Life (including HMP and custody for life)	297	16	313	3,488	125	3,613
In default of payment of a fine	5,427	354	5,781	123	5	128
Non-criminal prisoners	**3,063**	**141**	**3,204**	**547**	**25**	**571**
Held under the 1971 Immigration Act(³)	2,051	71	2,122	464	21	485
Others	1,012	70	1,082	83	4	87

(¹) The components do not always add to the totals because they have been rounded independently.

(²) Total receptions cannot be calculated by adding together receptions in each category, because there is double-counting (see paragraph 27 of the Notes). However double-counting has been allowed for in the figures of receptions of prisoners under remand. The total receptions figures given are estimates of initial receptions (see paragraph 1.18 and table 1(c) of the Commentary).

(³) Schedule 2, paragraph 16; Schedule 3, paragraph 2.

Table 1.2 Population in custody: by sex and type of custody, annual averages and month end figures

England and Wales
Males and females   Thousands(¹)

| | Prisoners on remand | | | | Male prisoners under sentence | | | | |
| | Males | | Females | | | | Adults by sentence length | | |
	Untried	Convicted unsentenced		All remand	Young offenders	Less than 12 months(²)	12 months less than 4 years	4 years & over (inc. life)	All sentenced adult males
Annual averages									
1993	7.69	2.59	0.40	10.67	4.99	3.89	9.60	13.70	27.19
1994	8.82	3.05	0.49	12.36	5.16	4.54	10.49	14.31	29.34
1995	8.08	2.81	0.49	11.37	5.62	4.96	11.49	15.51	31.97
1996	8.00	3.08	0.54	11.61	6.49	4.97	12.80	17.09	34.86
1997	8.06	3.50	0.60	12.13	7.56	5.17	14.36	19.27	38.81
Financial year averages									
1992–93	7.49	2.02	0.36	9.86	5.14	3.47	10.60	14.80	28.14
1993–94	8.08	2.72	0.43	11.24	5.08	4.19	9.84	13.75	27.77
1994–95	8.77	3.09	0.50	12.36	5.24	4.66	10.70	14.56	29.93
1995–96	7.92	2.79	0.48	11.20	5.77	4.92	11.71	15.85	32.54
1996–97	8.06	3.16	0.56	11.78	6.78	4.93	13.22	17.58	35.73
Month end figures									
1996 January	8.02	3.04	0.48	11.54	5.73	4.61	11.69	16.22	32.52
February	7.91	3.07	0.47	11.45	6.07	5.07	12.02	16.36	33.45
March	7.61	2.93	0.47	11.01	6.19	5.25	12.35	16.67	34.27
April	7.80	3.11	0.52	11.42	6.19	5.06	12.51	16.73	34.30
May	7.85	2.96	0.52	11.32	6.28	5.08	12.68	16.85	34.61
June	8.03	2.99	0.55	11.57	6.36	5.00	12.93	17.03	34.96
July	7.98	3.01	0.57	11.56	6.62	5.18	13.21	17.20	35.60
August	8.01	3.11	0.56	11.68	6.60	4.84	12.87	17.22	34.92
September	8.15	3.24	0.57	11.96	6.85	4.92	13.11	17.42	35.45
October	8.23	3.33	0.60	12.15	6.98	5.22	13.40	17.60	36.21
November	8.28	3.26	0.61	12.15	7.14	5.09	13.49	17.81	36.40
December	8.19	2.79	0.55	11.54	6.88	4.31	13.36	17.91	35.58
1997 January	8.15	3.43	0.60	12.18	6.93	4.45	13.46	18.12	36.03
February	7.99	3.47	0.54	12.00	7.26	5.02	13.70	18.35	37.07
March	8.05	3.22	0.55	11.82	7.28	5.01	13.90	18.67	37.58
April	7.98	3.38	0.59	11.96	7.26	5.26	14.16	18.92	38.34
May	7.90	3.24	0.56	11.70	7.42	5.21	14.24	19.16	38.60
June	8.13	3.38	0.59	12.11	7.70	5.35	14.41	19.28	39.04
July	8.19	3.34	0.62	12.14	7.82	5.57	14.60	19.51	39.68
August	8.29	3.46	0.63	12.38	7.59	5.23	14.53	19.53	39.28
September	8.35	3.45	0.63	12.43	7.73	5.32	14.72	19.71	39.75
October	7.97	3.91	0.63	12.50	7.90	5.43	14.80	19.86	40.09
November	7.94	3.97	0.67	12.58	7.90	5.37	15.03	19.99	40.40
December	7.74	3.44	0.59	11.78	7.80	4.86	14.82	20.12	39.80

(¹) The components do not always add up to the totals, because they have been rounded independently.
(²) Including fine defaulters and police cells.

Table 1.2 (Continued) Population in custody: by sex and type of custody, annual averages and month end figures

England and Wales
Males and females   Thousands(¹)   Number

	Prisoners under sentence			Non-criminal prisoners	All males	All females	Total in custody(¹)
	Males	Females	All sentenced				
Annual averages							
1993	32.18	1.14	33.32	0.57	43.01	1.56	44,566
1994	34.50	1.29	35.80	0.64	46.98	1.81	48,794
1995	37.59	1.46	39.06	0.62	49.07	1.98	51,047
1996	41.35	1.70	43.04	0.63	53.02	2.26	55,281
1997	46.36	2.05	48.41	0.57	58.44	2.68	61,114
Financial year averages							
1992–93	33.28	1.14	34.42	0.34	43.11	1.51	44,628
1993–94	32.85	1.17	34.02	0.64	44.26	1.64	45,895
1994–95	35.17	1.34	36.50	0.61	47.60	1.87	49,471
1995–96	38.31	1.51	39.82	0.63	49.63	2.01	51,644
1996–97	42.51	1.77	44.28	0.61	54.31	2.36	56,671
Month end figures							
1996 January	38.25	1.52	39.77	0.63	49.92	2.03	51,947
February	39.52	1.59	41.11	0.62	51.10	2.08	53,178
March	40.46	1.63	42.09	0.64	51.62	2.12	53,740
April	40.49	1.64	42.13	0.65	52.02	2.18	54,202
May	40.89	1.68	42.56	0.63	52.29	2.22	54,513
June	41.32	1.73	43.06	0.63	52.95	2.31	55,256
July	42.21	1.73	43.95	0.64	53.81	2.33	56,141
August	41.52	1.70	43.23	0.63	53.24	2.30	55,537
September	42.30	1.72	44.02	0.64	54.30	2.32	56,621
October	43.19	1.80	44.99	0.62	55.34	2.42	57,764
November	43.53	1.84	45.37	0.61	55.65	2.48	58,126
December	42.46	1.79	44.25	0.57	53.98	2.37	56,351
1997 January	42.96	1.83	44.79	0.59	55.10	2.46	57,560
February	44.34	1.90	46.23	0.59	56.37	2.45	58,820
March	44.85	1.93	46.78	0.56	56.66	2.50	59,161
April	45.60	1.99	47.60	0.58	57.52	2.61	60,131
May	46.02	2.04	48.07	0.57	57.70	2.63	60,335
June	46.74	2.07	48.81	0.56	58.80	2.67	61,467
July	47.50	2.11	49.60	0.58	59.57	2.75	62,324
August	46.87	2.11	48.98	0.58	59.17	2.77	61,940
September	47.48	2.15	49.63	0.60	59.85	2.80	62,652
October	47.98	2.15	50.14	0.59	60.42	2.80	63,226
November	48.39	2.20	50.59	0.55	60.83	2.89	63,715
December	47.60	2.16	49.75	0.51	59.28	2.77	62,040

(¹) The components do not always add up to the totals, because they have been rounded independently.
(²) Including fine defaulters and police cells.

Table 1.3   Average population in custody: by type of prisoner, type of establishment (including police cells) and sex

England and Wales 1997
Males   Number of persons[1]

Type of prisoner	All types of estab-lishment (including police cells)	Police cells	Remand centres	Local prisons	Training prisons		Young offender institutions		
					Open	Closed	Juvenile	Open	Closed
All males	**58,439**	–	**4,025**	**21,849**	**3,853**	**22,308**	**1,433**	**423**	**4,546**
Untried criminal prisoners	**8,057**	–	**1,572**	**6,334**	–	**40**	**85**	–	**27**
Aged 15 to 20	1,814	–	1,572	132	–	–	85	–	27
Aged 21 and over	6,243	–	–	6,202	–	40	–	–	–
Convicted unsentenced prisoners	**3,475**	–	**899**	**2,467**	–	**17**	**64**	–	**26**
Aged 15 to 20	1,065	–	899	75	–	–	64	–	26
Aged 21 and over	2,410	–	–	2,392	–	17	–	–	–
Sentenced prisoners	**46,360**	–	**1,240**	**12,824**	**3,848**	**22,248**	**1,284**	**423**	**4,492**
Young offenders	**7,556**	–	**1,220**	**131**	–	**5**	**1,284**	**423**	**4,492**
Less than 12 months[2]	1,744	–	488	53	–	–	470	155	578
12 months to less than 4 years	4,321	–	593	57	–	2	763	267	2,639
4 years to less than 10 years	1,320	–	121	15	–	2	50	1	1,131
10 years less than life	52	–	5	2	–	–	1	–	44
Life (including HMP and custody for life)	105	–	6	2	–	1	–	–	97
In default of payment of a fine	12	–	7	2	–	–	–	–	3
Adults	**38,805**	–	**20**	**12,693**	**3,848**	**22,243**	–	–	–
Less than 12 months[2]	5,049	–	–	3,524	973	552	–	–	–
12 months to less than 4 years	14,364	–	11	5,391	1,865	7,097	–	–	–
4 years to less than 10 years	12,873	–	9	2,753	623	9,488	–	–	–
10 years less than life	2,906	–	–	490	71	2,345	–	–	–
Life (including HMP and custody for life)	3,488	–	–	428	310	2,751	–	–	–
In default of payment of a fine	123	–	–	107	6	10	–	–	–
Non-criminal prisoners	**547**	–	**314**	**224**	**5**	**3**	–	–	**1**
Held under the 1971 Immigration Act	464	–	312	151	–	1	–	–	1
Others	83	–	2	73	5	2	–	–	–

(1) The components do not always add up to the totals, because they have been rounded independently.
(2) Excluding fine defaulters.

17

Table 1.3 Average population in custody: by type of prisoner, type of establishment (including police cells) and sex

England and Wales 1997
Females

Number of persons[1]

Type of prisoner	All types of establishment (including police cells)	Police cells	Remand centres	Local prisons	Training prisons Open	Training prisons Closed	Young offender institutions Open	Young offender institutions Closed
All females	**2,675**	–	–	**1,104**	**458**	**928**	**32**	**155**
Untried criminal prisoners	**396**	–	–	**362**	–	**30**	–	**4**
Aged 15 to 20	64	–	–	55	–	5	–	4
Aged 21 and over	332	–	–	307	–	25	–	–
Convicted unsentenced prisoners	**203**	–	–	**186**	–	**15**	–	**2**
Aged 15 to 20	39	–	–	34	–	3	–	2
Aged 21 and over	164	–	–	152	–	12	–	–
Sentenced prisoners	**2,052**	–	–	**533**	**458**	**881**	**32**	**149**
Young offenders	**278**	–	–	**48**	**15**	**34**	**32**	**149**
Less than 12 months[2]	76	–	–	23	4	7	13	29
12 months to less than 4 years	145	–	–	18	9	18	18	82
4 years to less than 10 years	46	–	–	6	2	8	1	29
10 years less than life	2	–	–	–	–	–	–	2
Life (including HMP and custody for life)	9	–	–	1	–	1	–	6
In default of payment of a fine	1	–	–	–	–	–	–	1
Adults	**1,774**	–	–	**485**	**443**	**847**	–	–
Less than 12 months[2]	379	–	–	171	134	74	–	–
12 months to less than 4 years	709	–	–	170	230	309	–	–
4 years to less than 10 years	475	–	–	85	55	335	–	–
10 years less than life	83	–	–	25	4	54	–	–
Life (including HMP and custody for life)	125	–	–	30	20	75	–	–
In default of payment of a fine	5	–	–	4	–	–	–	–
Non-criminal prisoners	**25**	–	–	**23**	–	**2**	–	–
Held under the 1971 Immigration Act	21	–	–	20	–	2	–	–
Others	4	–	–	3	–	–	–	–

[1] The components do not always add up to the totals, because they have been rounded independently.
[2] Excluding fine defaulters.

18

Table 1.4 Average population in custody: by type of custody and sex

England and Wales
Males and females

Number of persons[1]

Type of custody	1987	1988	1989	1990	1991	1992	1993	1994	1995	1996	1997
All males and females											
Population in custody of which:	**48,963**	**49,949**	**48,610**	**45,636**	**45,897**	**45,817**	**44,566**	**48,794**	**51,047**	**55,281**	**61,114**
Population in Prison Service establishments	48,426	48,872	48,500	44,975	44,809	44,719	44,552	48,621	50,962	55,281	61,114
Population in police cells[2]	537	1,077	110	661	1,088	1,098	14	173	85	–	–
All males											
Population in custody of which:	**47,191**	**48,160**	**46,843**	**44,039**	**44,336**	**44,240**	**43,005**	**46,983**	**49,068**	**53,019**	**58,439**
Population in Prison Service establishments	46,722	47,113	46,736	43,378	43,250	43,157	42,991	46,810	48,983	53,019	58,439
Population in police cells[2]	469	1,047	107	661	1,086	1,083	14	173	85	–	–
Prisoners on remand	**10,691**	**10,933**	**10,031**	**9,521**	**9,768**	**9,707**	**10,265**	**11,867**	**10,884**	**11,075**	**11,532**
Untried[2]	9,212	9,346	8,304	7,771	7,923	7,805	7,675	8,818	8,077	8,004	8,057
Convicted unsentenced	1,479	1,587	1,727	1,749	1,845	1,902	2,590	3,049	2,807	3,071	3,475
Prisoners under sentence	**36,234**	**37,006**	**36,599**	**34,322**	**34,274**	**34,230**	**32,183**	**34,505**	**37,593**	**41,346**	**46,360**
Young offenders	**8,557**	**8,156**	**7,056**	**6,121**	**5,723**	**5,336**	**4,994**	**5,164**	**5,619**	**6,489**	**7,556**
Detention in a young offender institution[3]	*	7,648[4]	6,878	5,928	5,518	5,169	4,836	5,020	5,486	6,389	7,439
Sentenced to detention centre	870	643[5]	*	*	*	*	*	*	*	*	*
Youth custody/borstal training[3]	7,499	7,440[5]	8	*	*	*	*	*	*	*	*
Life (incl HMP and custody for life)	105	105	109	115	122	105	84	84	81	80	105
In default of payment of a fine	83	75	69	78	82	62	74	60	52	20	12
Adults	**27,677**	**28,850**	**29,543**	**28,201**	**28,551**	**28,894**	**27,189**	**29,340**	**31,974**	**34,856**	**38,805**
Life (incl HMP and custody for life)	2,167	2,318	2,478	2,603	2,708	2,812	2,917	2,999	3,112	3,289	3,488
Immediate imprisonment (excl life)	25,076	26,149	26,687	25,325	25,573	25,830	23,874	25,977	28,528	31,417	35,194
In default of payment of a fine	434	383	378	273	271	252	398	364	334	150	123
Non-criminal prisoners	**266**	**221**	**214**	**197**	**294**	**303**	**543**	**611**	**591**	**599**	**547**
Held under the 1971 Immigration Act	164	140	154	141	218	224	405	464	464	494	464
Others	102	80	59	55	76	79	137	147	127	105	83
All females											
Population in custody of which:	**1,772**	**1,789**	**1,767**	**1,597**	**1,561**	**1,577**	**1,561**	**1,811**	**1,979**	**2,262**	**2,675**
Population in Prison Service establishments	1,704	1,759	1,764	1,597	1,559	1,562	1,561	1,811	1,979	2,262	2,675
Population in police cells[2]	68	30	3	–	2	15	–	–	–	–	–
Prisoners on remand	**471**	**507**	**468**	**384**	**389**	**383**	**395**	**490**	**491**	**537**	**599**
Untried[2]	399	430	375	300	292	271	285	351	344	371	396
Convicted unsentenced	72	77	93	84	97	112	110	139	147	167	203
Prisoners under sentence	**1,297**	**1,276**	**1,293**	**1,209**	**1,166**	**1,190**	**1,135**	**1,292**	**1,464**	**1,697**	**2,052**
Young offenders	**205**	**190**	**176**	**143**	**136**	**133**	**137**	**155**	**187**	**233**	**278**
Detention in a young offender institution[3]	*	185[4]	169	137	128	125	129	148	179	225	268
Youth custody/borstal training[3]	195	176[5]	*	*	*	*	*	*	*	*	*
Life (incl HMP and custody for life)	8	9	5	4	5	5	5	5	6	6	9
In default of payment of a fine	3	3	2	2	3	3	3	2	2	2	1
Adults	**1,092**	**1,086**	**1,117**	**1,066**	**1,030**	**1,057**	**998**	**1,137**	**1,277**	**1,464**	**1,774**
Life (incl HMP and custody for life)	65	69	80	86	92	95	102	104	108	117	125
Immediate imprisonment (excl life)	1,014	1,005	1,028	969	925	950	878	1,013	1,154	1,339	1,644
In default of payment of a fine	13	12	9	11	13	12	18	20	15	8	5
Non-criminal prisoners	**4**	**6**	**6**	**4**	**6**	**5**	**31**	**29**	**24**	**28**	**25**
Held under the 1971 Immigration Act	3	5	3	3	4	3	25	23	19	22	21
Others	1	1	2	1	2	2	6	6	5	6	4

[1] The components do not always add to the totals because they have been rounded independently.

[2] For 1987, all prisoners held in police cells are assumed to be untried prisoners.

[3] Persons detained under Section 53 of the Children and Young Persons Act 1933 (excluding lifers) are included with youth custody for 1986–88 and detention in a young offender institution subsequently.

[4] Average for 9 months January–September prior to 1988 CJA.

[5] Average for 3 months October–December following 1988 CJA.

Table 1.5 Population in prison under sentence by offence, type of establishment and sex

England and Wales 30 June 1997
Males

Number of persons

Offence	All types of establishment	Remand centres	Local prisons	Training prisons		Young offender institutions		
				Open	Closed	Open	Closed	Juvenile
All offences	**46,739**	**1,292**	**12,921**	**4,044**	**22,212**	**500**	**4,438**	**1,332**
Offences with immediate custodial sentence	**46,611**	**1,284**	**12,814**	**4,040**	**22,204**	**500**	**4,437**	**1,332**
Violence against the person	**10,033**	**192**	**2,367**	**792**	**5,657**	**47**	**787**	**164**
Murder	2,872	5	395	295	2,106	–	71	–
Other homicide and attempted homicide	1,285	11	238	111	838	6	78	3
Wounding	4,454	135	1,226	294	2,090	50	526	133
Assaults	499	26	243	54	100	14	46	16
Cruelty to children	40	–	18	2	19	–	1	–
Other offences of violence against the person	883	15	247	36	504	4	65	12
Sexual offences	**4,069**	**17**	**955**	**57**	**2,891**	**–**	**133**	**16**
Buggery and indecency between males	392	–	91	3	296	–	1	1
Rape	2,080	11	409	39	1,502	–	109	10
Gross indecency with children	455	1	124	–	324	–	5	1
Other sexual offences	1,142	5	331	15	769	–	18	4
Burglary	**7,976**	**363**	**2,288**	**472**	**3,230**	**165**	**1,060**	**398**
Robbery	**6,277**	**170**	**1,090**	**181**	**3,402**	**44**	**1,061**	**329**
Theft and handling	**3,929**	**191**	**1,456**	**767**	**946**	**74**	**327**	**168**
Taking and driving away	820	81	222	37	168	43	178	91
Other thefts	2,163	89	900	474	502	22	112	64
Handling stolen goods	946	21	334	256	276	9	37	13
Fraud and forgery	**1,104**	**6**	**343**	**493**	**243**	**5**	**13**	**1**
Frauds	1,042	6	325	471	225	5	9	1
Forgery	62	–	18	22	18	–	4	–
Drugs offences	**6,483**	**86**	**1,745**	**427**	**3,944**	**17**	**244**	**20**
Other offences	**5,046**	**183**	**2,084**	**723**	**1,376**	**94**	**439**	**147**
Arson	624	18	155	18	333	2	76	22
Criminal damage	218	11	80	18	62	3	23	21
In charge or driving under the influence of drink or drugs	357	3	229	105	12	4	4	–
Other motoring offences	1,530	80	814	282	185	39	99	31
Drunkenness	36	–	23	9	3	–	1	–
Blackmail	129	–	31	17	71	1	6	3
Kidnapping	157	2	34	2	96	–	20	3
Affray	511	23	193	64	131	19	59	22
Violent disorder	217	4	45	22	88	8	33	17
Perjury/libel/pervert the course of justice	225	7	91	49	50	6	21	1
Threatening/disorderly behaviour	82	3	43	7	17	1	9	2
Breach of court order	349	21	158	27	61	9	54	10
Other	620	11	188	103	267	2	34	15
Offence not recorded	**1,694**	**76**	**486**	**128**	**515**	**27**	**373**	**89**
In default of payment of a fine	**128**	**8**	**107**	**4**	**8**	**–**	**1**	**–**

Table 1.5 Population in prison under sentence by offence, type of establishment and sex

England and Wales 30 June 1997

Females — Number of persons

Offence	All types of estab-lishment	Remand centres	Local prisons	Training prisons Open	Training prisons Closed	Young offender institutions Open	Young offender institutions Closed
All offences	**2,066**	–	**587**	**476**	**848**	**31**	**124**
Offences with immediate custodial sentence	**2,063**	–	**584**	**476**	**848**	**31**	**124**
Violence against the person	**391**	–	**114**	**68**	**172**	**9**	**28**
Murder	112	–	28	20	58	–	6
Other homicide and attempted homicide	80	–	21	14	41	–	4
Wounding	147	–	48	24	51	9	15
Assaults	21	–	10	5	5	–	1
Cruelty to children	19	–	3	3	12	–	1
Other offences of violence against the person	12	–	4	2	5	–	1
Sexual offences	**8**	–	–	–	**7**	–	**1**
Buggery and indecency between males	–	–	–	–	–	–	–
Rape	3	–	–	–	3	–	–
Gross indecency with children	2	–	–	–	2	–	–
Other sexual offences	3	–	–	–	2	–	1
Burglary	**101**	–	**35**	**22**	**32**	**1**	**11**
Robbery	**161**	–	**30**	**17**	**65**	**7**	**42**
Theft and handling	**334**	–	**122**	**110**	**84**	**5**	**13**
Taking and driving away	3	–	1	–	–	1	1
Other thefts	280	–	104	94	68	3	11
Handling stolen goods	51	–	17	16	16	1	1
Fraud and forgery	**121**	–	**32**	**65**	**24**	–	–
Frauds	117	–	30	64	23	–	–
Forgery	4	–	2	1	1	–	–
Drugs offences	**691**	–	**141**	**148**	**376**	**6**	**20**
Other offences	**190**	–	**79**	**33**	**69**	**1**	**8**
Arson	51	–	22	3	22	–	4
Criminal damage	7	–	4	–	2	–	1
In charge or driving under the influence of drink or drugs	8	–	5	1	2	–	–
Other motoring offences	20	–	9	6	4	1	–
Drunkenness	–	–	–	–	–	–	–
Blackmail	7	–	1	1	4	–	1
Kidnapping	5	–	–	2	2	–	1
Affray	7	–	4	1	2	–	–
Violent disorder	6	–	3	2	1	–	–
Perjury/libel/ pervert the course of justice	18	–	5	5	8	–	–
Threat/disorderly behaviour	3	–	2	–	–	–	1
Breach of court order	18	–	10	3	5	–	–
Other	40	–	15	8	17	–	–
Offence not recorded	**66**	–	**31**	**13**	**19**	**2**	**1**
In default of payment of a fine	**3**	–	**3**	–	–	–	–

Table 1.6 Population in prison under sentence by offence group and sex

England and Wales 30 June
Males and females

Number of persons

Offence group	1987	1988	1989	1990	1991	1992	1993	1994	1995	1996	1997
All males and females	**39,303**	**38,548**	**38,013**	**35,220**	**35,114**	**35,564**	**33,046**	**35,763**	**39,379**	**43,055**	**48,805**
All males all offences	**37,916**	**37,292**	**36,734**	**33,967**	**33,966**	**34,389**	**31,897**	**34,474**	**37,897**	**41,323**	**46,739**
Offences with immediate custodial sentence([1])	**37,318**	**36,743**	**36,274**	**33,526**	**33,569**	**34,030**	**31,375**	**33,960**	**37,407**	**41,187**	**46,611**
Violence against the person	8,037	8,586	8,449	7,477	6,945	6,893	7,273	7,715	8,491	9,230	10,033
Rape	884	1,069	1,343	1,441	1,508	1,582	1,593	1,638	1,781	1,926	2,080
Other sexual offences	1,433	1,608	1,639	1,577	1,585	1,564	1,572	1,629	1,875	2,013	1,989
Burglary	8,852	7,857	7,038	5,885	5,082	5,349	4,690	5,096	5,896	6,342	7,976
Robbery	3,764	3,915	4,151	4,052	3,990	4,174	4,856	5,090	5,264	5,591	6,277
Theft and handling	6,701	4,499	4,073	3,042	2,910	2,910	2,578	3,030	3,450	3,591	3,929
Fraud and forgery		943	937	795	791	800	826	879	1,071	1,099	1,104
Drugs offences	3,100	2,893	2,896	2,829	2,584	2,899	2,900	3,186	3,858	5,269	6,483
Other offences	3,689	4,240	4,127	3,280	3,172	3,457	3,293	3,828	4,174	4,672	5,046
Offence not recorded	858	1,133	1,621	3,148	5,002	4,402	1,794	1,869	1,547	1,454	1,694
In default of payment of a fine	**598**	**549**	**460**	**441**	**397**	**359**	**522**	**514**	**490**	**136**	**128**
All females all offences	**1,387**	**1,256**	**1,279**	**1,253**	**1,148**	**1,175**	**1,149**	**1,289**	**1,482**	**1,732**	**2,066**
Offences with immediate custodial sentence([1])	**1,359**	**1,229**	**1,255**	**1,228**	**1,136**	**1,152**	**1,125**	**1,266**	**1,456**	**1,727**	**2,063**
Violence against the person	202	247	218	201	189	184	216	277	290	355	391
Rape	3	6	7	3	1	2	1	1	2	3	3
Other sexual offences	9	9	16	8	15	8	14	11	10	9	5
Burglary	102	57	68	51	39	51	39	39	57	80	101
Robbery	83	73	82	51	46	56	77	95	108	124	161
Theft and handling	460	238	230	203	175	190	207	227	279	314	334
Fraud and forgery		75	63	50	42	53	64	65	96	119	121
Drugs offences	356	314	317	318	272	259	308	326	398	486	691
Other offences	131	170	176	212	176	158	125	132	132	164	190
Offence not recorded	13	40	78	131	181	191	74	93	84	73	66
In default of payment of a fine	**28**	**27**	**24**	**25**	**12**	**23**	**24**	**23**	**26**	**5**	**3**

([1]) Figures for particular offence groups are understated because they do not include those for which the offences were not recorded, the numbers of which were particularly high for 1990, 1991 and 1992.

Table 1.7 Population in prison under sentence[1] by length of sentence and sex

England and Wales 30 June
Males and females

Number of persons

Type of prisoner	1987	1988	1989	1990	1991	1992	1993	1994	1995	1996	1997
Males											
All offenders	**37,916**	**37,292**	**36,734**	**33,967**	**33,966**	**34,389**	**31,897**	**34,474**	**37,897**	**41,323**	**46,739**
Up to and including 3 months	2,168	1,604	1,378	1,274	1,396	1,461	1,591	1,567	1,644	1,363	1,448
Over 3 months up to 6 months	3,507	2,436	2,194	1,800	2,109	2,004	2,015	2,652	2,969	3,087	3,287
Over 6 months less than 12 months }	5,980	4,572	4,062	1,613	1,811	1,817	1,860	1,959	2,085	2,210	2,309
12 months				1,789	1,684	1,727	1,647	1,648	1,801	1,866	1,817
Over 12 months up to 18 months	4,195	4,500	3,776	3,539	3,504	3,540	2,658	2,821	3,146	3,416	3,639
Over 18 months up to 3 years	9,288	9,917	9,815	8,322	7,720	8,027	6,645	7,373	8,277	9,532	11,180
Over 3 years less than 4 years }	3,369	3,585	3,765	1,210	1,126	1,191	1,130	1,252	1,388	1,602	2,329
4 years				2,234	2,127	2,068	2,077	2,158	2,432	2,812	3,371
Over 4 years up to 5 years	2,391	2,526	2,678	2,583	2,574	2,563	2,501	2,652	3,062	3,504	4,156
Over 5 years up to 10 years	3,960	4,789	5,375	5,711	5,846	5,710	5,408	5,802	6,327	6,873	7,735
Over 10 years less than life	793	936	1,099	1,188	1,269	1,377	1,375	1,509	1,590	1,693	1,884
Life	2,265	2,427	2,592	2,704	2,800	2,904	2,990	3,081	3,176	3,365	3,584
Females											
All offenders	**1,387**	**1,256**	**1,279**	**1,253**	**1,148**	**1,175**	**1,149**	**1,289**	**1,482**	**1,732**	**2,066**
Up to and including 3 months	116	75	62	67	60	79	121	70	94	102	117
Over 3 months up to 6 months	151	113	110	97	85	77	94	139	148	171	208
Over 6 months less than 12 months }	276	175	148	82	95	71	88	101	125	166	166
12 months				88	54	74	83	82	88	116	96
Over 12 months up to 18 months	176	149	154	122	113	136	126	135	146	173	186
Over 18 months up to 3 years	319	336	314	273	214	232	201	265	315	359	476
Over 3 years less than 4 years }	115	124	123	31	29	25	21	34	42	48	73
4 years				83	78	70	52	80	86	92	135
Over 4 years up to 5 years	77	101	120	111	104	91	71	91	110	115	146
Over 5 years up to 10 years	76	97	144	187	203	202	167	158	188	230	279
Over 10 years less than life	7	10	19	21	17	22	20	23	27	36	47
Life	74	76	85	91	96	96	105	111	113	124	137

[1] Including persons imprisoned or detained in default of payment of a fine.
[2] Includes detention centre trainees up to 1988.

Table 1.8 Population in prison under sentence[1] by age and sex

England and Wales 30 June
Males and females

Age in years	1987	1988	1989	1990	1991	1992	1993	1994	1995	1996	1997
All males										Number	of persons
15–17[2]	788[2]	547[2]	445[2]	896	726	711	754	813	957	1,262	1,620
18–20[3]	8,068[3]	7,171[3]	6,121[3]	4,811	4,634	3,881	3,830	3,944	4,187	4,315	5,092
21–24	8,689	8,668	8,554	7,456	7,305	7,667	6,490	6,919	7,305	7,739	8,685
25–29	7,370	7,748	7,986	7,509	7,703	7,904	7,233	7,704	8,390	8,928	10,162
30–39	7,923	8,058	8,242	7,887	8,081	8,476	7,932	8,954	10,184	11,507	12,801
40–49	3,579	3,569	3,752	3,712	3,743	3,818	3,673	4,019	4,460	4,826	5,189
50–59	1,195	1,198	1,289	1,341	1,378	1,490	1,543	1,599	1,827	2,047	2,370
60 and over	304	333	345	355	396	442	442	522	587	699	820
All ages	**37,916**	**37,292**	**36,734**	**33,967**	**33,966**	**34,389**	**31,897**	**34,474**	**37,897**	**41,323**	**46,739**
											Percentage
15–17[2]	2.1[2]	1.5[2]	1.2[2]	2.6	2.1	2.1	2.3	2.4	2.5	3.1	3.5
18–20[3]	21.3[3]	19.2[3]	16.7[3]	14.2	13.6	11.3	12.0	11.4	11.1	10.4	10.9
21–24	22.9	23.2	23.3	22.0	21.5	22.3	20.4	20.1	19.3	18.7	18.6
25–29	19.4	20.8	21.7	22.1	22.7	23.0	22.7	22.3	22.1	21.6	21.7
30–39	20.9	21.6	22.4	23.2	23.8	24.6	24.9	26.0	26.9	27.8	27.4
40–49	9.4	9.6	10.2	10.9	11.0	11.1	11.5	11.7	11.8	11.7	11.1
50–59	3.2	3.2	3.5	3.9	4.1	4.3	4.8	4.6	4.8	5.0	5.1
60 and over	0.8	0.9	0.9	1.0	1.2	1.3	1.4	1.5	1.5	1.7	1.7
All ages	**100**	**100**	**100**	**100**	**100**	**100**	**100**	**100**	**100**	**100**	**100**
All females										Number	of persons
15–17[2]	10[2]	9[2]	14[2]	28	16	18	15	27	31	57	53
18–20[3]	200[3]	156[3]	148[3]	109	99	101	117	105	129	169	165
21–24	306	274	258	228	211	178	193	238	237	265	377
25–29	303	299	304	293	253	274	256	295	331	374	457
30–39	369	333	354	368	351	378	333	382	451	544	627
40–49	137	129	148	169	162	166	166	175	227	231	278
50–59	51	43	44	48	44	48	61	53	60	81	92
60 and over	11	13	9	10	12	12	8	14	16	11	17
All ages	**1,387**	**1,256**	**1,279**	**1,253**	**1,148**	**1,175**	**1,149**	**1,289**	**1,482**	**1,732**	**2,066**
											Percentage
15–17[2]	0.7[2]	0.7[2]	1.1[2]	2.2	1.4	1.5	1.3	2.1	2.1	3.3	2.6
18–20[3]	14.4[3]	12.4[3]	11.6[3]	8.7	8.6	8.7	10.2	8.1	8.7	9.8	8.0
21–24	22.1	21.8	20.2	18.2	18.4	15.1	16.8	18.5	16.0	15.3	18.2
25–29	21.8	23.8	23.8	23.4	22.0	23.3	22.3	22.9	22.3	21.6	22.1
30–39	26.6	26.5	27.7	29.4	30.6	32.2	29.0	29.6	30.4	31.4	30.3
40–49	9.9	10.3	11.6	13.5	14.1	14.1	14.4	13.6	15.3	13.3	13.5
50–59	3.7	3.4	3.4	3.8	3.8	4.1	5.3	4.1	4.1	4.7	4.5
60 and over	0.8	1.0	0.7	0.8	1.0	1.0	0.7	1.1	1.1	0.6	0.8
All ages	**100**	**100**	**100**	**100**	**100**	**100**	**100**	**100**	**100**	**100**	**100**

[1] Including persons committed in default of payment of a fine.
[2] 14–16 up to 1989.
[3] 17–20 up to 1989.

Table 1.9 Receptions into prison by type of custody and sex

England and Wales
Males and females   Number of persons

Type of custody	1987	1988	1989	1990	1991	1992	1993	1994	1995	1996	1997
Males											
Untried	56,515	55,009	55,708	50,431	51,997	47,501	50,918	54,157	52,347	55,545	58,092
Convicted unsentenced	17,269	16,222	16,744	19,229	18,828	20,051	28,593	32,751	30,261	32,993	33,988
Under sentence	82,355	78,087	72,912	64,550	69,080	66,630	69,312	79,251	84,342	78,390	81,949
Young offenders	27,480	24,799	20,672	17,359	18,648	16,941	15,973	17,570	18,400	17,727	18,427
Young offender institution	*	4,556	17,013	13,851	14,509	12,691	12,423	14,058	15,318	16,328	17,325
Detention centre	7,964	5,131	*	*	*	*	*	*	*	*	*
Youth custody	15,128	11,134	*	*	*	*	*	*	*	*	*
Immediate imprisonment (excl life)([1])	152	169	132	111	83	107	327	357	333	494	499
Life (incl HMP and custody for life)	39	54	39	37	27	32	36	32	29	59	66
In default of payment of a fine	4,197	3,755	3,488	3,360	4,029	4,111	3,187	3,123	2,720	846	537
Adults	54,875	53,288	52,240	47,191	50,432	49,689	53,339	61,681	65,942	60,663	63,522
Immediate imprisonment (excl life)	41,069	40,981	39,420	34,557	36,258	34,828	35,240	43,608	49,645	53,147	57,798
Life	199	181	191	180	206	190	189	181	230	268	297
In default of payment of a fine	13,607	12,126	12,629	12,454	13,968	14,671	17,910	17,892	16,067	7,248	5,427
Non-criminal	3,320	2,949	2,917	2,238	2,680	2,968	4,756	4,217	3,611	2,994	3,063
Held under the 1971 Immigration Act	1,324	1,309	1,400	893	1,185	1,221	1,773	1,593	1,776	1,810	2,051
Others	1,996	1,640	1,517	1,345	1,495	1,747	2,983	2,624	1,835	1,184	1,012
Females											
Untried	2,695	2,867	3,081	2,704	2,679	2,368	2,647	2,922	2,940	3,343	3,974
Convicted unsentenced	1,066	1,058	1,056	1,181	1,099	1,199	1,505	1,812	1,778	1,994	2,436
Under sentence	4,003	3,749	3,518	2,960	3,233	3,202	3,654	4,406	4,831	4,471	5,219
Young offenders	904	800	673	543	589	515	585	654	690	751	871
Young offender institution	*	136	483	371	401	339	406	492	544	700	830
Youth custody	696	442	*	*	*	*	*	*	*	*	*
Immediate imprisonment (excl life)([1])	3	7	7	8	4	5	8	16	17	11	18
Life (incl HMP and custody for life)	2	2	–	2	4	–	5	1	3	1	5
In default of payment of a fine	203	213	183	162	180	171	166	145	126	39	18
Adults	3,099	2,949	2,845	2,417	2,644	2,687	3,069	3,752	4,141	3,720	4,348
Immediate imprisonment (excl life)	2,378	2,214	2,147	1,724	1,839	1,800	1,916	2,435	2,879	3,288	3,978
Life	5	12	13	10	9	14	13	8	18	10	16
In default of payment of a fine	716	723	685	683	796	873	1,140	1,309	1,244	422	354
Non–criminal	79	83	104	76	111	141	317	290	178	134	141
Held under the 1971 Immigration Act	15	24	48	23	40	51	64	48	49	47	71
Others	64	59	56	53	71	90	253	242	129	87	70

([1]) Persons detained under Section 53(2) of the Children and Young Persons Act 1933.

25

Table 1.10 Receptions and population under sentence in prison by court sentencing

England and Wales
Males and females

Number of persons

Court sentencing(1)	1987(2)	1988(2)	1989(2)	1990(2)	1991(2)	1992(2)	1993	1994	1995	1996	1997
Receptions											
All receptions	**86,358**	**81,836**	**76,430**	**67,510**	**72,313**	**69,832**	**72,996**	**83,657**	**89,173**	**82,861**	**87,168**
Crown Court	**44,187**	**44,293**	**37,643**	**34,962**	**35,293**	**32,732**	**29,189**	**31,133**	**34,996**	**40,063**	**42,424**
Young offenders	13,375	12,855	9,766	9,116	8,751	7,592	6,149	6,072	6,839	8,704	9,412
Adults	30,540	31,159	27,803	25,738	26,280	24,865	22,892	24,971	28,070	31,300	32,961
In default of payment of a fine	272	279	74	108	262	275	148	90	87	59	51
Magistrates' courts	**41,998**	**37,399**	**38,745**	**32,488**	**36,923**	**36,962**	**43,625**	**52,339**	**53,981**	**42,628**	**44,509**
Young offenders	10,581	8,758	7,901	5,258	6,268	5,568	7,038	8,864	9,380	8,870	9,301
Adults	13,013	12,141	13,947	10,712	11,989	11,899	14,396	21,133	24,566	25,286	28,945
In default of payment of a fine	18,404	16,500	16,897	16,518	18,666	19,495	22,191	22,342	20,035	8,472	6,263
Other courts	**173**	**144**	**42**	**60**	**97**	**138**	**152**	**185**	**196**	**170**	**235**
Young offenders	28	18	7	6	9	14	18	20	25	19	30
Adults	98	88	21	21	43	68	70	128	136	127	183
In default of payment of a fine	47	38	14	33	45	56	64	37	35	24	22
Population at 30 June											
Total population	**39,303**	**38,548**	**38,013**	**35,220**	**35,114**	**35,564**	**33,046**	**35,763**	**39,379**	**43,055**	**48,805**
Crown Court	**33,458**	**33,787**	**34,087**	**31,412**	**31,115**	**30,835**	**29,372**	**31,001**	**34,613**	**37,975**	**43,437**
Young offenders	7,135	6,758	5,788	5,109	4,535	4,151	3,851	3,829	4,539	5,220	6,496
Adults	26,303	27,001	28,273	26,275	26,565	26,667	25,500	27,163	30,057	32,747	36,931
In default of payment of a fine	20	28	26	28	15	17	21	9	17	8	10
Magistrates' courts	**5,268**	**3,716**	**3,219**	**2,271**	**2,437**	**3,114**	**3,504**	**4,603**	**4,534**	**4,858**	**5,084**
Young offenders	2,180	1,368	1,113	662	719	937	1,124	1,363	1,208	1,319	1,370
Adults	2,514	1,866	1,719	1,369	1,506	1,941	1,930	2,775	2,917	3,437	3,634
In default of payment of a fine	574	482	387	240	212	236	450	465	409	102	80
Other courts	**121**	**105**	**115**	**90**	**12**	**14**	**21**	**21**	**23**	**12**	**49**
Young offenders	14	10	9	8	2	5	2	3	3	2	19
Adults	106	95	104	81	8	8	15	17	20	10	30
In default of payment of a fine	1	—	2	1	2	1	4	1	–	—	—
Not recorded	**456**	**940**	**592**	**1,447**	**1,550**	**1,601**	**149**	**138**	**209**	**210**	**235**
Young offenders	87	182	166	504	445	397	3	7	17	59	49
Adults	338	692	357	746	925	1,076	75	69	102	120	145
In default of payment of a fine	31	66	69	197	180	128	71	62	90	31	41

(1) Type of court originally awarding a custodial sentence; further sentences may have been awarded at a different court.
(2) The receptions data for 1987 to 1992 include estimates for cases where the type of court is not recorded. The breakdown by type of court in 1990, 1991 and 1992 is subject to a wider margin of error than in previous years because the numbers of cases where the type of court is not recorded are particularly high.

26

Table 1.11   Fine defaulters: population, receptions and estimated average time spent in prison by sex

England and Wales
Fine defaulters   Numbers/days

	1987	1988	1989	1990	1991	1992	1993	1994	1995	1996	1997
Population at 30 June											
All fine defaulters	**626**	**576**	**484**	**466**	**409**	**382**	**546**	**537**	**516**	**141**	**131**
Males	598	549	460	441	397	359	522	514	490	136	128
Females	28	27	24	25	12	23	24	23	26	5	3
Total sentenced population	39,303	38,548	39,013	35,220	35,114	35,564	33,046	35,763	39,379	43,055	48,805
Fine defaulters as a percentage of total sentenced population	1.6	1.5	1.3	1.3	1.2	1.1	1.7	1.5	1.3	0.3	0.3
Population serving sentences of imprisonment if 6 months or less[1]	4,856	3,563	3,744	3,238	3,650	3,621	3,821	4,428	4,855	4,723	5,060
Fine defaulters as a percentage of population serving sentences of imprisonment of 6 months or less	12.9	16.2	12.9	14.4	11.2	10.5	14.3	12.1	10.6	3.0	2.6
Receptions											
All fine defaulters	**18,723**	**16,817**	**16,985**	**16,659**	**18,973**	**19,826**	**22,403**	**22,469**	**20,157**	**8,555**	**6,336**
Males	17,804	15,881	16,117	15,814	17,997	18,782	21,097	21,015	18,787	8,094	5,964
Females	919	936	868	845	976	1,044	1,306	1,454	1,370	461	372
All receptions under sentence	86,358	81,836	76,430	67,510	72,313	69,832	72,966	83,657	89,173	82,861	87,168
Fine defaulters as a percentage of all receptions under sentence	21.7	20.5	22.2	24.7	26.2	28.4	30.7	26.9	22.6	10.3	7.3
All receptions under sentence of imprisonment of 6 months or less[1]	41,446	39,391	42,209	36,813	41,245	40,509	46,240	54,503	57,318	47,507	49,408
Fine defaulters as a percentage of all receptions serving sentences of imprisonment of 6 months or less	45.2	42.7	40.2	45.3	46.0	48.9	48.4	41.2	35.2	18.0	12.8
Average time served (days)[2]											
Males	10.9	9.9	8.1	7.0	7.5	7.3[3]	7.0	7.0	7.0	7.0	7.0
Females	8.4	7.1	6.0	6.0	6.8	6.8[3]	6.0	5.0	5.0	5.0	5.0

[1] Excludes detention centre trainees; includes youth custody trainees and persons sentenced to detention in a young offender institution.
[2] Excluding those remaining in custody as fine defaulters on completion of a custodial sentence for a criminal offence.
[3] January to June.

27

Table 1.12 Receptions of fine defaulters into prison by age, offence group and sex

England and Wales
Males

Number of persons

Offence group	1987	1988	1989	1990	1991	1992	1993	1994	1995	1996	1997
All ages 18 and over(1)	**17,804**	**15,881**	**16,117**	**15,814**	**17,997**	**18,782**	**21,097**	**21,015**	**18,787**	**8,094**	**5,964**
Violence against the person	1,022	968	883	986	1,177	1,247	1,446	1,203	1,040	454	331
Sexual offences	34	44	36	40	35	29	27	13	17	11	8
Burglary/Robbery	1,465	1,223	1,155	934	1,128	1,318	1,440	1,109	879	338	232
Theft and handling	4,684	3,888	3,690	2,844	3,074	3,335	3,802	3,189	2,738	1,076	733
Fraud and forgery				53	557	598	602	548	406	179	131
Drunkenness	834	794	753	719	655	540	633	486	417	216	188
Motoring offences	5,739	4,769	4,497	4,562	5,180	6,139	8,141	7,383	6,789	2,976	2,263
Using a TV without a licence	...	...	...	...	258	405	547	487	493	238	171
Other offences	3,908	3,814	3,992	3,632	3,836	4,164	4,377	3,950	3,584	1,699	1,308
Offence not recorded	118	381	111	1,544	2,355	1,412	82	2,647	2,406	907	599
Aged under 21(1)	**4,197**	**3,755**	**3,488**	**3,360**	**4,029**	**4,111**	**3,187**	**3,123**	**2,720**	**846**	**537**
Violence against the person	291	290	216	236	276	255	231	216	184	53	34
Sexual offences	6	8	6	10	10	3	3	1	1	1	–
Burglary/Robbery	582	474	445	312	456	497	415	278	225	67	32
Theft and handling	1,192	979	867	738	923	961	752	605	457	156	76
Fraud and forgery				63	54	52	31	30	27	7	4
Drunkenness	150	153	116	87	85	62	55	49	36	24	15
Motoring offences	1,064	839	705	716	873	1,055	973	851	777	236	163
Using a TV without a licence	...	...	...	...	5	10	8	4	7	3	–
Other offences	903	949	833	868	926	850	707	584	540	169	111
Offence not recorded	9	63	300	330	421	366	12	505	466	130	102
Aged 21–29	**8,349**	**7,530**	**7,877**	**8,084**	**9,035**	**9,369**	**11,284**	**10,895**	**9,549**	**4,116**	**2,996**
Violence against the person	530	487	488	552	628	699	809	625	537	235	172
Sexual offences	17	21	15	14	15	15	8	9	6	4	5
Burglary/Robbery	674	557	547	506	527	625	767	631	508	200	147
Theft and handling	2,069	1,727	1,721	1,407	1,439	1,622	2,042	1,676	1,439	552	395
Fraud and forgery				241	251	271	284	244	168	75	54
Drunkenness	256	241	272	294	260	191	248	164	147	79	69
Motoring offences	2,979	2,535	2,402	2,498	2,753	3,187	4,516	4,005	3,576	1,569	1,163
Using a TV without a licence	...	...	...	...	106	159	188	168	164	86	61
Other offences	1,764	1,780	1,941	1,801	1,906	2,109	2,383	2,071	1,855	870	655
Offence not recorded	60	182	491	771	1,256	650	39	1,302	1,151	446	275
Aged 30 and over	**5,285**	**4,596**	**4,752**	**4,370**	**4,933**	**5,302**	**6,626**	**6,997**	**6,518**	**3,132**	**2,431**
Violence against the person	201	191	179	198	273	293	406	362	319	166	125
Sexual offences	11	15	15	16	10	11	16	3	10	6	3
Burglary/Robbery	209	192	163	116	145	196	258	200	166	71	53
Theft and handling	1,423	1,182	1,102	699	712	752	1,008	908	842	368	262
Fraud and forgery				249	252	275	287	274	211	97	73
Drunkenness	428	400	365	338	310	287	330	273	234	113	104
Motoring offences	1,696	1,395	1,390	1,348	1,554	1,897	2,652	2,527	2,436	1,171	937
Using a TV without a licence	...	...	...	...	147	236	351	315	322	149	110
Other offences	1,214	1,085	1,218	963	999	1,195	1,287	1,295	1,189	660	542
Offence not recorded	49	136	320	443	678	396	31	840	789	331	222

(1) Includes those aged 17 up to 1992.

Table 1.12   Receptions of fine defaulters into prison by age, offence group and sex

England and Wales
Females

Number of persons

Offence group	1987	1988	1989	1990	1991	1992	1993	1994	1995	1996	1997
All ages 18 and over[1]	**919**	**936**	**868**	**845**	**976**	**1,044**	**1,306**	**1,454**	**1,370**	**461**	**372**
Violence against the person	28	33	25	42	38	59	60	73	54	21	20
Sexual offences	1	4	1	1	1	1	–	–	–	1	–
Burglary/Robbery	26	29	16	22	14	15	22	21	21	8	2
Theft and handling }	241	223	175	{ 155	158	174	265	238	222	59	63
Fraud and forgery }				35	74	71	87	82	58	14	9
Drunkenness	14	17	29	27	32	27	24	17	25	5	9
Motoring offences	70	59	84	66	113	156	202	214	288	93	68
Using a TV without a licence	...	...	...	...	136	163	278	243	235	89	61
Other offences	535	246	505	441	404	456	352	444	360	136	111
Offence not recorded	4	25	33	56	142	95	16	122	107	35	29
Aged under 21[1]	**203**	**213**	**183**	**162**	**180**	**171**	**166**	**145**	**126**	**39**	**18**
Violence against the person	10	14	8	12	10	14	11	16	10	3	3
Sexual offences	–		–	–	1	–	–	–	–		
Burglary/Robbery	9	11	8	7	2	8	4	3	5	3	1
Theft and handling }	72	65	50	{ 38	49	51	57	44	30	7	7
Fraud and forgery }				3	7	5	8	8	11	2	–
Drunkenness	6	4	7	10	6	6	5	1	2	1	2
Motoring offences	13	10	10	9	17	18	20	13	20	6	1
Using a TV without a licence	...	...	...	...	8	6	15	4	9	3	–
Other offences	92	104	94	72	57	53	44	41	33	13	4
Offence not recorded	1	5	6	11	31	16	2	15	6	1	
Aged 21–29	**435**	**426**	**402**	**392**	**453**	**512**	**664**	**730**	**627**	**210**	**179**
Violence against the person	13	12	13	20	20	29	36	37	27	12	11
Sexual offences	–	2	1	1	–	1	–	–	–	–	–
Burglary/Robbery	13	11	4	9	8	3	12	14	8	2	–
Theft and handling }	98	87	77	{ 76	67	74	133	117	100	32	32
Fraud and forgery }				18	31	36	47	40	27	7	5
Drunkenness	2	10	12	9	7	9	8	10	8	–	4
Motoring offences	34	25	43	31	53	59	99	108	146	44	38
Using a TV without a licence	...	...	...	...	60	89	129	120	102	37	25
Other offences	273	263	236	208	198	249	190	222	159	55	48
Offence not recorded	2	16	16	20	69	52	10	62	50	21	16
Aged 30 and over	**281**	**297**	**283**	**291**	**343**	**361**	**476**	**579**	**617**	**212**	**175**
Violence against the person	5	7	4	10	8	16	13	20	17	6	6
Sexual offences	1	2	–	–	–	–	–	–	–	1	–
Burglary/Robbery	4	7	4	6	4	4	6	4	8	3	1
Theft and handling }	71	71	48	{ 41	42	94	75	77	92	20	24
Fraud and forgery }				14	36	30	32	34	20	5	4
Drunkenness	6	3	10	8	19	12	11	6	15	4	3
Motoring offences	23	24	31	26	43	69	83	93	122	43	29
Using a TV without a licence	...	...	...	...	68	68	134	119	124	49	36
Other offences	170	179	175	161	149	164	118	181	168	68	59
Offence not recorded	1	4	11	25	42	27	4	45	51	13	13

[1] Includes those aged 17 up to 1992.

Table 1.13   Non-criminal prisoners: population in prison by sex and type of committal

England and Wales 30 June
Non-criminal prisoners

Number of persons

Type of committal	1987	1988	1989	1990	1991	1992	1993	1994	1995	1996	1997
All males and females	**293**	**216**	**255**	**189**	**377**	**363**	**568**	**623**	**649**	**633**	**557**
All males	**288**	**211**	**254**	**186**	**368**	**361**	**539**	**599**	**628**	**606**	**538**
Committed for non payment of:											
Wife maintenance (including wife and child maintenance)	42	19	8	4	19	9	14	9	7	2	–
Child maintenance	–	1	1	3	4	6	8	4	4	1	–
Arrears under an affiliation order	4	–	1	–	1	–	1	–	2	1	–
Rates	12	12	5	3	6	6	6	2	4	1	–
Community charge/council tax	*	*	*	–	4	16	32	43	44	21	18
Other debts	–	1	3	–	3	–	3	1	3	–	1
In contempt of court	49	30	23	20	29	36	38	58	52	57	49
Persons held under the 1971 Immigration Act[1]	167	143	205	132	280	264	405	460	488	499	457
Others	3	1	1	3	–	1	6	1	2	1	1
Committal type not recorded	11	4	7	21	22	23	26	21	22	24	12
All females	**5**	**5**	**1**	**3**	**9**	**2**	**29**	**24**	**21**	**27**	**19**
Committed for non payment of:											
Child maintenance	–	–	–	–	–	–	–	–	–	–	–
Rates	–	2	–	–	–	–	2	–	–	–	–
Community charge/council tax	*	*	*	–	–	–	–	3	–	2	–
Other debts	–	–	–	–	–	–	–	–	–	–	–
In contempt of court	2	–	–	–	1	–	3	–	4	4	–
Persons held under the 1971 Immigration Act[1]	3	3	–	1	8	2	24	20	17	20	19
Others	–	–	–	–	–	–	–	–	–	–	–
Committal type not recorded	–	–	1	2	–	–	–	1	–	1	–

[1] The figures do not include persons held in detention centres controlled by the Immigration Service.

30

Table 1.14   Non-criminal prisoners: receptions into prison by sex and type of committal

England and Wales
Non-criminal prisoners   Number of persons

Type of committal	1987	1988	1989	1990	1991	1992	1993	1994	1995	1996	1997
All males and females	**3,399**	**3,032**	**3,021**	**2,314**	**2,791**	**3,109**	**5,073**	**4,507**	**3,789**	**3,128**	**3,204**
All males	**3,320**	**2,949**	**2,917**	**2,238**	**2,680**	**2,968**	**4,756**	**4,217**	**3,611**	**2,994**	**3,063**
Committed for non payment of:											
Wife maintenance (including wife and child maintenance)	516	382	271	192	240	167	207	148	79	35	14
Child maintenance	18	17	12	51	58	80	104	80	55	26	26
Arrears under an affiliation order	70	36	33	27	20	3	21	12	10	5	1
Rates	336	253	181	172	198	188	173	100	31	18	18
Community charge/council tax	*	*	*	1	104	476	1,249	1,175	727	413	327
Other debts	65	59	55	69	73	37	68	27	38	26	18
In contempt of court	924	810	798	550	584	532	716	772	680	533	540
Persons held under the 1971 Immigration Act[1]	1,324	1,309	1,400	893	1,185	1,221	1,773	1,593	1,776	1,810	2,051
Others	51	48	68	95	78	36	86	40	67	42	24
Committal type not recorded	16	35	99	188	140	228	359	270	148	86	44
All females	**79**	**83**	**104**	**76**	**111**	**141**	**317**	**290**	**178**	**134**	**141**
Committed for non payment of:											
Child maintenance	–	–	–	–	–	1	–	–	–	–	–
Rates	14	11	16	22	30	24	21	16	2	4	–
Community charge/council tax	*	*	*	–	9	28	177	188	85	46	30
Other debts	3	–	–	2	2	–	1	–	–	1	–
In contempt of court	41	43	22	16	23	22	36	24	31	31	36
Persons held under the 1971 Immigration Act	15	24	48	23	40	51	64	48	49	47	71
Others	4	4	16	8	2	4	4	2	2	2	3
Committal type not recorded	2	1	2	5	5	11	14	12	9	3	1

Table 1.15 Average population in custody and certified normal accommodation: by type of establishment

England and Wales
Males and females

Number of persons

Type of establishment	1987	1988	1989	1990	1991	1992	1993	1994	1995	1996	1997
Average population											
Population in custody	**48,963**	**49,949**	**48,610**	**45,636**	**45,897**	**45,817**	**44,566**	**48,794**	**51,047**	**55,281**	**61,114**
All establishments	**48,426**	**48,872**	**48,500**	**44,975**	**44,809**	**44,719**	**44,552**	**48,621**	**50,962**	**55,281**	**61,114**
Male establishments, of which											
Remand centres	4,077	3,992	3,079	2,299	2,304	2,678	3,172	3,202	2,697	3,118	4,025
Local prisons	17,711	17,298	17,354	15,551	15,208	14,948	15,112	17,309	18,484	19,672	21,849
Open prisons	3,156	3,141	3,252	3,187	3,246	3,206	3,159	3,341	3,240	3,576	3,853
Closed training prisons	14,193	15,252	16,543	16,651	17,172	17,484	17,152	18,319	19,436	20,953	22,308
All young offender institutions	**7,585**	**7,160**	**6,509**	**5,690**	**5,319**	**4,840**	**4,396**	**4,640**	**5,128**	**5,701**	**6,402**
Junior detention centres	261	201(⁴)	*	*	*	*	*	*	*	*	*
Senior detention centres	607	438(⁴)	*	*	*	*	*	*	*	*	*
Open youth custody centres	1,316	1,300(⁴)	*	*	*	*	*	*	*	*	*
Closed youth custody centres	5,401	5,268(⁴)	*	*	*	*	*	*	*	*	*
Juvenile young offender institutions	*	293(⁵)	330	285	314	276	437	704	1,013	1,360	1,433
Short sentence young offender institutions	*	438(⁵)	340	296	290	303	*	*	*	*	*
Other open young offender institutions	*	1,174(⁵)	976	877	793	604	565	446	339	377	423
Other closed young offender institutions	*	5,102(⁵)	4,863	4,232	3,923	3,657	3,395	3,490	3,776	3,964	4,546
Female establishments	1,704	1,759	1,763	1,597	1,559	1,562	1,561	1,811	1,979	2,262	2,675
Certified normal accommodation (CNA) on 30 June											
All establishments	**41,994**	**44,179**	**45,427**	**42,804**	**43,875**	**46,239**	**46,646**	**48,291**	**50,239**	**53,152**	**56,329**
Male establishments of which											
Remand centres	2,794	3,388	2,809	2,133	2,117	2,994	3,268	3,341	2,992	3,041	3,754
Local prisons	11,625	11,237	12,347	11,460	11,706	12,571	12,938	14,762	16,041	16,359	17,549
Open prisons	3,481	3,312	3,700	3,496	3,434	3,674	3,581	3,745	3,682	3,834	4,068
Closed training prisons	13,896	16,090	17,086	17,073	18,602	19,487	19,210	19,206	20,314	21,929	22,007
All young offender institutions	**8,560**	**8,303**	**7,626**	**6,869**	**6,240**	**5,748**	**5,867**	**5,374**	**5,150**	**5,785**	**6,258**
Junior detention centres	536	414	*	*	*	*	*	*	*	*	*
Senior detention centres	824	798	*	*	*	*	*	*	*	*	*
Open youth custody centres	1,538	1,532	*	*	*	*	*	*	*	*	*
Closed youth custody centres	5,662	5,559	*	*	*	*	*	*	*	*	*
Juvenile young offender institutions	*	(502)	409	398	378	244	486	747	842	1,088	1,202
Short sentence young offender institutions	*	(694)	570	448	384	619	*	*	*	*	*
Other open young offender institutions	*	(1,472)	1,456	1,312	1,222	833	1,138	706	450	552	548
Other closed young offender institutions	*	(5,361)	5,191	4,711	4,256	4,052	4,243	3,921	3,858	4,145	4,508
Female establishments	1,638	1,849	1,859	1,773	1,776	1,765	1,782	1,863	2,060	2,204	2,693
Excess of average population over CNA											
Population in custody	**6,969**	**5,770**	**3,183**	**2,832**	**2,022**	**(422)(³)**	**(2,080)(³)**	**503**	**808**	**2,129**	**4,785**
All establishments	**6,432**	**4,693**	**3,075**	**2,171**	**934**	**(1,520)(³)**	**(2,095)(³)**	**330**	**723**	**2,129**	**4,785**
Male establishments, of which											
Remand centres	1,283	604	270	166	187	(316)(³)	(96)(³)	(139)(³)	(295)(³)	77	271
Local prisons	6,086	6,061	5,007	4,091	3,502	2,377	2,174	2,547	2,443	3,313	4,300

(¹) CNA figures for 30 June 1989 are derived from baseline figures calculated following a special census of the Prison Service estate in March 1989 and amended to take account of changes reported by establishments each subsequent month. These may not be consistent with those previously recorded, as the revised CNA was about 500 places lower than the previous estimates. CNA was redefined in September 1992 to exclude accommodation in new establishments which is not yet operational.

(²) Figures in brackets show the certified normal accommodation on 31 December 1988.

(³) Excess of CNA over average population.

(⁴) Average 9 months January–September prior to 1988 CJA.

(⁵) Average of 3 months October–December following 1988 CJA.

Table 1.16 International prison population comparison([1])

Country	1995	1996	1997	% change 1996–97	Rate([2]) of occupancy in 1997 (per 100 places)	Rate([3]) per 100,000 population in 1997
England & Wales([4])([5])	51,265	55,537	61,940	12	109	120
Northern Ireland	1,740	1,640	1,581	–4	..	95
Scotland([6])	5,626	5,862	6,082	4	104	119
Austria	6,180	6,778	6,946	2	86([7])	86
Belgium([6])	7,693	7,935	8,522	7	112([7])	84
Czech Republic([9])	19,508	20,860	21,560	3	114	209
Denmark	3,421	3,194	3,170	–1	91	60
Finland	3,092	3,248	2,974	–8	79	58
France([10])	53,178	54,014	54,442	1	109	90
Germany	68,408	71,047	..	4([8])	95([7])	87([7])
Greece	5,831	5,270	5,577	6	129	53
Hungary	12,455	12,763	13,405	5	123	132
Ireland (Eire)	2,032	2,139	2,424	13	102	67
Italy	49,102	48,747	50,197	3	100	87
Netherlands	10,329	11,931	11,770	–1	96	75
Norway	2,605	2,558	..	–2([8])	84([7])	58([7])
Poland	65,819	57,320	57,424	0	89	149
Portugal	11,829	13,743	14,167	3	132	142
Russia([9])	1,017,372	1,051,515	1,009,863	–4	103	687
Spain([9])	44,956	42,105	..	–6([8])	..	106([7])
Sweden	6,285	5,757	5,181	–10	80	59
Switzerland	5,655	6,047	5,980	–1	89	84
Australia([6])	16,142	16,922	17,667	4	..	96
Canada([11])	33,759	33,785	34,166	1	–	114
Japan([9])	46,535	48,395	50,600	5	79	40
New Zealand([12])	4,685	4,983	5,152	3	96	137
USA([13])	1,585,589	1,630,940	1,725,842	6	..	645

([1]) At 1 September.
([2]) Rate of occupancy: number of prisoners including pre-trial detainees in relation to the number of places available.
([3]) Based on estimates of national population.
([4]) At 31 August.
([5]) Includes prisoners held in police cells.
([6]) Average daily population.
([7]) In 1996.
([8]) 1995–96.
([9]) At 31 December.
([10]) Metropolitan and overseas departments.
([11]) Annual average by financial year.
([12]) Annual averages.
([13]) At 30 June.
Source: Mainly statistical contacts in each country.

CHAPTER 2

REMAND PRISONERS

Key points

- Receptions of remand prisoners increased by 7.2 per cent between 1996 and 1997. Receptions for almost all offence categories increased, particularly those for drug offences which rose by just over 14 per cent and sexual offences which rose by just over 12 per cent.

- The average remand population in 1997 was 12,100, over 500 higher than in 1996. Females accounted for 4.9 per cent of the average remand population, continuing the gradual rise seen since 1993.

- Untried prisoners accounted for 70 per cent of the remand population in 1997, similar to the proportions in each year since 1994.

- The average time spent in custody in 1997 by both male and female untried prisoners was at the lowest levels seen during the last decade, 51 and 36 days respectively.

- An average of 3,700 remand prisoners were convicted, awaiting sentence in 1997, a rise of 400 from 1996.

- The total number of convicted unsentenced receptions during 1997 was at an all-time high of 36,400, 4 per cent higher than the previous high in 1996. Within this rise, the number of females received increased by 22 per cent compared to an increase of 3 per cent in the number of males received.

- Of male prisoners received on remand, 46 per cent were subsequently received with a custodial sentence in 1997; for females the proportion was 31 per cent. Around 23 per cent of males and females remanded in custody were acquitted, or the proceedings were terminated early.

Population (Table 2.1)

2.1   The average remand population in 1997 was 12,100, over 500 higher than in 1996 but over 200 lower than the record high in 1994. Females accounted for 4.9 per cent of the average remand population, continuing the gradual rise seen since 1993 when females accounted for 3.7 per cent.

2.2   The average population of untried prisoners was 8,550 in 1997, accounting for 70 per cent of the remand population. This proportion was similar to those in each year since 1994, but a fall from 80 per cent in 1992. The percentage of untried prisoners who were involved in proceedings at magistrates' courts has increased from 50 per cent in 1995 to nearly 56 per cent in 1997.

2.3   An average of 3,700 remand prisoners were convicted, awaiting sentence in 1997, a rise of 400 from 1996. Of the 3,700, 6 per cent were females.

2.4   As in 1996, no remand prisoners were accommodated in police cells to allay overcrowding in 1997; females have not been accommodated in police cells since 1992.

2.5   The average age of the remand population on 30 June 1997 was 28 years. Just under 25 per cent of remand prisoners were aged under 21 in 1997, similar to the proportion in 1995 and 1996. Further details of young remand prisoners are given in Chapter 3.

Figure 2.1

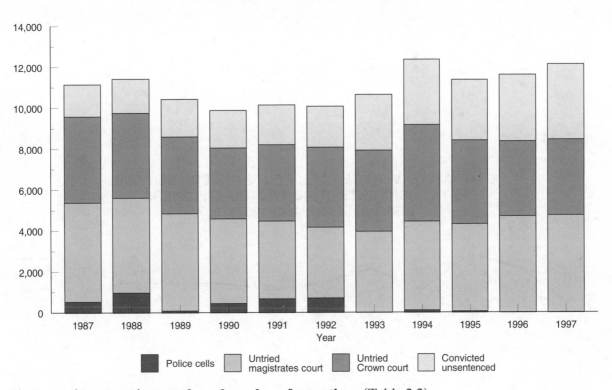

AVERAGE POPULATION OF REMAND PRISONERS BY TYPE OF COMMITTAL, 1987–1997

Average time spent in custody and number of receptions (Table 2.2)

2.6   The average time spent in custody in 1997 by both male and female untried prisoners was at the lowest levels seen during the last decade, 51 and 36 days respectively. The average population of untried males rose by less than 1 per cent over the year, but the number of male receptions—at 58,100—rose by 4.6 per cent. Female receptions rose by 18.9 per cent.

2.7   Convicted unsentenced males spent an average of 37 days in custody in 1997; a rise from the average of 33-34 days in the previous five years. Females spent an average of 30 days in custody.

2.8   The total number of convicted unsentenced receptions during 1997 was at an all-time high of 36,400, 4 per cent higher than the previous high in 1996. Within this rise, the number of females received increased by 22 per cent compared to an increase of 3 per cent in the number of males received.

Figure 2.2

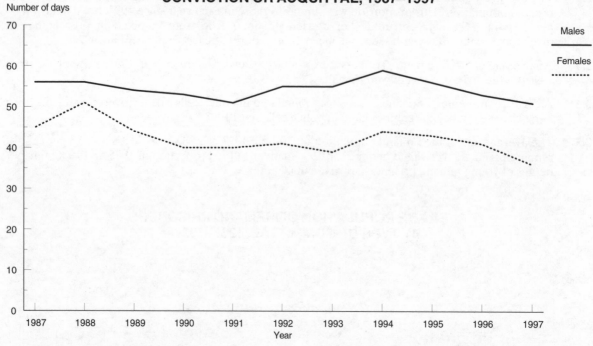

ESTIMATED AVERAGE TIME SPENT IN PRISON SERVICE
ESTABLISHMENTS BY UNTRIED PRISONERS BEFORE
CONVICTION OR ACQUITTAL, 1987–1997

Figure 2.3

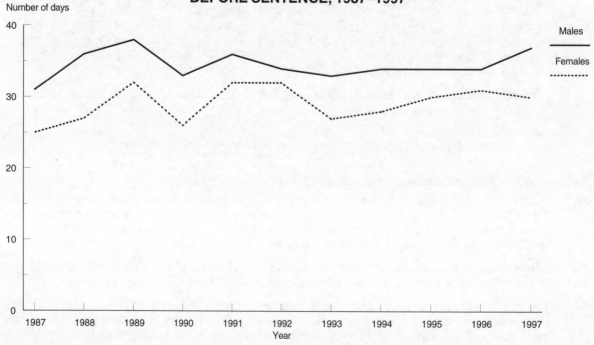

ESTIMATED AVERAGE TIME SPENT IN PRISON SERVICE
ESTABLISHMENTS BY CONVICTED PRISONERS
BEFORE SENTENCE, 1987–1997

Length of time since first reception as remand prisoner (Tables 2.3, 2.4, 2.5)

2.9   The untried population on 30 June 1997 (8,550) included 1,050 prisoners who were first received as a remand prisoner more than 6 months previously; this represented 12 per cent of the total untried population, compared to 14 per cent on 30 June 1996. 1,400 untried prisoners were first received between 3 and 6 months earlier—100 less than in 1996 and 650 less than in 1994.

2.10   For convicted unsentenced prisoners, the length of time since first remand into a Prison Service establishment in 1997 was similar to 1996. Almost 35 per cent had first been remanded in custody up to one month earlier and a further 48 per cent between one and six months earlier.

Remand disposals (Table 2.6, provisional data)

2.11   Of males received on remand, 46 per cent subsequently received a custodial sentence in 1997; for females the proportion was 31 per cent. These proportions are similar to those recorded in 1995 and 1996 for male prisoners, but show a small fall of one percentage point in both 1996 and 1997 for female prisoners.

2.12   Around 23 per cent of males and females remanded in custody were acquitted, or the proceedings were terminated early, a small fall of one percentage point on 1996. A further 15 per cent of males and 23 per cent of females received a community sentence.

Persons received with a custodial sentence previously remanded in custody (Table 2.7)

2.13   Of those received under a custodial sentence, 51 per cent of males and 38 per cent of females had previously been remanded in custody. Prisoners with longer sentences were more likely to have been remanded in custody; 89 per cent of males sentenced to over four years were known to have been previously remanded in custody compared to 33 per cent of those sentenced to three months or less.

2.14   The percentage previously remanded in custody also depends on the offence committed; 81 per cent of males sentenced for robbery offences and 76 per cent sentenced for burglary offences were previously received on remand, compared with 34 per cent of those sentenced for fraud and forgery.

Remand population and receptions by offence (Tables 2.8 and 2.9)

2.15   The remand population, at 12,100, increased by 4.6 per cent over the year to 30 June 1997. Within this increase, recorded sexual offences rose by 17 per cent and recorded drug offences by 15 per cent. The only category where the proportion committed fell was where the offence was not recorded on the Prison Service's computer system. This would have resulted in increases in the numbers included in the other offence categories.

2.16   Just under 21 per cent of the male remand population on 30 June 1997 were held for burglary offences and 18 per cent for violence. Burglary offences only accounted for 5 per cent of the female remand population, whereas 22 per cent of females were being held for theft and handling and 21 per cent for drug offences. Figure 2.4 shows the *untried* population breakdown by gender.

Figure 2.4

POPULATION OF UNTRIED PRISONERS
BY OFFENCE AND SEX, 30 JUNE 1997

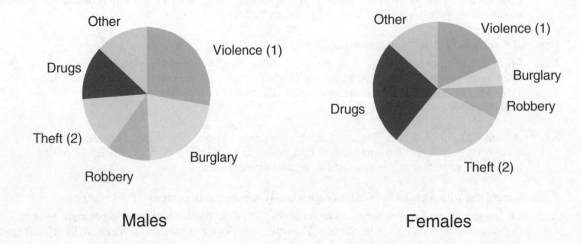

Males

Females

(1) Including sexual offences

(2) Theft, handling, fraud & forgery

2.17   Receptions of remand prisoners increased by 7.2 per cent between 1996 and 1997. Within this increase, receptions for all offence categories apart from robbery increased. In particular, drug offences rose by just over 14 per cent and sexual offences by just over 12 per cent.

2.18   Over 26 per cent of male remand receptions in 1997 were for theft and fraud, compared to just under 47 per cent of female receptions. Burglary offences made up 18 per cent of male receptions but under 6 per cent of female receptions. Figure 2.5 highlights these differences.

Figure 2.5

**RECEPTIONS OF UNTRIED PRISONERS
BY OFFENCE AND SEX, 1997**

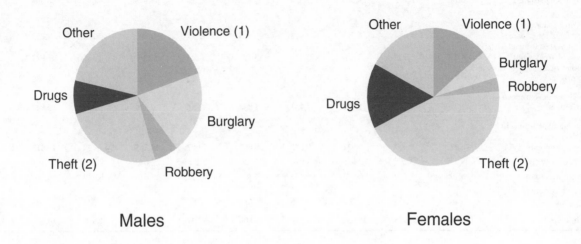

Males   Females

(1) Including sexual offences

(2) Theft, handling, fraud & forgery

2.19 Violent, robbery and drug offences accounted for a greater proportion of the remand population than of receptions; this indicates that remand prisoners held for these offences spend relatively longer in custody. However, theft and fraud offences are a greater proportion of receptions than of the population.

Waiting times at magistrates' courts (Tables 2.1 and 2.10)

2.20 In 1997, 6 per cent of defendants proceeded against for indictable offences in magistrates' courts were remanded in custody throughout the proceedings, ie. from first listing to completion; they spent an average of 7 weeks in custody. A further 6 per cent were remanded in custody for part of the period spending on average 5 weeks in custody. The majority (65 per cent) were remanded on bail only.

2.21 In 1997, defendants who were remanded in custody throughout the proceedings, had an average first listing to completion time of 51 days, compared to 53 days in 1996. The average time for all defendants in indictable cases was 60 days with an average of 2.6 adjournments—unchanged from 1996 and 1995.

2.22 Defendants remanded in custody for magistrates' court proceedings in 1997 accounted for a prison population of 4,700 untried inmates, and a proportion of the 3,700 convicted but unsentenced inmates.

Waiting times at the Crown Court (Tables 2.11 and 2.12)

2.23 The number of cases outstanding at the Crown Court rose by 900 during 1997 to 25,900, after falling by over 30 per cent during 1995. Of these cases, 6,300 (24 per cent) involved defendants who were remanded in custody, a fall of 200 on the previous year. Around 90,100 cases were disposed of during the year, 6,800 more than in 1996 and the largest number since 1992.

2.24 The average time between committal and start of trial for defendants remanded in custody was 8.7 weeks in 1997; a reduction of almost one week over the year and of almost five weeks since the 1994 high.

Table 2.1   Average population of remand prisoners in custody: by type of committal, age and sex

England and Wales
Males and females   Number of persons

Type of prisoner	1987	1988	1989	1990	1991	1992	1993	1994	1995	1996	1997
Males											
All untried prisoners	**8,743**	**8,395**	**8,204**	**7,324**	**7,253**	**7,122**	**7,675**	**8,696**	**8,008**	**8,004**	**8,057**
Involved in proceedings at Magistrates' courts	4,695	4,449	4,555	3,973	3,655	3,337	3,806	4,125	4,053	4,459	4,502
Committed for trial to the Crown Court	4,039	3,935	3,580	3,331	3,592	3,774	3,839	4,536	3,922	3,506	3,521
Other untried prisoners	9	11	68	21	8	12	31	36	33	39	34
Convicted unsentenced prisoners	**1,479**	**1,583**	**1,727**	**1,731**	**1,834**	**1,885**	**2,590**	**3,042**	**2,807**	**3,071**	**3,475**
All remand prisoners in Prison Service establishments	**10,222**	**9,977**	**9,931**	**9,055**	**9,087**	**9,007**	**10,265**	**11,738**	**10,815**	**11,075**	**11,532**
Aged 14–20(¹)	3,322	3,199	3,056	2,816	2,730	2,486	2,649	2,919	2,701	2,848	2,879
Aged 21 and over	6,900	6,779	6,875	6,239	6,357	6,521	7,616	8,819	8,114	8,227	8,653
Remand prisoners in police cells(²)	469	955	100	465	681	700	14	129	68	–	–
All in custody	**10,691**	**10,933**	**10,031**	**9,521**	**9,800**	**9,707**	**10,279**	**11,867**	**10,884**	**11,075**	**11,532**
Females											
All untried prisoners	**331**	**403**	**372**	**300**	**291**	**264**	**285**	**350**	**344**	**371**	**396**
Involved in proceedings at Magistrates' courts	165	194	197	167	150	126	152	172	170	204	224
Committed for trial to the Crown Court	165	209	175	133	141	136	127	170	163	148	165
Other untried prisoners	–	–	–	–	–	2	6	8	10	19	7
Convicted unsentenced prisoners	**72**	**77**	**93**	**84**	**96**	**104**	**110**	**139**	**147**	**167**	**203**
All remand prisoners in Prison Service establishments	**402**	**480**	**465**	**384**	**387**	**368**	**395**	**490**	**491**	**538**	**599**
Aged 14–20(¹)	83	80	94	79	79	65	67	74	88	93	99
Aged 21 and over	319	400	371	305	308	303	327	416	403	445	500
Remand prisoners in police cells(²)	68	27	3	–	2	15	–	–	–	–	–
All in custody	**471**	**507**	**468**	**384**	**389**	**383**	**395**	**490**	**491**	**538**	**599**

(¹) 14 year olds have not been held in custody since October 1993.
(²) Estimated. Up to 1987 all prisoners in police cells are assumed to be remand prisoners.

Table 2.2 Untried and convicted unsentenced prisoners in prison: average population, receptions and estimated average time spent in custody

England and Wales
Males and females   Number of persons/days

Type of prisoner	1987	1988	1989	1990	1991	1992	1993	1994	1995	1996	1997
Untried prisoners											
Males											
Average population	8,743	8,395	8,204	7,324	7,253	7,122	7,675	8,696	8,008	8,004	8,057
Receptions	56,515	55,009	55,708	50,431	51,997	47,501	50,918	54,157	52,347	55,545	58,092
Average number of days in custody[1]	56	56	54	53	51	55	55	59	56	53	51
Females											
Average population	331	403	372	300	291	264	285	351	344	371	396
Receptions	2,695	2,867	3,081	2,704	2,679	2,368	2,647	2,922	2,940	3,343	3,974
Average number of days in custody[1][3]	45	51	44	40	40	41	39	44	43	41	36
Convicted unsentenced prisoners											
Males											
Average population	1,479	1,583	1,727	1,731	1,834	1,885	2,590	3,042	2,807	3,071	3,475
Receptions	17,269	16,222	16,744	19,229	18,828	20,051	28,593	32,751	30,261	32,993	33,988
Average number of days in custody[2]	31	36	38	33	36	34	33	34	34	34	37
Females											
Average population	72	77	93	84	96	104	110	139	147	167	203
Receptions	1,066	1,058	1,056	1,181	1,099	1,199	1,505	1,812	1,778	1,994	2,436
Average number of days in custody[2][3]	25	27	32	26	32	32	27	28	30	31	30

[1] Time spent in Prison Service establishments before conviction, acquittal etc.
[2] Time spent in Prison Service establishments after conviction.
[3] Averages are subject to wide variation because of the small population on which they are based.

41

Table 2.3 Untried prisoners in prison by length of time since first reception([1])

England and Wales 30 June
Males and females   Number of persons([2])

Length of time since first remand into a Prison Service establishment	1987	1988	1989	1990	1991	1992	1993	1994	1995	1996	1997
All lengths	**9,150**	**9,000**	**8,300**	**7,300**	**7,400**	**7,550**	**7,850**	**9,200**	**7,950**	**8,450**	**8,550**
Less than 1 week	850	700	800	700	900	700	750	700	600	950	700
1 week	150	150	50	–	10	100	100	100	100	–	200
More than 1 week up to and including one month	2,000	2,000	1,800	1,600	1,700	1,500	1,800	1,850	1,900	1,900	2,000
More than 1 month up to and including 3 months	3,250	3,300	2,900	2,300	2,400	2,700	2,600	3,000	2,400	2,900	3,200
More than 3 months up to and including 6 months	2,000	1,950	1,800	1,700	1,450	1,500	1,700	2,050	1,650	1,500	1,400
More than 6 months up to and including 12 months	750	900	850	900	800	900	800	1,250	1,050	950	850
More than 12 months	100	100	100	100	100	100	150	250	250	250	200

([1]) Time since first reception on remand into a Prison Service establishment. This includes any intervening time spent on bail, but excludes time spent in police cells beforehand.
([2]) Rounded estimates which therefore may not add to the totals.

Table 2.4 Convicted unsentenced prisoners in prison by length of time since first reception([1])

England and Wales 30 June
Males and females   Number of persons([2])

Length of time since first remand into a Prison Service establishment	1987	1988	1989	1990	1991	1992	1993	1994	1995	1996	1997
All lengths	**1,550**	**1,750**	**1,950**	**1,800**	**1,900**	**2,000**	**2,800**	**3,300**	**3,100**	**3,150**	**3,550**
Less than 1 week	100	100	150	150	150	150	200	250	250	300	250
1 week	–	50	–	–	–	– ·	50	50	50	–	100
More than 1 week up to and including one month	450	500	550	500	450	400	750	850	850	750	900
More than 1 month up to and including 3 months	400	500	500	450	550	550	600	750	700	750	850
More than 3 months up to and including 6 months	300	350	450	400	400	550	650	750	700	800	850
More than 6 months up to and including 12 months	200	250	300	350	350	400	400	650	450	450	500
More than 12 months							100	–	100	100	100

([1]) Time since first reception on remand into a Prison Service establishment. This includes any intervening time spent on bail, but excludes time spent in police cells beforehand.
([2]) Rounded estimates which therefore may not add to the totals.

Table 2.5 All remand prisoners in prison by length of time since first reception(¹)

England and Wales 30 June
Males and females   Number of persons(²)

Length of time since first remand into a Prison Service establishment	1995	1996	1997
All lengths	**11,050**	**11,600**	**12,100**
Less than 1 week	850	1,250	950
1 week	150	–	300
More than 1 week up to and including one month	2,750	2,650	2,900
More than 1 month up to and including 3 months	3,100	3,650	4,050
More than 3 months up to and including 6 months	2,350	2,300	2,250
More than 6 months up to and including 12 months	1,500	1,400	1,350
More than 12 months	350	350	300

(¹) Time since first reception on remand into a Prison Service establishment. This includes any intervening time spent on bail, but excludes time spent in police cells beforehand.
(²) Rounded estimates which therefore may not add to the totals.

Table 2.6   Final court outcome for persons remanded in custody at some stage in magistrates' court proceedings(¹)

England and Wales   *Estimated percentages*

Final court outcome(²)	Males			Females		
	1995(³)	1996	1997(⁴)	1995(³)	1996	1997(⁴)
Acquitted, etc	24	24	23	24	24	22
Convicted(⁵):	76	76	77	76	76	78
Discharge	4	4	4	7	7	7
Fine	5	5	6	7	6	7
Community sentence(⁶)	16	15	15	22	22	23
Fully suspended sentence	–	–	–	1	1	1
Immediate custody(⁷)	46	46	46	33	32	31
Total	100	100	100	100	100	100

(¹) Includes persons remanded in custody by magistrates during proceedings or on committal.
(²) Includes estimated outcome at the Crown Court for those committed for trial or sentence.
(³) Uses Crown Court (CREST) data from 1 July to 31 December 1995.
(⁴) Provisional figures
(⁵) Includes offences otherwise dealt with.
(⁵) Includes CSO, probation, supervision orders, attendance centre orders.
(⁷) Includes detention in a young offender institution and unsuspended imprisonment.

Table 2.7   Receptions into prison under an immediate custodial sentence: proportion known to have been previously remanded in custody: by sex, offence and length of sentence

England and Wales 1997
Males and females   *Percentage*

		Length of Sentence						
Offence group	All sentence lengths	Up to and including 3 months	Over 3 months up to 6 months	Over 6 months less than 12 months	12 months	Over 12 months up to 18 months	Over 18 months up to 4 years	4 years	Over 4 years (including life)
All males and females	*50*	*33*	*44*	*49*	*48*	*57*	*72*	*80*	*89*
All males	*51*	*34*	*44*	*49*	*49*	*58*	*72*	*80*	*89*
Violence against the person	49	29	38	43	47	57	72	79	92
Sexual offences	60	42	38	36	37	48	62	67	79
Burglary	76	64	65	69	70	79	89	92	96
Robbery	81	82	70	71	63	72	79	88	96
Theft and handling	59	43	59	69	69	75	86	90	96
Fraud and forgery	34	24	30	28	29	47	59	83	79
Drugs offences	63	50	39	35	45	51	69	83	94
Other offences	39	23	39	58	64	72	83	91	95
Offence not recorded	21	16	13	14	15	21	31	48	52
All females	*38*	*24*	*36*	*40*	*38*	*43*	*62*	*81*	*85*

44

Table 2.8   Population of untried and convicted unsentenced prisoners in prison by offence and sex

England and Wales 30 June
Males and females   Number of persons

	1996			1997		
Offence	Untried	Convicted Unsentenced	Total	Untried	Convicted Unsentenced	Total
Males						
All offences	**8,028**	**2,994**	**11,022**	**8,134**	**3,384**	**11,518**
Violence against the person	1,646	369	2,015	1,659	455	2,114
Sexual offences	443	91	534	522	103	625
Burglary	1,547	630	2,177	1,649	733	2,382
Robbery	839	249	1,088	858	300	1,158
Theft and handling	885	569	1,454	912	664	1,576
Fraud and forgery	149	51	200	150	52	202
Drugs offences	868	252	1,120	1,017	279	1,296
Other offences	1,052	582	1,634	1,028	622	1,650
Offence not recorded	599	201	800	339	176	515
Females						
All offences	**404**	**142**	**546**	**429**	**158**	**587**
Violence against the person	86	35	121	73	28	101
Sexual offences	2	1	3	4	–	4
Burglary	24	5	29	24	8	32
Robbery	32	6	38	34	6	40
Theft and handling	74	34	108	100	49	149
Fraud and forgery	11	4	15	18	4	22
Drugs offences	98	17	115	106	18	124
Other offences	66	31	97	56	37	93
Offence not recorded	11	9	20	14	8	22

Table 2.9   Receptions(¹) of untried and convicted unsentenced prisoners into prison by offence and sex

England and Wales
Males and females   Number of persons

Offence	1996			1997		
	Untried	Convicted Unsentenced	Total	Untried	Convicted Unsentenced	Total
Males						
All offences	**55,545**	**32,993**	**66,384**	**58,092**	**33,988**	**70,540**
Violence against the person	8,316	3,356	9,241	8,823	3,529	9,928
Sexual offences	2,162	815	2,382	2,440	772	2,677
Burglary	11,295	6,349	12,487	11,413	6,131	12,792
Robbery	3,789	1,752	3,991	3,463	1,492	3,693
Theft and handling	12,385	9,093	15,705	13,015	9,873	16,983
Fraud and forgery	1,182	608	1,433	1,290	658	1,559
Drugs offences	4,129	1,916	4,607	4,645	2,041	5,289
Other offences	11,000	8,076	14,630	12,223	8,706	16,251
Offence not recorded	1,287	1,028	1,908	780	786	1,368
Females						
All offences	**3,343**	**1,994**	**4,221**	**3,974**	**2,436**	**5,124**
Violence against the person	391	161	443	511	222	593
Sexual offences	15	5	17	22	7	23
Burglary	215	98	244	256	110	280
Robbery	141	68	159	125	58	145
Theft and handling	1,226	934	1,713	1,513	1,241	2,164
Fraud and forgery	162	104	207	184	109	236
Drugs offences	528	212	575	594	196	652
Other offences	573	339	717	660	408	859
Offence not recorded	92	73	146	109	85	172

(¹) Total receptions cannot be calculated by adding together receptions in each category, because there is double counting (see paragraph 27 of the Notes).

Table 2.10   Average time for indictable proceedings in magistrates' courts from first listing to completion and weeks in court custody

England and Wales   Days and weeks

	1989	1990	1991	1992	1993	1994	1995	1996	1997
Defendants remanded in custody throughout proceedings:									
Days from first listing to completion	51	52	49	47	51	49	51	53	51
Weeks in court custody	7	7	7	6	7	7	7	7	7
Defendants remanded in custody for part of proceedings:									
Days from first listing to completion	116	123	116	123	109	112	110	106	106
Weeks in court custody	5	4	4	4	4	5	4	5	5

Source: Time intervals for criminal proceedings in magistrates' courts October 1997.
Lord Chancellor's Department Information bulletin 1/98.

Table 2.11   Committal for trial cases dealt with by the Crown Court. Total cases outstanding and cases in custody at end December

                                                                                                                        Thousands

	1989	1990	1991	1992	1993	1994	1995	1996	1997
Cases outstanding	23.8	26.7	29.4	29.2	30.4	32.8	25.0	25.0	25.9
Of which, cases in custody	5.0	5.1	6.3	5.8	7.5	7.9	6.1	6.5	6.3
Cases disposed of during the year	101.2	100.0	102.0	100.7	85.5	87.0	89.0	83.3	90.1

Source: Court Service.

Table 2.12   Average waiting time for defendants committed for trial in custody at the Crown Court

                                                                                                                        Weeks

	1989	1990	1991	1992	1993	1994	1995	1996	1997
Waiting time	10	10	10	11[1]	12.5[1]	13.5[1]	12.4[1]	9.5[1]	8.7[1]

Source: Court Service.
[1] Figures affected by the introduction of a new recording system.

CHAPTER 3

YOUNG OFFENDERS UNDER SENTENCE

Key points

Population

- The population of young offenders under sentence, which fell by a half between 1980 and 1993, rose by nearly 60 per cent in the four years to 1997. It reached 7,949 in mid-1997.

- At mid-1997, 1,673 young offenders under sentence were aged 17 years or under and 251 were female.

Receptions

- 19,300 young offenders were received into Prison Service establishments under sentence in 1997: 1,600 more than in 1996.

- 5,600 offenders aged 17 years or under and 870 females were received in 1997.

Discharges

- The average sentence length of male young offenders discharged in 1997 was 11.3 months. It was 8.6 months for females.

- Average time served by male young offenders discharged in 1997 was 4.7 months, compared with 4.4 months in 1996.

- On average male young offenders discharged in 1997 had served 42 per cent of their sentence and females 43 per cent.

Population (Tables 3.1–3.7)

3.1   Young offenders are those given a custodial sentence when aged under 21 who have not subsequently been reclassified as adults. The treatment of young offenders has been much affected by legislative and administrative changes over the last 10 years. In October 1992, under the Criminal Justice Act 1991, 17 year olds were brought within the jurisdiction of the juvenile court (which was renamed the youth court) and the sentence of detention in young offender institutions for 14 year old males was abolished.

3.2   The 1994 Criminal Justice and Public order Act influenced the sentencing of young offenders in 1995. From 9 January 1995 the provisions of section 53 of the Children and Young Persons Act 1933 for 10 to 13 year olds were extended, but this had only a minor effect on the figures for 1995. Of greater effect was the provision of the 1994 Act which increased the maximum sentence length for 15 to 17 years from 1 to 2 years, which came into effect from 3 February 1995.

3.3   The total number of sentenced young offenders in Prison Service custody on 30 June 1997 was 7,949. This was 1,300 more than a year earlier, continuing the firm upward trend since 1993. 251 sentenced young offenders were female, the same as in 1996.

Figure 3.1

**PRISON POPULATION OF SENTENCED YOUNG OFFENDERS
ON 30 JUNE: 1987–1997: BY SEX**

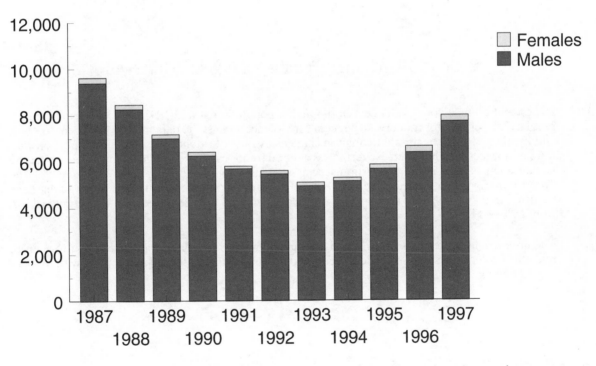

3.4   1,673 sentenced young offenders were aged 17 years or under, a rise of around a quarter over mid-1996. A further 800 of the young offenders held on remand or convicted unsentenced were 17 years or under.

Sentence length

3.5   In mid-1997 just over 40 per cent of young offenders with immediate custodial sentences were serving sentences of up to 18 months, just under a third (32 per cent) were serving sentences of 18 months to 3 years and the remaining quarter were serving sentences of longer than 3 years. Over recent years there has been an increase in the proportion of those serving over 18 months.

49

Figure 3.2

**YOUNG OFFENDER PRISON POPULATION UNDER SENTENCE
ON 30 JUNE 1997 BY SENTENCE LENGTH**

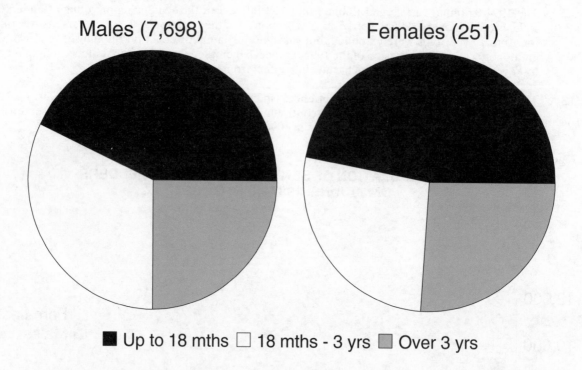

Males (7,698)   Females (251)

■ Up to 18 mths □ 18 mths - 3 yrs ■ Over 3 yrs

3.6 28 per cent of male young offenders in the prison population at mid-1997 had been sentenced for burglary, 23 per cent for robbery, 18 per cent for violence against the person and 11 per cent for theft and handling. It may be unsafe to analyse changes by type of offence because the proportion with offence not recorded has risen. Nevertheless general trends can be seen. The main increase over the last decade has been in the proportion serving sentences for robbery (up from 11% to 23%): the proportions for drugs offences have risen but still account for only 5 per cent. Falls, as for adults, have occurred in the proportions sentenced for burglary (from 38% to 28%) and theft and fraud (down from 18% to 11%).

3.7 The proportions for females, being based on small numbers vary considerably from year to year. In mid-1997 violent and sexual offenders accounted for 26% of the sentenced population, with robbery accounting for 28%.

Figure 3.3

**YOUNG OFFENDER PRISON POPULATION UNDER SENTENCE
ON 30 JUNE 1997 BY OFFENCE GROUP***

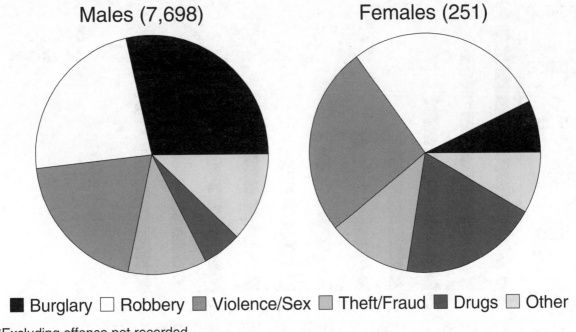

Males (7,698)   Females (251)

■ Burglary ☐ Robbery ▤ Violence/Sex ▥ Theft/Fraud ■ Drugs ☐ Other

*Excluding offence not recorded

Receptions (Tables 3.8–3.13)

3.8 In 1997 19,300 young offenders were received into Prison Service establishments under an immediate custodial sentence. This excludes fine defaulters. Nearly 5,600 were aged 17 years or under and 870 were female.

Figure 3.4

RECEPTIONS OF SENTENCED YOUNG OFFENDERS UNDER
AN IMMEDIATE CUSTODIAL SENTENCE 1987–1997

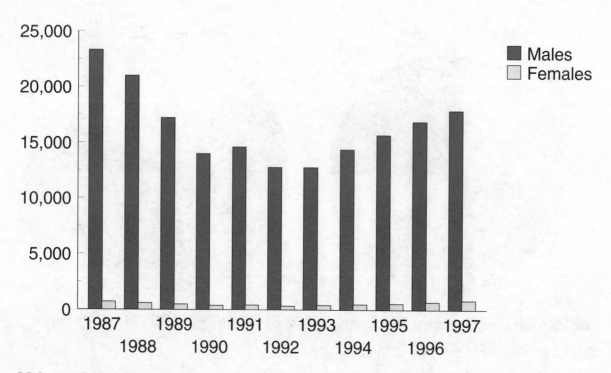

Males aged 15 to 17

3.9 Receptions of sentenced males aged 17 years or under were 5,620 in 1997. 517 males were received under Section 53(2) of the Children and Young Persons Act 1933 with sentence lengths of greater than a year for very serious offences other than murder. This was slightly up on 1996.

3.10 1,180 males aged 17 or under received in 1997 were sentenced up to 3 months; 1,560 were sentenced to over 3 and up to 6 months and 2,130 were sentenced to over 6 months, similar proportions to 1996. The average sentence length for all males aged 15 to 17 years received in 1997 was 11.6 months. This was an average rise of 0.5 months over 1996, which reflects the provisions of the Criminal Justice and Public Order Act 1994 which raised the maximum sentence length for 15 to 17 year olds to 2 years from 3 February 1995. (See paragraph 15(ii) of the Notes).

3.11 The main two offence groups of males received in 1997 aged 15 to 17 years were burglary and theft and handling (both around a quarter). Violence and robbery each accounted for around 13 per cent of all males received in 1997.

Males aged 18 to 20

3.12 Receptions of sentenced males aged 18 to 20 were 12,500 in 1997. Some 9,750 were sentenced to up to 18 months, 1,900 sentenced to over 18 months to up to 3 years and 870 were sentenced to over 3 years. Theft and handling accounted for 23 per cent of receptions of 18-20 year olds: 'other offences' (including motoring offences and criminal damage) accounted for a further quarter and burglary for 20 per cent.

Females aged 15 to 17

3.13 Receptions of sentenced females aged 15 to 17 were 250 in 1997: 94 were received with sentences of up to 3 months and 64 with sentences between 3 and 6 months. 18 were received under section 53(2) of the Children and Young persons Act 1933. The main offences were violence, robbery and theft and handling but as numbers are small any further analysis would be misleading.

Females aged 18 to 20

3.14   Receptions of sentenced females aged 18 to 20 were 600 in 1997. 510 were sentenced to up to 18 months. The main offence group for females aged 18 to 20 received in 1997 was theft and handling (27 per cent), followed by violence against the person (24 per cent) and 'other' offences including motoring offences and criminal damage (15 per cent).

Discharges (Tables 3.14–3.15)

3.15   In 1997 15,450 young offenders were discharged from Prison Service custody, excluding those with life sentences. The average sentence length of those discharged was 11.3 months for males and 8.6 months for females: the average time served under determinate sentences was 4.7 months for males, compared to 4.4 months in 1996. It was 3.7 months for females, compared to 3.6 months in 1996.

Table 3.1 Population in prison under sentence by type of custody, sex, offence group and length of sentence

England and Wales 30 June 1997
Young offenders

Number of persons

Offence group	All custody types	In default of payment of a fine	Detention in a young offender institution						
			All sentence lengths	Length of sentence					
				Up to and including 3 months	Over 3 months up to 6 months	Over 6 months less than 12 months	12 months	Over 12 months up to 18 months	Over 18 months up to 3 years
All males and females	7,949	15	7,082	324	830	682	481	977	2,325
All males	7,698	14	6,850	304	805	663	466	939	2,262
Offences with immediate custodial sentence	**7,684**	–	**6,850**	**304**	**805**	**663**	**466**	**939**	**2,262**
Violence against the person	1,254	–	1,031	51	109	72	83	118	319
Rape	126	–	65	–	1	–	–	1	7
Other sexual offences	34	–	31	3	4	4	1	5	6
Burglary	2,018	–	1,917	43	150	203	156	353	760
Robbery	1,663	–	1,366	10	32	44	47	137	572
Theft and handling	744	–	742	83	211	133	59	93	139
Fraud and forgery	26	–	26	2	4	4	1	7	6
Drugs offences	385	–	365	7	29	28	30	46	125
Other offences	860	–	822	103	242	135	53	73	148
Offence not recorded	574	–	485	2	23	40	36	106	180
In default of payment of a fine	**14**	**14**	–	–	–	–	–	–	–
All females	251	1	232	20	25	19	15	38	63
Offences with immediate custodial sentence	**250**	–	**232**	**20**	**25**	**19**	**15**	**38**	**63**
Violence against the person	61	–	51	5	8	6	4	7	9
Rape	1	–	1	–	–	–	–	–	–
Other sexual offences	–	–	–	–	–	–	–	–	–
Burglary	17	–	16	2	1	3	1	5	2
Robbery	68	–	64	1	1	1	4	12	33
Theft and handling	26	–	26	6	7	3	3	4	2
Fraud and forgery	2	–	2	–	1	–	–	–	1
Drugs offences	47	–	47	1	3	3	2	6	12
Other offences	20	–	17	5	2	3	–	2	2
Offence not recorded	8	–	8	–	2	–	1	2	2
In default of payment of a fine	**1**	**1**	–	–	–	–	–	–	–

54

Table 3.1 Population in prison under sentence by type of custody, sex, offence group and length of sentence

England and Wales 30 June 1997

Young offenders

Number of persons

| Offence group | Detention in a young offender institution | | | | | | Detained under S53 C&YP Act 1933 | | |
| | Length of sentence | | | | | | S53(1) HMP | S53(2) Life | S53(2) Determinate |
	Over 3 years less than 4 years	4 years	Over 4 years up to 5 years	Over 5 years up to 10 years	Over 10 years less than life	Custody for life			
All males and females	**376**	**357**	**371**	**338**	**21**	**30**	**63**	**16**	**743**
All males	**368**	**339**	**354**	**329**	**21**	**30**	**57**	**13**	**734**
Offences with immediate custodial sentence	**368**	**339**	**354**	**329**	**21**	**30**	**57**	**13**	**734**
Violence against the person	47	68	68	88	8	22	54	4	143
Rape	2	5	17	28	4	3	1	2	55
Other sexual offences	–	3	3	2	–	–	–	–	3
Burglary	105	71	49	25	2	–	–	2	99
Robbery	121	117	148	135	3	2	–	2	293
Theft and handling	14	2	6	2	–	–	–	–	2
Fraud and forgery	1	–	–	1	–	–	–	–	–
Drugs offences	30	30	20	19	1	–	–	2	18
Other offences	20	19	16	12	1	3	–	1	34
Offence not recorded	28	24	27	17	2	–	2	–	87
In default of payment of a fine	–	–	–	–	–	–	–	–	–
All females	**8**	**18**	**17**	**9**	**–**	**–**	**6**	**3**	**9**
Offences with immediate custodial sentence	**8**	**18**	**17**	**9**	**–**	**–**	**6**	**3**	**9**
Violence against the person	2	4	5	1	–	–	6	3	1
Rape	–	–	–	1	–	–	–	–	–
Other sexual offences	–	–	–	–	–	–	–	–	–
Burglary	2	–	–	–	–	–	–	–	1
Robbery	2	6	3	1	–	–	–	–	4
Theft and handling	–	–	–	1	–	–	–	–	–
Fraud and forgery	–	–	–	–	–	–	–	–	–
Drugs offences	2	6	7	5	–	–	–	–	–
Other offences	–	2	1	–	–	–	–	–	3
Offence not recorded	–	–	1	–	–	–	–	–	–
In default of payment of a fine	–	–	–	–	–	–	–	–	–

Table 3.2 Population of young offenders in prison by sex, age and type of custody

England and Wales 30 June 1997
Young offenders

Number of persons

Sex and age	All custody types	Type of custody				
		Detention in a young offender institution	Section 53 C&YP Act 1933 and custody for life	In default of payment of fine	Untried	Convicted unsentenced
All males and females	**10,922**	**7,082**	**852**	**15**	**1,881**	**1,092**
All males	**10,564**	**6,850**	**834**	**14**	**1,803**	**1,063**
Aged 15	254	140	40	–	46	28
Aged 16	643	354	118	–	114	57
Aged 17	1,511	713	255	–	297	246
Aged 18	2,126	1,180	236	3	453	254
Aged 19	2,547	1,738	93	4	465	247
Aged 20	2,497	1,781	52	5	428	231
Aged 21	986	944	40	2	–	–
All females	**358**	**232**	**18**	**1**	**78**	**29**
Aged 15	9	7	2	–	–	–
Aged 16	12	12	–	–	–	–
Aged 17	50	29	3	–	11	7
Aged 18	77	41	6	1	24	5
Aged 19	91	62	2	–	16	11
Aged 20	86	52	1	–	27	6
Aged 21	33	29	4	–	–	–

Table 3.3 Population of prisoners aged 17 and under held in prison under sentence by sex, offence group and type of custody

England and Wales 30 June 1997
Youths

Number of persons

Sex and offence	Type of custody		
	All custody types	Detention in a young offender institution	Section 53 C&YP Act 1933
All youths([1])	**1,673**	**1,255**	**418**
All males	**1,620**	**1,207**	**413**
Violence against the person	213	138	75
Sexual offences	40	9	31
Burglary	447	387	60
Robbery	425	263	162
Theft and handling	178	177	1
Fraud and forgery	–	–	–
Other offences	182	155	27
Offence not recorded	135	78	57
All females	**53**	**48**	**5**
Violence against the person	18	15	3
Sexual offences	–	–	–
Burglary	5	5	–
Robbery	18	17	1
Theft and handling	3	3	–
Fraud and forgery	–	–	–
Other offences	9	8	1
Offence not recorded	–	–	–

([1]) Youths are inmates aged 15, 16 or 17.

Table 3.4 Population of prisoners aged 17 and under held in prison by type of custody and sex

England and Wales 30 June
Youths   Number of persons

	1993	1994	1995	1996	1997
Male youths					
Aged 15					
Total	126	167	181	217	254
Untried	29	35	34	35	46
Convicted unsentenced	6	22	20	39	28
Detention in a young offender institution	87	101	115	129	140
Detained under Section 53 C&YP Act 1933	4	9	12	14	40
Aged 16					
Total	279	408	453	582	643
Untried	58	109	104	133	114
Convicted unsentenced	28	59	51	64	57
Detention in a young offender institution	165	217	256	309	354
Detained under Section 53 C&YP Act 1933	28	23	42	76	118
Aged 17					
Total	870	916	992	1,225	1,511
Untried	276	293	260	304	297
Convicted unsentenced	123	158	200	187	246
Detention in a young offender institution	372	335	390	580	713
Detained under Section 53 C&YP Act 1933	98	130	142	154	255
In default of payment of a fine	1	–	–	–	–
Aged 15 to 17					
Total	1,275	1,491	1,626	2,024	2,408
Untried	363	437	398	472	457
Convicted unsentenced	157	239	271	290	331
Detention in a young offender institution	624	653	761	1,018	1,207
Detained under Section 53 C&YP Act 1933	130	162	196	244	413
In default of payment of a fine	1	–	–	–	–
Female youths					
Aged 15					
Total	2	5	1	7	9
Untried	–	–	–	–	–
Convicted unsentenced	–	–	–	–	–
Detention in a young offender institution	2	4	1	7	7
Detained under Section 53 C&YP Act 1933	–	1	–	–	2
Aged 16					
Total	7	11	13	17	12
Untried	1	–	–	–	–
Convicted unsentenced	–	–	1	–	–
Detention in a young offender institution	6	10	8	16	12
Detained under Section 53 C&YP Act 1933	–	1	4	1	–
Aged 17					
Total	20	19	35	45	50
Untried	11	4	11	8	11
Convicted unsentenced	2	4	6	4	7
Detention in a young offender institution	6	11	16	32	29
Detained under Section 53 C&YP Act 1933	1	–	2	1	3
In default of payment of a fine	–	–	–	–	–
Aged 15 to 17					
Total	29	35	49	69	71
Untried	12	4	11	8	11
Convicted unsentenced	2	4	7	4	7
Detention in a young offender institution	14	25	25	55	48
Detained under Section 53 C&YP Act 1933	1	2	6	2	5
In default of payment of a fine	–	–	–	–	–

Table 3.5 Population in prison under sentence by sex and offence group

England and Wales 30 June
Young offenders

Number of persons

Offence group	1987	1988	1989	1990	1991	1992	1993	1994	1995	1996	1997
All males and females	**9,556**	**8,446**	**7,170**	**6,401**	**5,793**	**5,572**	**5,081**	**5,276**	**5,842**	**6,615**	**7,949**
All males	**9,329**	**8,263**	**6,997**	**6,247**	**5,683**	**5,443**	**4,925**	**5,137**	**5,659**	**6,363**	**7,698**
Offences with immediate custodial											
sentence	**9,197**	**8,141**	**6,910**	**6,134**	**5,592**	**5,354**	**4,830**	**5,064**	**5,587**	**6,349**	**7,684**
Violence against the person	1,695	1,719	1,344	1,019	852	715	838	846	983	1,114	1,254
Rape	134	136	157	159	123	118	91	89	89	101	126
Other sexual offences	67	78	73	58	53	43	58	40	51	51	34
Burglary	3,394	2,648	2,070	1,653	1,337	1,360	1,217	1,356	1,462	1,657	2,018
Robbery	1,044	969	978	900	791	797	854	828	978	1,245	1,663
Theft and handling }	1,597	1,182	952	650	640	524	587	641	716	697	744
Fraud and forgery }				23	26	19	10	10	16	20	26
Drugs offences	140	133	89	90	108	123	161	136	199	304	385
Other offences	960	1,068	893	629	611	640	566	606	667	715	860
Offence not recorded	166	208	354	953	1,051	1,015	448	512	426	445	574
In default of payment of a fine([1])	**132**	**122**	**87**	**113**	**91**	**79**	**95**	**73**	**72**	**14**	**14**
											Percentage([2])
Violence against the person	18.8	21.7	20.5	19.7	18.8	16.4	19.1	18.5	19.1	18.9	17.6
Rape	1.5	1.7	2.4	3.0	2.7	2.7	2.1	2.0	1.7	1.7	1.8
Other sexual offences	0.7	1.0	1.1	1.1	1.2	1.0	1.3	0.9	1.0	0.9	0.5
Burglary	37.6	33.4	31.5	31.9	29.4	31.3	28.1	29.8	28.3	28.1	28.4
Robbery	11.6	12.2	14.9	17.4	17.4	18.3	19.4	18.2	18.9	21.1	23.3
Theft and handling }	17.7	14.9	14.5	12.5	14.1	12.1	13.3	14.1	13.9	11.8	10.5
Fraud and forgery }				0.4	0.6	0.4	0.2	0.2	0.3	0.3	0.4
Drugs offences	1.5	1.7	1.4	1.7	2.4	2.8	3.7	3.0	3.9	5.1	5.4
Other offences	10.6	13.8	13.6	12.1	13.5	14.7	12.9	13.3	12.9	21.1	12.1
Total	100	100	100	100	100	100	100	100	100	100	100
All females	**227**	**183**	**173**	**154**	**110**	**139**	**156**	**139**	**183**	**252**	**251**
Offences with immediate custodial sentence	**219**	**177**	**166**	**149**	**109**	**136**	**150**	**138**	**180**	**251**	**250**
Violence against the person	37	56	38	31	19	26	38	39	39	67	61
Rape	1	1	2	–	–	–	–	–	–	1	1
Other sexual offences	–	–	–	2	1	1	1	–	3	1	–
Burglary	35	21	16	11	5	11	12	9	14	28	17
Robbery	27	25	27	20	17	19	22	23	36	45	68
Theft and handling }	69	35	35	21	9	18	18	17	22	34	26
Fraud and forgery }				1	2	1	3	–	1	2	2
Drugs offences	26	9	12	15	12	14	18	13	36	35	47
Other offences	21	24	23	24	15	15	23	24	15	28	20
Offence not recorded	3	6	13	24	29	31	15	13	14	10	8
In default of payment of a fine([1])	**8**	**6**	**7**	**5**	**1**	**3**	**6**	**1**	**3**	**1**	**1**
											Percentage([2])
Violence against the person	17.1	32.7	24.8	24.8	23.7	24.8	28.1	31.2	23.5	27.9	25.2
Rape	0.5	0.6	1.3	–	–	–	–	–	–	0.4	0.4
Other sexual offences	–	–	–	1.6	1.2	1.0	0.7	–	1.8	0.4	–
Burglary	16.2	12.3	10.5	8.8	6.2	10.5	8.9	7.2	8.4	11.7	7.0
Robbery	12.5	14.6	17.6	16.0	21.2	18.1	16.3	18.4	21.7	18.6	28.1
Theft and handling }	31.9	20.5	22.9	16.8	11.2	17.1	13.3	13.6	13.3	14.1	10.8
Fraud and forgery }				0.8	2.5	1.0	2.2	–	0.6	0.8	0.8
Drugs offences	12.0	5.3	7.8	12.0	15.0	13.3	13.3	10.4	21.7	14.5	19.4
Other offences	9.7	14.0	15.0	19.2	18.7	14.3	17.0	19.2	9.0	11.6	8.3
Total	100	100	100	100	100	100	100	100	100	100	100

([1]) Including detention in default.
([2]) Excluding offence not recorded.

58

Table 3.6 Population of male young offenders in prison under sentence by number of previous convictions([1])([2])

England and Wales 30 June
Young male offenders

| Year | All young offenders | Previous convictions not found([4]) | Percentage([3]) | | | | |
| | | | Number of previous convictions | | | | |
			Nil	1-2	3-6	7-10	11 and over
1993	4,830	4	18	22	36	14	6
1994	5,064	4	15	23	33	19	7
1995	5,587	5	18	22	29	17	9
1996	6,349	10	21	21	27	13	8

([1]) Excludes fine defaulters.

([2]) Based on a samples of 2,072, 2,069, 2,562 and 3,281 prisoners respectively in the years 1993, 1994, 1995 and 1996.

([3]) Rounded estimates which therefore may not add to 100.

([4]) From 1996 more stringent criteria for accepting a possible match to records on the Home Office Offenders Index have been applied that will have tended to increase the number of instances where previous convictions are not found.

Table 3.7   Population in prison under sentence by sex, type of custody and length of sentence

England and Wales 30 June
Young offenders

Number of persons

Sex, type of custody and length of sentence	1987	1988	1989	1990	1991	1992	1993	1994	1995	1996	1997
All males and females	**9,556**	**8,446**	**7,170**	**6,401**	**5,793**	**5,572**	**5,081**	**5,276**	**5,842**	**6,615**	**7,949**
All males	**9,329**	**8,263**	**6,997**	**6,247**	**5,683**	**5,433**	**4,925**	**5,137**	**5,659**	**6,363**	**7,698**
Detention centre	**1,086**	**665**	*	*	*	*	*	*	*	*	*
Up to and including 2 months	199	124	*	*	*	*	*	*	*	*	*
Over 2 months and up to 3 months	415	248	*	*	*	*	*	*	*	*	*
Over 3 months	472	293	*	*	*	*	*	*	*	*	*
Detention in a young offender institution/youth custody/ imprisonment/Section 53 C&YP Act 1933	**8,111**	**7,476**	**6,910**	**6,134**	**5,592**	**5,354**	**4,830**	**5,064**	**5,587**	**6,349**	**7,684**
Up to and including 3 months	52	33	327	266	318	337	304	280	270	288	304
Over 3 months up to 6 months	1,025	660	765	611	677	621	603	705	747	706	806
Over 6 months less than 12 months }	2,222	1,639	1,344	{ 517	529	479	610	660	636	615	664
12 months				624	526	482	480	433	448	499	466
Over 12 months up to 18 months	1,367	1,407	1,039	1,022	891	844	543	540	681	830	943
Over 18 months up to 3 years	2,229	2,377	2,117	1,810	1,527	1,567	1,334	1,374	1,563	1,994	2,519
Over 3 years less than 4 years }	538	565	527	{ 202	152	150	149	188	210	265	445
4 years				312	302	282	265	270	329	393	497
Over 4 years up to 5 years	271	309	313	309	276	245	224	252	250	342	475
Over 5 years up to 10 years	283	359	344	317	278	248	226	264	351	320	436
Over 10 years less than life	18	21	31	23	16	12	15	15	19	22	29
Life[1]	106	106	103	121	100	87	77	83	83	75	100
In default of payment of a fine	**132**	**122**	**87**	**113**	**91**	**79**	**95**	**73**	**72**	**14**	**14**
All females	**227**	**183**	**173**	**154**	**100**	**139**	**156**	**139**	**183**	**252**	**251**
Detention in a young offender institution/youth custody/ imprisonment/Section 53 C&YP Act 1933	**219**	**177**	**166**	**149**	**109**	**136**	**150**	**138**	**180**	**251**	**250**
Up to and including 3 months	23	11	5	4	5	8	20	14	10	21	20
Over 3 months up to 6 months	41	28	26	16	9	20	20	21	26	44	26
Over 6 months less than 12 months }	59	34	33	{ 16	12	9	16	13	20	28	19
12 months				21	7	7	16	13	15	25	15
Over 12 months up to 18 months	36	28	30	23	13	18	14	20	16	23	38
Over 18 months up to 3 years	27	42	48	42	37	45	37	22	51	60	67
Over 3 years less than 4 years }	11	10	7	{ 7	5	3	3	5	7	10	8
4 years				7	6	10	6	12	16	9	19
Over 4 years up to 5 years	8	10	8	4	4	6	4	8	8	16	19
Over 5 years up to 10 years	6	4	4	5	6	6	10	5	6	10	10
Over 10 years less than life	–	–	–	–	–	–	–	–	–	–	–
Life[1]	8	10	5	4	5	4	4	5	5	5	9
In default of payment of a fine	**8**	**6**	**7**	**5**	**1**	**3**	**6**	**1**	**3**	**1**	**1**

[1] Includes HMP, detention for life and custody for life.

60

Table 3.8 Receptions into prison under sentence: by age, sex and offence

England and Wales 1997
Young offenders   Number of persons

Offence	Immediate custodial sentence						In default of payment of a fine		
	Males			Females			Males	Females	All
	15–17	18–20	All	15–17	18–20	All			
All offences	**5,365**	**12,525**	**17,890**	**252**	**601**	**853**	**537**	**18**	**555**
Violence against the person	**715**	**1,835**	**2,550**	**83**	**147**	**230**	**34**	**3**	**37**
Murder	11	34	45	1	3	4	–	–	–
Manslaughter	9	26	35	–	2	2	–	–	–
Other homicide and attempted homicide	26	91	117	1	5	6	–	–	–
Wounding	453	1,063	1,516	51	78	129	15	–	15
Assaults	169	438	607	29	50	79	15	3	18
Cruelty to children	–	4	4	–	4	4	–	–	–
Other offences of violence against the person	47	179	226	1	5	6	4	–	4
Sexual offences	**65**	**108**	**173**	**–**	**–**	**–**	**–**	**–**	**–**
Buggery and indecency between males	1	2	3	–	–	–	–	–	–
Rape	40	47	87	–	–	–	–	–	–
Gross indecency with children	1	14	15	–	–	–	–	–	–
Other sexual offences	23	45	68	–	–	–	–	–	–
Burglary	**1,421**	**2,495**	**3,916**	**15**	**35**	**50**	**32**	**1**	**33**
Robbery	**777**	**1,019**	**1,796**	**66**	**45**	**111**	**–**	**–**	**–**
Theft & handling	**1,230**	**2,802**	**4,032**	**42**	**166**	**208**	**76**	**7**	**83**
Taking and driving away	665	1,089	1,754	2	5	7	13	–	13
Other thefts	504	1,527	2,031	39	145	184	56	7	63
Handling stolen goods	61	186	247	1	16	17	7	–	7
Fraud and forgery	**15**	**110**	**125**	**1**	**25**	**26**	**4**	**–**	**4**
Frauds	14	100	114	1	24	25	4	–	4
Forgery	1	10	11	–	1	1	–	–	–
Drugs offences	**74**	**558**	**632**	**8**	**81**	**89**	**8**	**–**	**8**
Other offences	**857**	**3,165**	**4,022**	**30**	**89**	**119**	**281**	**7**	**288**
Arson	32	77	109	2	2	4	–	–	–
Criminal damage	79	182	261	3	8	11	39	2	41
In charge or driving under the influence of drink or drugs	10	90	100	–	1	1	9	–	9
Other motoring offences	269	1,340	1,609	–	11	11	154	1	155
Drunkeness	4	21	25	–	–	–	15	2	17
Blackmail	6	13	19	–	1	1	–	–	–
Kidnapping	5	34	39	1	–	1	–	–	–
Affray	96	272	368	6	5	11	8	–	8
Violent disorder	52	119	171	–	5	5	1	–	1
Perjury/libel/pervert the course of Justice	25	103	128	–	7	7	3	–	3
Threat/disorderly behaviour	52	130	182	5	6	11	9	–	9
Breach or Court Order	157	609	766	2	25	27	24	–	24
Other	70	175	245	11	18	29	19	2	21
Offence not recorded	**211**	**433**	**644**	**7**	**13**	**20**	**102**	**–**	**102**

Table 3.9 Receptions into prison under immediate custodial sentence: by age, sex, offence group, type of custody and length of sentence

England and Wales 1997
Young offenders

Number of persons

Sex, age and offence	All custody types	All sentence lengths	Detention in a young offender institution — Length of sentence												Custody for life	S53(1) HMP	S53(2) Life	S53(2) (Determinate sentence)
			Up to and including 3 months	Over 3 months up to 6 months	Over 6 months less than 12 months	12 months	Over 12 months up to 18 months	Over 18 months up to 3 years	Over 3 years less than 4 years	4 years	Over 4 years up to 5 years	Over 5 years up to 10 years	Over 10 years less than life				
All males and females	18,743	18,155	4,641	5,049	2,175	1,273	1,749	2,407	244	224	191	188	14	32	21	18	517
All males	17,890	17,325	4,305	4,864	2,101	1,220	1,674	2,322	241	220	183	181	14	29	19	18	499
Aged 15–17	5,365	4,862	1,173	1,562	759	402	522	444	–	–	–	–	–	–	9	15	479
Violence against the person	715	628	201	191	84	38	55	59	–	–	–	–	–	–	9	2	76
Sexual offences	65	34	6	9	1	3	3	12	–	–	–	–	–	–	–	1	30
Burglary	1,421	1,347	247	386	254	145	195	120	–	–	–	–	–	–	–	2	72
Robbery	777	559	69	94	61	64	130	141	–	–	–	–	–	–	–	7	211
Theft & handling	1,230	1,208	325	485	203	79	63	53	–	–	–	–	–	–	–	–	22
Fraud and forgery	15	15	4	5	2	1	3	–	–	–	–	–	–	–	–	–	–
Drugs offences	74	61	7	24	6	8	7	9	–	–	–	–	–	–	–	1	12
Other offences	857	821	259	315	120	52	39	36	–	–	–	–	–	–	–	2	34
Offence not recorded	211	189	55	53	28	12	27	14	–	–	–	–	–	–	–	–	22
Aged 18–20	12,525	12,463	3,132	3,302	1,342	818	1,152	1,878	241	220	183	181	14	29	10	3	20
Violence against the person	1,834	1,796	450	434	191	125	162	277	36	36	34	47	4	25	10	1	2
Sexual offences	108	105	8	18	10	4	12	10	3	9	15	13	3	–	–	–	3
Burglary	2,495	2,494	359	457	306	236	387	597	63	44	29	16	–	–	–	–	1
Robbery	1,019	1,011	82	90	59	57	101	374	72	58	54	60	4	–	–	–	8
Theft & handling	2,802	2,799	828	936	373	143	207	235	26	22	18	9	2	1	–	1	1
Fraud and forgery	110	110	44	25	14	4	11	10	1	–	1	–	–	–	–	–	–
Drugs offences	558	556	77	94	58	53	59	137	16	29	14	19	–	–	–	–	2
Other offences	3,165	3,158	1,155	1,126	274	161	181	196	21	18	12	13	1	3	–	1	3
Offence not recorded	434	434	129	122	57	35	32	42	3	4	6	4	–	–	–	–	–
All females	853	830	336	185	74	53	75	85	3	4	8	7	–	3	2	–	18
Aged 15–17	252	233	94	64	20	19	18	18	–	–	–	–	–	–	1	–	18
Violence against the person	83	80	35	29	9	4	2	1	–	–	–	–	–	–	1	–	2
Sexual offences	–	–	–	–	–	–	–	–	–	–	–	–	–	–	–	–	–
Burglary	15	15	4	4	4	–	1	2	–	–	–	–	–	–	–	–	–
Robbery	66	60	15	7	4	11	12	11	–	–	–	–	–	–	–	–	6
Theft & handling	42	40	26	11	–	–	1	2	–	–	–	–	–	–	–	–	2
Fraud and forgery	1	1	1	–	–	–	–	–	–	–	–	–	–	–	–	–	–
Drugs offences	8	6	–	4	1	–	–	1	–	–	–	–	–	–	–	–	2
Other offences	30	25	10	7	2	4	1	1	–	–	–	–	–	–	–	–	5
Offence not recorded	7	6	3	2	–	–	1	–	–	–	–	–	–	–	–	–	1
Aged 18–20	601	597	242	121	54	34	57	67	3	4	8	7	–	3	1	–	–
Violence against the person	147	143	67	29	9	10	12	12	1	–	2	1	–	3	1	–	–
Sexual offences	–	–	–	–	–	–	–	–	–	–	–	–	–	–	–	–	–
Burglary	35	35	4	10	6	3	9	3	–	–	–	–	–	–	–	–	–
Robbery	45	45	4	3	3	5	10	16	2	2	–	–	–	–	–	–	–
Theft & handling	166	166	80	43	22	7	6	8	–	–	–	–	–	–	–	–	–
Fraud and forgery	25	25	15	3	2	2	1	2	–	–	–	–	–	–	–	–	–
Drugs offences	81	81	17	10	5	6	13	17	–	2	5	6	–	–	–	–	–
Other offences	89	89	49	18	7	1	5	9	–	–	–	–	–	–	–	–	–
Offence not recorded	13	13	6	5	–	–	1	–	–	–	1	–	–	–	–	–	–

Table 3.10 Receptions([1]) into prison by age, sex and type of custody

England and Wales 1997
Young offenders   Number of persons

Sex and type of custody	All young offenders	Age on sentence					
		15	16	17	18	19	20
All males and females on remand([1])	**20,455**	**677**	**1,298**	**4,650**	**4,988**	**4,606**	**4,236**
All males and females under sentence	**19,298**	**859**	**1,721**	**3,037**	**4,362**	**4,749**	**4,570**
All males on remand([1])	**19,395**	**677**	**1,293**	**4,424**	**4,703**	**4,335**	**3,963**
Untried	16,238	634	1,161	3,797	3,940	3,535	3,171
Convicted unsentenced	10,562	346	705	2,473	2,539	2,360	2,139
All males under sentence	**18,427**	**801**	**1,644**	**2,920**	**4,168**	**4,541**	**4,353**
Detention in a young offender institution	17,325	731	1,476	2,655	4,037	4,335	4,091
Custody for life	29	–	–	–	4	10	15
In default of payment of a fine	537	–	–	–	101	190	246
Section 53(1) C&YP Act 1933	19	1	5	3	7	3	–
Section 53(2) C&YP Act 1933	517	69	163	262	19	3	1
All females on remand([1])	**1,060**	**–**	**5**	**226**	**285**	**271**	**273**
Untried	811	–	3	187	218	198	205
Convicted unsentenced	533	–	4	107	142	140	140
All females under sentence	**871**	**58**	**77**	**117**	**194**	**208**	**217**
Detention in a young offender institution	830	48	73	112	193	199	205
Custody for life	3	–	–	–	–	1	2
In default of payment of a fine	18	–	–	–	1	7	10
Section 53(1) C&YP Act 1933	2	–	–	1	–	1	–
Section 53(2) C&YP Act 1933	18	10	4	4	–	–	–

([1]) Total receptions cannot be calculated by adding together receptions in each category because there is double-counting (See paragraph 27 of the Notes). However double-counting has been allowed for in the figures of receptions of prisoners under remand where the figures for "all remand" record only once a person received as an untried prisoner who is subsequently received also as a convicted unsentenced prisoner.

63

Table 3.11   Receptions into prison under an immediate custodial sentence: by age, sex and offence group

England and Wales
Male young offenders   Number of persons

Age and offence group	1987	1988	1989	1990	1991	1992	1993	1994	1995	1996	1997
All males	**23,283**	**21,044**	**17,184**	**13,999**	**14,619**	**12,830**	**12,786**	**14,447**	**15,680**	**16,881**	**17,890**
Aged under 21	**23,283**	**21,044**	**17,184**	**13,999**	**14,619**	**12,830**	**12,786**	**14,447**	**15,680**	**16,881**	**17,890**
Violence against the person	4,223	3,954	2,412	1,734	1,570	1,593	1,646	1,802	1,980	2,288	2,549
Sexual offences	262	245	231	185	174	137	155	114	165	152	173
Burglary	8,353	6,805	5,154	3,889	3,842	3,608	3,405	3,746	3,923	3,752	3,916
Robbery	1,276	1,133	1,122	1,057	941	1,024	1,039	1,047	1,247	1,681	1,796
Theft and handling	5,440	4,643	3,733	2,741	3,127	2,463	3,087	3,778	4,005	3,912	4,032
Fraud and forgery				76	80	49	70	89	80	137	125
Drugs offences	285	273	170	215	233	335	319	322	434	581	632
Other offences	3,328	3,540	3,395	2,327	2,597	2,444	2,653	3,141	3,533	3,622	4,022
Offence not recorded([1])	116	451	967	1,775	2,055	1,177	412	408	313	756	645
Aged under 18([2])	**3,825**	**3,120**	**2,131**	**3,709**	**3,621**	**3,344**	**3,564**	**3,971**	**4,505**	**5,071**	**5,365**
Violence against the person	516	523	207	350	309	385	425	424	546	665	715
Sexual offences	32	35	33	52	44	35	47	33	46	62	65
Burglary	1,683	1,312	806	1,203	1,112	1,056	1,070	1,211	1,258	1,284	1,421
Robbery	257	197	165	314	276	293	330	378	521	704	777
Theft and handling	853	615	433	761	874	726	1,004	1,192	1,268	1,219	1,230
Fraud and forgery				7	2	4	4	10	8	14	15
Drugs offences	14	20	8	22	19	36	32	26	43	63	74
Other offences	460	385	378	507	545	543	555	625	721	789	857
Offence not recorded([1])	10	33	101	493	440	266	97	72	94	271	211
Aged 18–20([3])	**19,458**	**17,924**	**15,053**	**10,290**	**10,998**	**9,486**	**9,222**	**10,476**	**11,175**	**11,810**	**12,525**
Violence against the person	3,707	3,431	2,205	1,384	1,261	1,208	1,221	1,378	1,434	1,623	1,834
Sexual offences	230	210	198	133	130	102	108	81	119	90	108
Burglary	6,670	5,493	4,348	2,686	2,730	2,552	2,335	2,535	2,665	2,468	2,495
Robbery	1,019	936	957	743	665	731	709	669	726	977	1,019
Theft and handling	4,587	4,028	3,300	1,980	2,253	1,737	2,083	2,586	2,737	2,693	2,802
Fraud and forgery				69	78	45	66	79	72	123	110
Drugs offences	271	253	162	193	214	299	287	296	391	518	558
Other offences	2,868	3,155	3,017	1,820	2,052	1,901	2,098	2,516	2,812	2,833	3,165
Offence not recorded([1])	106	418	866	1,282	1,615	911	315	336	219	485	434

([1]) See paragraph 19 of the Notes.
([2]) 14–16 up to 1989.
([3]) 17–20 up to 1989.

Table 3.11   Receptions into prison under an immediate custodial sentence: by age, sex and offence group

England and Wales
Female young offenders   Number of persons

Age and offence group	1987	1988	1989	1990	1991	1992	1993	1994	1995	1996	1997
All females	**701**	**587**	**490**	**381**	**409**	**344**	**419**	**509**	**564**	**712**	**853**
Aged under 21	**701**	**587**	**490**	**381**	**409**	**344**	**419**	**509**	**564**	**712**	**853**
Violence against the person	138	115	79	58	55	59	93	128	115	149	230
Sexual offences	1	1	1	4	3	2	–	–	4	–	–
Burglary	104	78	51	26	38	26	39	45	51	49	50
Robbery	46	59	42	38	41	32	46	58	60	86	111
Theft and handling	287	210	171	100	96	87	106	144	168	222	208
Fraud and forgery				11	11	12	16	9	23	25	26
Drugs offences	48	25	20	26	26	27	26	34	47	62	89
Other offences	75	83	99	65	51	51	68	69	76	92	119
Offence not recorded(¹)	2	16	27	53	88	48	25	22	20	27	20
Aged under 18(²)	**59**	**60**	**45**	**95**	**97**	**79**	**102**	**149**	**166**	**214**	**252**
Violence against the person	19	17	11	20	13	18	34	54	48	68	83
Sexual offences	–	–	–	–	1	–	–	–	3	–	–
Burglary	15	8	2	7	14	8	4	15	21	15	15
Robbery	6	13	9	14	18	15	22	28	28	40	66
Theft and handling	12	14	11	23	20	15	20	31	39	43	42
Fraud and forgery				–	–	2	3	–	–	2	1
Drugs offences	1	–	–	–	3	4	2	3	4	4	8
Other offences	6	7	11	13	8	6	15	13	20	31	30
Offence not recorded(¹)	–	1	1	18	20	11	2	5	3	11	7
Aged 18–20(³)	**642**	**527**	**445**	**286**	**312**	**265**	**317**	**360**	**398**	**498**	**601**
Violence against the person	119	98	68	38	42	41	59	74	67	81	147
Sexual offences	1	1	1	4	2	2	–	–	1	–	–
Burglary	89	70	49	19	24	18	35	30	30	34	35
Robbery	40	46	33	24	23	17	24	30	32	46	45
Theft and handling	275	196	160	77	76	72	86	113	129	179	166
Fraud forgery				11	11	10	13	9	23	23	25
Drugs offences	47	25	20	26	23	23	24	31	43	58	81
Other offences	69	76	88	52	43	45	53	56	56	61	89
Offence not recorded(¹)	2	15	26	35	68	37	23	17	17	16	13

(¹) See paragraph 19 of the Notes.
(²) 14–16 up to 1989.
(³) 17–20 up to 1989.

Table 3.12 Receptions into prison under an immediate custodial sentence: by sex, age, type of custody and length of sentence

England and Wales
Male young offenders

Number of persons

Sex, age, type of custody and length of sentence	1987	1988	1989	1990	1991	1992	1993	1994	1995	1996	1997
All males	**23,283**	**21,044**	**17,184**	**13,999**	**14,619**	**12,830**	**12,786**	**14,447**	**15,680**	**16,881**	**17,890**
Detained under Section 53(2) C&YP Act 1933([1])	**154**	**169**	**122**	**113**	**85**	**108**	**327**	**357**	**339**	**502**	**517**
Section 53([2]) Life	**4**	**2**	**3**	**2**	**2**	**1**	–	–	**6**	**8**	**18**
Section 53([2]) Determinate sentence	**150**	**167**	**119**	**111**	**83**	**107**	**327**	**357**	**333**	**494**	**499**
Less than 12 months	3	10	7	6	8	12	1	8	2	–	–
12 months							3	2	1	1	–
Over 12 months up to 18 months	–	–	–	–	–	–	24	14	4	5	4
Over 18 months up to 3 years	98	117	88	85	60	70	212	243	182	242	203
Over 3 years less than 4 years	24	22	14	14	10	11	10	12	38	50	61
4 years							30	38	41	79	103
Over 4 years up to 5 years	13	11	8	2	2	7	19	10	36	59	78
Over 5 years up to 10 years	11	6	–	3	2	3	28	29	29	53	43
Over 10 years less than life	1	–	1	–	–	3	–	1	–	5	7
Life	–	1	1	1	1	1	–	–	–	–	–
Aged under 21											
Detention centre	**7,964**	**5,131**	*	*	*	*	*	*	*	*	*
Detention in a young offender institution/youth custody/ imprisonment	**15,165**	**15,744**	**17,062**	**13,886**	**14,534**	**12,722**	**12,459**	**14,090**	**15,341**	**16,379**	**17,373**
Up to and including 3 months	490	1,308	3,915	2,659	3,230	2,823	2,841	3,538	3,972	3,916	4,305
Over 3 months up to 6 months	3,955	3,919	4,440	3,462	3,922	3,272	3,875	4,451	4,701	4,714	4,864
Over 6 months less than 12 months	5,123	5,004	4,069	1,909	1,896	1,722	1,841	2,135	2,221	2,145	2,101
12 months				1,576	1,465	1,344	1,178	1,166	1,185	1,201	1,220
Over 12 months up to 18 months	2,370	2,385	1,906	1,822	1,599	1,389	988	973	1,214	1,562	1,674
Over 18 months up to 3 years	2,482	2,425	2,065	1,857	1,835	1,614	1,213	1,278	1,524	2,070	2,322
Over 3 years less than 4 years	356	334	306	111	127	87	94	130	113	187	241
4 years				190	172	165	149	133	166	199	220
Over 4 years up to 5 years	179	144	169	136	132	108	121	107	128	182	183
Over 5 years up to 10 years	167	161	146	124	124	153	116	139	91	134	181
Over 10 years less than life	8	13	11	5	7	14	7	8	3	18	14
Life([2])	35	51	35	35	25	31	36	32	23	51	48

([1]) Those detained under Section 53 of the C and YP Act 1933 applied to 14–16 year olds for any offence (15–16 for females) up to 30 September 1992. Thereafter it applies to 15–17 year olds.
([2]) Includes HMP, Section 53(1), detention for life and custody for life.

66

Table 3.12 **Receptions into prison under an immediate custodial sentence: by sex, age, type of custody, and length of sentence**

England and Wales
Female young offenders   Number of persons

Sex, age, type of custody and length of sentence	1987	1988	1989	1990	1991	1992	1993	1994	1995	1996	1997
All females	**701**	**587**	**490**	**381**	**409**	**344**	**419**	**509**	**564**	**712**	**853**
Detained under Section 53(2) C&YP Act 1933(1)	**3**	**8**	**7**	**8**	**4**	**5**	**8**	**16**	**18**	**12**	**18**
Section 53(2) Life	–	–	–	–	–	–	–	–	**1**	**1**	–
Section 53(2) Determinate sentence	**3**	**8**	**7**	**8**	**4**	**5**	**8**	**16**	**17**	**11**	**18**
Up to and including 18 months	–	–	1	–	–	–	–	2	1	–	2
Over 18 months up to 3 years	3	5	6	6	4	5	8	10	11	8	8
Over 3 years up to 4 years	–	1	–	2	–	–	–	3	2	2	4
Over 4 years up to 5 years	–	1	–	–	–	–	–	–	2	–	1
Over 5 years up to 10 years	–	–	–	–	–	–	–	1	1	1	3
Over 10 years less than life	–	–	–	–	–	–	–	–	–	–	–
Life	–	1	–	–	–	–	–	–	–	–	–
Aged under 21											
Imprisonment/youth custody/ detention in a young offender institution	**698**	**579**	**483**	**373**	**405**	**339**	**411**	**493**	**546**	**700**	**835**
Up to and including 3 months	236	158	140	90	132	99	145	183	213	238	336
Over 3 months up to 6 months	214	186	144	93	85	101	109	137	142	196	185
Over 6 months less than 12 months	133	117	99	55	46	38	55	68	57	76	74
12 months				35	22	27	32	36	39	54	53
Over 12 months up to 18 months	60	50	48	47	42	32	22	26	31	48	75
Over 18 months up to 3 years	36	56	40	36	54	28	27	25	46	65	85
Over 3 years less than 4 years	9	6	6	4	1	4	4	2	2	2	3
4 years				6	7	1	5	8	4	9	4
Over 4 years up to 5 years	6	1	4	2	5	1	3	7	5	8	8
Over 5 years up to 10 years	2	4	2	3	7	7	4	–	5	4	7
Over 10 years less than life	–	–	–	–	–	1	–	–	–	–	–
Life(2)	2	1	–	2	4	–	5	1	2	–	5

(1) Those detained under Section 53 of the C and YP Act 1933 applied to 14–16 year olds for any offence (15–16 for females) up to 30 September 1992. Thereafter it applies to 15–17 year olds.

(2) Includes HMP, Section 53(1), detention for life and custody for life.

Table 3.13   Average time served in prison under sentence by prisoners discharged from determinate sentences on completion of sentence or on licence: by sex and length of sentence

England and Wales 1997
Young offenders

Length of sentence(¹)	Number of persons discharged(²)	Months			Percentage of sentence served under sentence	
		Average length of sentence	Average time served under sentence			
			Including remand time	Excluding remand time	Including remand time	Excluding remand time
Males						
Detention in a young offender institution(³)						
All lengths of sentence less than life	**14,800**	**11.3**	**6.1**	**4.7**	*53*	*42*
Up to and including 3 months	3,250	2.3	1.1	1.0	*49*	*43*
Over 3 months up to 6 months	4,050	5.0	2.6	2.1	*51*	*41*
Over 6 months less than 12 months	2,000	8.8	4.6	3.6	*53*	*42*
12 months	1,100	12.0	6.5	4.9	*54*	*41*
Over 12 months up to 18 months	1,650	16.7	9.0	6.7	*54*	*40*
Over 18 months up to 3 years	2,300	27.0	14.4	11.2	*53*	*42*
Over 3 years less than 4 years	200	41.5	24.2	17.4	*53*	*42*
4 years	120	48.0	27.5	24.1	*57*	*50*
Over 4 years less than life	100	61.3	36.6	31.5	*57*	*51*
Females						
Detention in a young offender institution(³)						
All lengths of sentence less than life	**650**	**8.6**	**4.5**	**3.7**	*52*	*43*
Up to and including 3 months	260	2.1	1.0	0.9	*47*	*41*
Over 3 months up to 6 months	170	4.8	2.4	2.2	*49*	*45*
Over 6 months less than 12 months	60	8.7	5.2	3.8	*51*	*43*
12 months	40	12.0	6.2	5.1	*52*	*43*
Over 12 months up to 18 months	50	17.2	9.2	7.5	*54*	*44*
Over 18 months less than life	70	32.9	18.0	14.3	*54*	*43*

(¹) On discharge: the sentence may change after reception if there are further charges or an appeal.

(²) Excludes discharges following recall after release on licence, non-criminals, persons committed to custody for non-payment of a fine and persons reclassified as adult prisoners. A further 142 males and 10 females died or were discharged for other reasons such as transfers to other establishments or successful appeals. Figures have been rounded to the nearest fifty except for the two longest male sentence bands and all female sentence bands where the rounding is to the nearest ten.

(³) Includes detention under Section 53(2), Children and Young Persons Act 1933.

Table 3.14 Average time served in prison under sentence(¹) by prisoners discharged(²) from determinate sentences on completion of sentence or on licence: by sex and length of sentence, 1989–97

England and Wales
Young offenders

Length of sentence(³)	1989	1990	1991	1992	1993	1994	1995	1996	1997
Males									Months
Average time served under sentence									
Youth custody/detention in a young offender institution(⁴)									
Up to and including 3 months	0.9	0.9	0.9	0.9	1.1	1.1	1.0	1.0	1.0
Over 3 months up to 6 months	2.2	2.2	2.2	2.2	2.2	2.1	2.1	2.1	2.1
Over 6 months less than 12 months	} 4.1	4.1	3.8	3.6	3.8	3.7	3.6	3.6	3.6
12 months		4.1	4.7	4.7	5.1	4.9	4.8	4.8	4.9
Over 12 months up to 18 months	6.9	6.9	7.2	7.4	7.0	6.6	6.4	6.5	6.7
Over 18 months up to 3 years	11.6	11.0	10.9	11.0	11.7	11.7	11.3	11.0	11.2
Over 3 years less than 4 years	} 20.7	17.5	17.8	18.6	18.0	19.7	18.3	17.1	17.4
4 years		23.5	22.8	22.4	21.0	23.2	24.4	22.9	24.1
Over 4 years less than life	30.8	29.1	27.1	28.1	29.4	29.4	31.6	31.1	31.5
									Percentage
Percentage of sentence served under sentence									
Youth custody/detention in a young offender institution(⁴)									
Up to and including 3 months	*43*	*43*	*43*	*43*	*44*	*44*	*44*	*44*	*43*
Over 3 months up to 6 months	*42*	*42*	*43*	*42*	*42*	*42*	*41*	*41*	*41*
Over 6 months less than 12 months	} *40*	*42*	*42*	*40*	*42*	*42*	*41*	*41*	*42*
12 months		*35*	*39*	*39*	*42*	*41*	*40*	*40*	*41*
Over 12 months up to 18 months	*42*	*42*	*44*	*43*	*42*	*39*	*39*	*39*	*40*
Over 18 months up to 3 years	*42*	*40*	*40*	*41*	*43*	*42*	*41*	*41*	*42*
Over 3 years less than 4 years	} *45*	*42*	*43*	*45*	*43*	*47*	*44*	*41*	*42*
4 years		*49*	*48*	*47*	*44*	*48*	*51*	*48*	*50*
Over 4 years less than life	*47*	*46*	*42*	*46*	*44*	*48*	*51*	*50*	*51*
Females									Months
Average time served under sentence									
Youth custody/detention in a young offender institution(⁴)									
Up to and including 3 months	0.7	0.7	0.9	0.8	1.0	1.0	0.9	0.9	0.9
Over 3 months up to 6 months	2.4	2.3	2.4	2.2	2.3	2.3	2.2	2.1	2.2
Over 6 months less than 12 months	} 4.0	4.4	4.9	4.2	4.0	3.9	3.9	3.8	3.8
12 months					5.2	5.4	4.9	5.3	5.1
Over 12 months up to 18 months	6.9	6.6	6.8	8.2	7.2	8.4	6.6	7.6	7.0
Over 18 months less than life	13.4	13.5	11.6	12.0	14.7	13.6	13.4	13.1	14.3
									Percentage
Percentage of sentence served under sentence									
Youth custody/detention in a young offender institution(⁴)									
Up to and including 3 months	*40*	*37*	*44*	*44*	*44*	*46*	*43*	*45*	*41*
Over 3 months up to 6 months	*47*	*46*	*47*	*44*	*45*	*46*	*44*	*43*	*45*
Over 6 months less than 12 months	} *40*	*44*	*46*	*42*	*45*	*44*	*44*	*44*	*43*
12 months					*44*	*45*	*41*	*44*	*43*
Over 12 months up to 18 months	*42*	*40*	*40*	*49*	*44*	*49*	*40*	*46*	*44*
Over 18 months less than life	*39*	*42*	*34*	*39*	*32*	*46*	*43*	*42*	*43*

(¹) Excluding time served on remand awaiting trial or sentence, which counts towards the discharge of sentence.

(²) Excludes discharges following recall after release on licence, non-criminals, persons committed to custody for non-payment of a fine and persons reclassified as adult prisoners.

(³) On discharge; the sentence may change after reception if there are further charges or an appeal.

(⁴) Includes imprisonment and detention under Section 53(2), Children and Young Persons Act 1933. Detention in a young offender institution from 1 October 1988.

Table 3.15 **Average sentence length of receptions into prison under an immediate custodial sentence([1]): by sex, age, type of custody and court sentencing**

England and Wales
Young offenders

Months

Year and age	Type of custody			Court sentencing([2])		
	Detention centre	Youth custody([3])	Young offender institution([3])	Crown Court	Magistrate's courts	All courts
All males						
Aged 15–17([5])						
1988 (Jan-Sept)	2.5	11.5	* }	12.9	4.1	6.2
(Oct-Dec)	*	*	7.4			
1989	*	*	5.6	9.2	4.8	5.6
1990([4])	*	*	6.2	10.5	5.0	6.2
1991([4])	*	*	6.5	12.1	4.6	6.5
1992([4])	*	*	9.2	14.8	4.6	9.2
1993	*	*	8.6	16.4	5.1	8.6
1994	*	*	8.5	16.5	5.2	8.5
1995	*	*	9.6	17.3	5.2	9.6
1996	*	*	11.1	20.0	5.5	11.1
1997	*	*	11.6	20.5	5.4	11.6
Aged 18–20([5])						
1988 (Jan-Sept)	2.6	15.5	* }	16.2	4.4	12.2
(Oct-Dec)	*	*	13.0			
1989	*	*	12.3	17.1	4.3	12.3
1990([4])	*	*	13.6	18.2	4.7	13.6
1991([4])	*	*	12.4	17.9	4.3	12.4
1992([4])	*	*	14.0	19.3	4.0	14.0
1993	*	*	12.7	19.0	4.3	12.7
1994	*	*	12.4	19.6	4.4	12.4
1995	*	*	12.7	20.9	4.1	12.7
1996	*	*	13.2	20.4	4.8	13.2
1997	*	*	13.4	21.2	4.6	13.4
All females						
Aged 15–17([5])						
1988 (Jan-Sept)	*	7.5	* }	15.2	5.0	9.5
(Oct-Dec)	*	*	15.7			
1989	*	*	5.5	6.6	4.6	5.5
1990([4])	*	*	7.2	11.8	4.5	7.2
1991([4])	*	*	7.5	12.0	4.8	7.5
1992([4])	*	*	8.1	11.4	4.2	8.1
1993	*	*	6.9	13.3	3.7	6.9
1994	*	*	8.2	14.8	4.1	8.2
1995	*	*	10.0	18.5	3.5	10.0
1996	*	*	8.3	15.1	4.3	8.3
1997	*	*	9.6	15.6	3.7	9.6
Aged 18–20([5])						
1988 (Jan-Sept)	*	9.8	* }	14.5	3.8	10.0
(Oct-Dec)	*	*	10.7			
1989	*	*	9.5	14.4	3.1	9.5
1990([4])	*	*	11.8	16.1	3.6	11.8
1991([4])	*	*	12.9	19.3	3.1	12.9
1992([4])	*	*	11.5	16.1	3.3	11.5
1993	*	*	11.0	16.8	3.8	11.0
1994	*	*	9.9	15.4	3.9	9.9
1995	*	*	10.4	16.3	3.4	10.4
1996	*	*	10.8	16.5	3.3	10.8
1997	*	*	10.3	17.4	3.1	10.3

([1]) Excluding those sentenced to life.
([2]) Type of court originally imposing the sentence; further sentences may have been awarded at a different court.
([3]) Includes persons sentenced to detention under Section 53(2), Children and Young Persons Act 1933.
([4]) Figures for 1990, 1991 and 1992 are subject to a wider margin of error than those for earlier years because of a particularly large number of cases with court not recorded; such cases are included in the "All courts" column.
([5]) The age ranges "under 17" and "18–20" up to 1990 refer to those aged 14–16 and 17–20.

CHAPTER 4

ADULT PRISONERS UNDER SENTENCE

Key points

Population

- The population of adult prisoners under sentence was 40,860 on 30 June 1997, a 12 per cent increase on 1996.

- Between mid 1993 and mid 1997 the population rose by 46 per cent.

- Males accounted for 96 per cent of the sentenced adult population, but the rate of increase for females has been much higher than for males in the last four years.

- The proportion of the adult male population serving a sentence of over 4 years has increased from 31 per cent in 1987 to 42 per cent in 1997. The proportion serving sentences of up to 12 months has decreased from 24 per cent to 17 per cent over this period.

- The distribution of sentence lengths for adult females is generally shorter than for males, but by 1997 nearly one third of the population had sentences of 4 years or more.

- In 1997 nearly a quarter of adult males for whom offence type was recorded were serving sentences for offences of violence against the person, 16 per cent for drug offences, 16 per cent for burglary and 12 per cent for robbery.

- Over a third (37 per cent) of adult females for whom offence type was recorded were serving a sentence for drug offences, 24 per cent for theft and fraud offences and 19 per cent for violence against the person.

Receptions

- Nearly 62,100 adults were received under sentence in 1997, 9 per cent higher than in 1996.

- Female receptions were up by 21 per cent in 1997.

- Receptions have risen each year since 1992 when there were under 37,000.

- The average sentence length male adults received in 1997 was 16.2 months.

- The female adult average sentence in 1997 was 12.2 months.

- Adult male receptions were not concentrated in a small group of offences whereas nearly half of females were received for theft handling, fraud and forgery offences.

- Drugs offences accounted for 17 per cent of female receptions and 10 per cent of male receptions.

Discharges

- Nearly 58,000 adults were discharged from determinate sentences in 1997.

- On average about 55 per cent of sentence was served before discharge.

Population (Tables 4.1–4.4)

4.1   There were 40,860 sentenced adults in prison on 30 June 1997 (adults are those aged 21 years and over). This was 4,400 (12 per cent) more than a year earlier and the highest mid-year population of the decade.

4.2   Since 1987 the population has increased every year, apart from 1990 and 1993. In 1990 there was a substantial decrease (2,000) which can be partly attributed to the effect on sentencing practice of the Strangeways riot and to the increased use of community penalties. The decrease between mid-1992 and mid-1993 reflected the effects of the Criminal Justice Act 1991 (see notes). In the four years to mid-1997 there was a sustained increase of 46 per cent in the sentenced adult population.

4.3   Males accounted for 39,040 (96 per cent) of the sentenced adult population having increased by 45 per cent since mid-1993. The 1,815 females in mid-1997 accounted for 4 per cent of the total, but the increase since 1992 of 83 per cent has been much faster than for males.

Figure 4.1

**PRISON POPULATION OF SENTENCED* ADULT MALES
BY LENGTH OF SENTENCE, 30 JUNE 1987–1997**

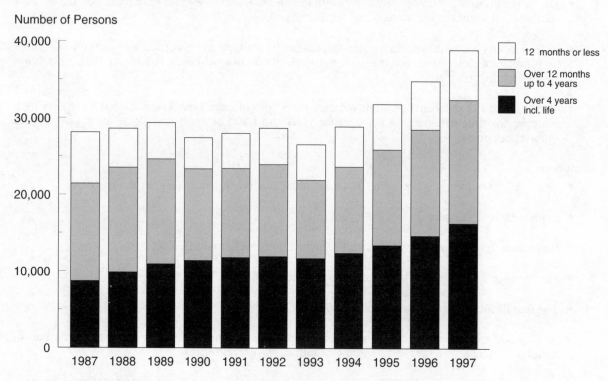

* Excluding fine defaulters

72

Figure 4.2

PRISON POPULATION OF SENTENCED* ADULT FEMALES
BY LENGTH OF SENTENCE, 30 JUNE 1987–1997

Number of Persons

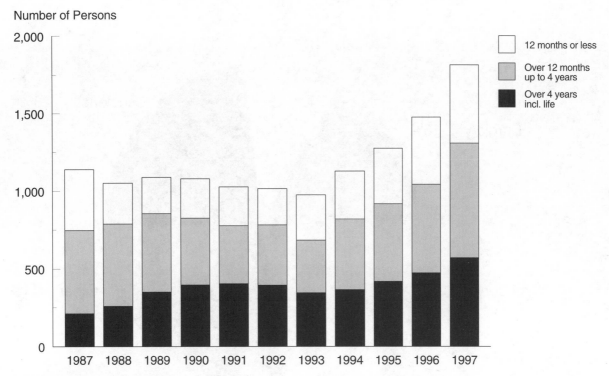

* Excluding fine defaulters

4.4   Estimates based on a sample of the prison population (see paragraph 22 of the notes) show that about 22 per cent of adult males and 37 per cent of adult females had no previous convictions in 1996, the latest year for which data are available.

Sentence length

4.5   In mid-1997 about one sixth (17 per cent) of adult male prisoners with immediate custodial sentences were serving sentences of 12 months or less, two fifths (41 per cent) were serving medium sentences (over 12 months up to 4 years) and just over two fifths (42 per cent were serving long sentences (over 4 years including life); the corresponding figures for 1987 were 24 per cent, 45 per cent and 31 per cent. All of these figures exclude fine defaulters. The last decade has seen a general decrease in the proportion serving short sentences and a corresponding increase in those serving long sentences.

4.6   The distribution of sentence lengths for sentenced females is generally shorter than that for males. In mid-1997 over a quarter (28 per cent) of adult female prisoners with immediate custodial sentences were serving sentences of 12 months or less, two fifths (41 per cent) were serving medium sentences (over 12 months up to 4 years) and one third (31 per cent) were serving long sentences (over 4 years including life). However the last decade has also seen a general increase in the proportion of females serving long sentences and a corresponding decrease in the proportion serving short sentences.

Offence type

4.7   The main offence groups for adult males at mid-1997 were violence against the person (23 per cent of offences excluding offences not recorded), drugs offences (16 per cent), burglary (16 per cent) and robbery (12 per cent). It is difficult to analyse changes over time in the population in custody by type of offence because the proportion with offence not recorded has varied from 2 per cent to 14 per cent. Nevertheless general trends can be seen: the main increase over the last decade has been in the proportion serving sentences for drug offences (up from 11 to 16 per cent); the main decreases have been for burglary (down from 20 to 16 per cent) and theft and fraud (from 19 to 11 per cent).

73

Figure 4.3

**PRISON POPULATION OF SENTENCED ADULT MALES
BY TYPE OF OFFENCE* 1997**

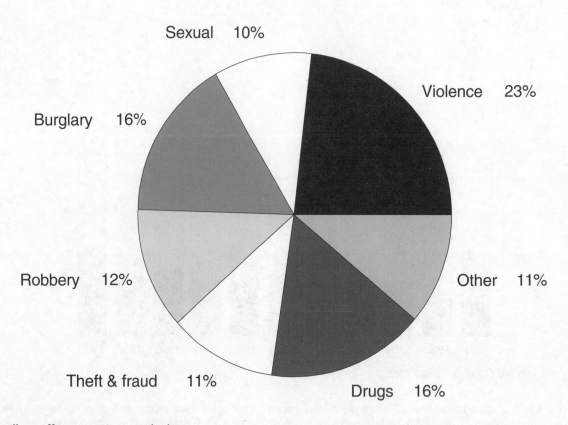

* Excluding offence not recorded

4.8 The main offence groups for adult females at mid-1997 were drug offences (37 per cent of all offences excluding offences not recorded), theft and fraud (24 per cent) and violence against the person (19 per cent). The main changes over the last decade have been that the proportion serving sentences for violent and drug offences has increased while the proportion serving sentences for theft and fraud has decreased.

Figure 4.4

**PRISON POPULATION OF SENTENCED ADULT FEMALES
BY TYPE OF OFFENCE* 1997**

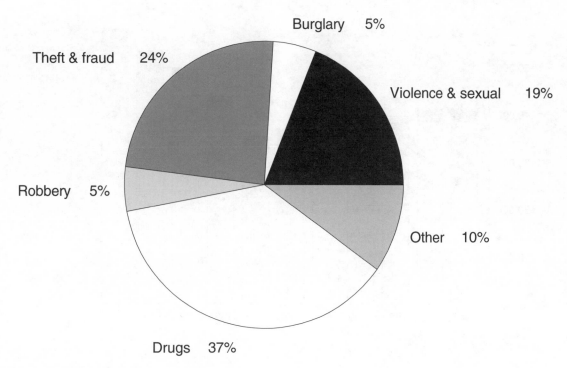

* Excluding offence not recorded

Receptions (Tables 4.5–4.11)

4.9 In 1997 nearly 62,100 adults were received under sentence of immediate imprisonment into Prison Service establishments. This excludes fine defaulters. Receptions in 1997 were 9 per cent higher than in 1996 and have risen continuously since 1992 when there were under 37,000. There were 58,100 receptions of male adults (up 9 per cent on 1996) and 4,000 receptions of female adults (up 21 per cent on 1996).

4.10 Over half (55 per cent) of males received under sentence were aged 21 to 29 and a further 30 per cent were aged 30 to 39. Females received tended to be slightly older: 51 per cent were aged 21 to 29 and 33 per cent were aged 30 to 39. The age distributions of both male and female receptions have shifted upwards in the last decade: in 1986 some 61 per cent of males and 57 per cent of females received were aged 21 to 29.

Sentence length

4.11 The proportion of adult males received with sentences of 12 months or less fell from 61 per cent in 1987 to 57 per cent in 1990, but increased thereafter and was 67 per cent in 1997. A further 26 per cent had sentences of over 12 months up to 4 years and 7 per cent had sentences of over 4 years (including life). The proportion of adult females received with sentences of 12 months or less fell from 69 per cent in 1987 to 66 per cent by 1990, but increased to 76 per cent by 1997. A further 19 per cent of females received had sentences of over 12 months up to 4 years and 5 per cent had sentences of 4 years or more.

Figure 4.5

**RECEPTIONS INTO PRISON OF SENTENCED* ADULT MALES
BY LENGTH OF SENTENCE, 1987–1997**

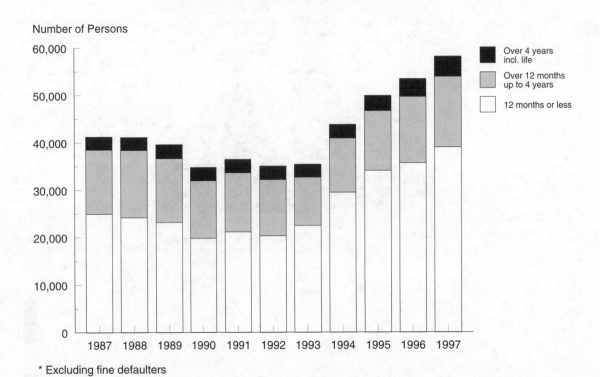

* Excluding fine defaulters

Figure 4.6

**RECEPTIONS INTO PRISON OF SENTENCED* ADULT FEMALES
BY LENGTH OF SENTENCE, 1987–1997**

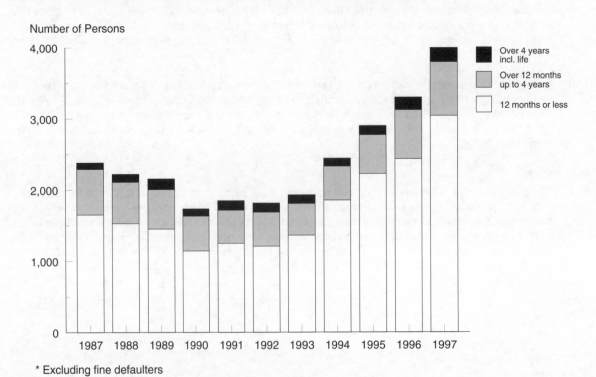

* Excluding fine defaulters

Average sentence length

4.12 Crown Court sentences for adult males received into Prison Service establishments averaged 26.9 months in 1997. The average sentence for those received from magistrates' courts was 4 months and the overall average was 16.2 months. The average sentence for adult females received from the Crown Court in 1997 was 21.4 months. Those received from magistrates' courts had an average sentence of 3.2 months and the overall average was 12.2 months.

Figure 4.7

AVERAGE SENTENCE LENGTH OF PRISON RECEPTIONS OF ADULT MALES, 1987–1997: BY TYPE OF COURT

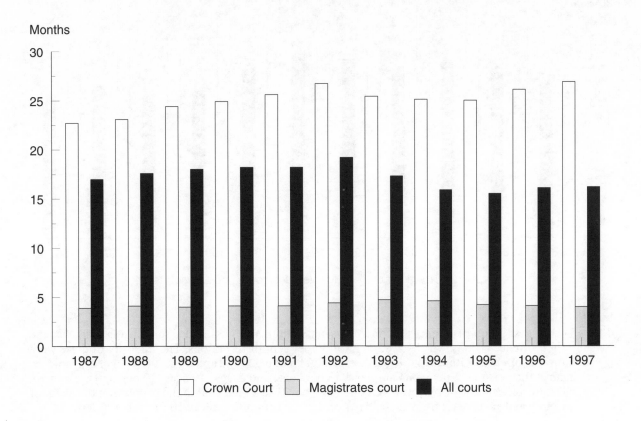

Figure 4.8

AVERAGE SENTENCE LENGTH OF PRISON RECEPTIONS OF ADULT FEMALES, 1987–1997: BY TYPE OF COURT

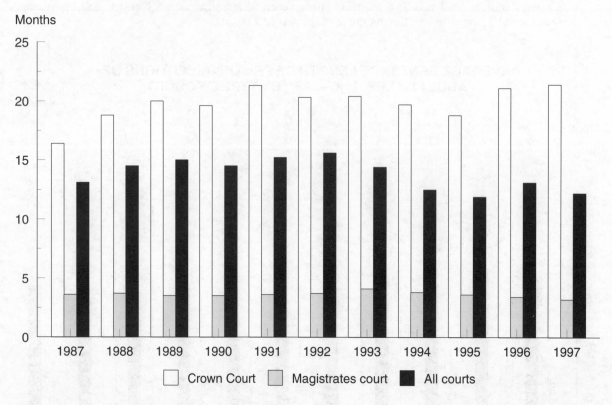

Offence type

4.13 The biggest group of offences recorded for male adults received under sentence in 1997 was the 'other' offence groups, which accounted for 30 per cent of receptions. The majority of these were motoring offences. Other large groups were: theft handling, fraud and forgery (24 per cent), violence against the person (15 per cent) burglary (13 per cent) and drugs offences (10 per cent). The main changes compared with 1987 were a reduction from 21 to 13 per cent in the proportion received for burglary and an increase from 19 to 30 per cent in the proportion received for 'other' offences.

Figure 4.9

**RECEPTIONS OF ADULT SENTENCED MALES
BY OFFENCE GROUP AND SENTENCE LENGTH, 1997**

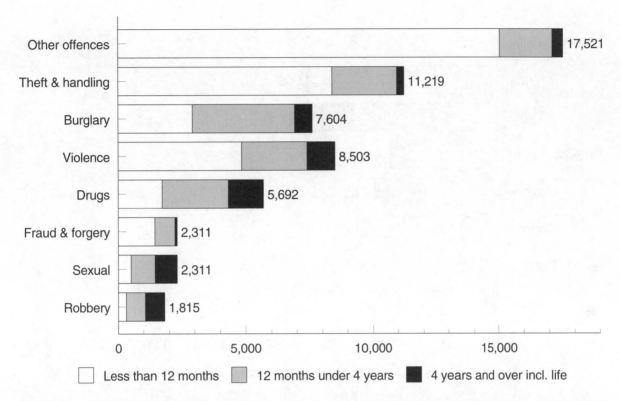

4.14 Theft handling and fraud and forgery accounted for 49 per cent of female adult sentenced receptions in 1997, compared with 51 per cent in 1987. Drugs offences accounted for 17 per cent of female adult receptions in 1997 compared to 10 per cent for male receptions.

Figure 4.10

**RECEPTIONS OF ADULT SENTENCED FEMALES
BY OFFENCE GROUP AND SENTENCE LENGTH, 1997**

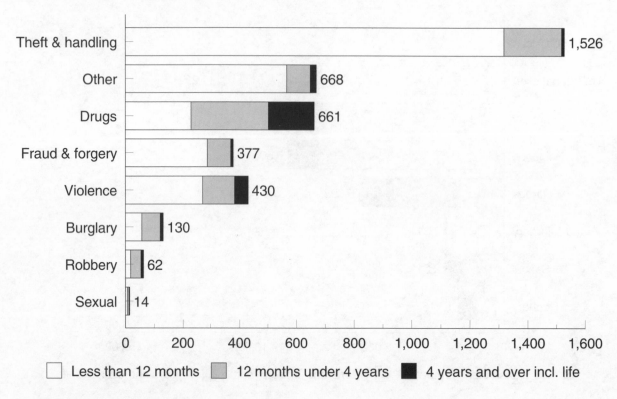

4.15 Robbery, sexual and drug offences all had high proportions of long sentences (4 years or more) compared with the other groups of offences.

Discharges (Tables 4.12–4.14)

4.16 Nearly 58,000 adults were discharged from determinate sentences in 1997, 54,200 males and 3,740 females.

4.17 The average length of sentence for males was 15.1 months of which 8.4 months (55 per cent) were served in total (including remand) and 7 months (46 per cent) were served under sentence. The equivalent figures for adult females were: an average sentence of 10.5 months of which 5.6 months (53 per cent) were served in total and 4.7 months (45 per cent) were served since the date of sentence.

4.18 Under the 1991 Criminal Justice Act (see notes) prisoners sentenced to less than four years are released automatically at the half way point subject to additional days awarded for disciplinary offences whilst in custody. Those sentenced to four years or more are eligible for parole half way through their sentence and if parole is not granted they are released automatically at the two-thirds point, subject to additional days. The average times served by those released in 1997 reflect these arrangements. Those discharged from sentences of under four years had generally served just over 50 per cent of the sentence length, whilst for longer sentences the proportion rose to about 55 per cent for females and the low sixties for males.

Table 4.1   Population in prison under sentence by offence group and length of sentence

England and Wales 30 June 1997
All adults

Number of persons

Offence group	All sentence lengths	Up to 3 months	Over 3 months up to 6 months	Over 6 months less than 12 months	12 months	Over 12 months up to 18 months	Over 18 months up to 3 years	Over 3 years less than 4 years	4 years	Over 4 years up to 5 years	Over 5 years up to 10 years	Over 10 years less than life	Life
All Adults													
All offences	**40,856**	**1,226**	**2,663**	**1,792**	**1,432**	**2,844**	**9,070**	**1,949**	**2,990**	**3,808**	**7,568**	**1,902**	**3,612**
Offences with immediate custodial sentence	**40,740**	**1,115**	**2,658**	**1,792**	**1,432**	**2,844**	**9,070**	**1,949**	**2,990**	**3,808**	**7,568**	**1,902**	**3,612**
Violence against the person	9,109	158	373	244	198	457	1,284	275	553	715	1,306	344	3,202
Rape	1,956	–	1	2	1	3	30	19	87	185	1,062	348	218
Other sexual offences	1,960	12	27	44	64	104	415	86	232	274	600	66	36
Burglary	6,042	33	173	231	274	652	2,680	576	507	496	371	38	11
Robbery	4,707	3	10	14	23	66	652	242	493	753	1,864	555	32
Theft and handling	3,493	313	548	496	261	498	949	139	110	93	83	3	–
Fraud and forgery	1,197	42	102	135	109	157	396	54	69	74	55	4	–
Drugs offences	6,742	41	150	177	226	418	1,525	391	692	912	1,759	448	3
Other offences	4,356	480	1,197	361	196	380	773	120	185	199	302	53	110
Offence not recorded	1,178	33	77	88	80	109	366	47	62	107	166	43	–
In default of payment of a fine	**116**	**111**	**5**	**–**	**–**	**–**	**–**	**–**	**–**	**–**	**–**	**–**	**–**
Adult males													
All offences	**39,041**	**1,130**	**2,481**	**1,645**	**1,351**	**2,696**	**8,661**	**1,884**	**2,874**	**3,681**	**7,299**	**1,855**	**3,484**
Offences with immediate custodial sentence	**38,927**	**1,021**	**2,476**	**1,645**	**1,351**	**2,696**	**8,661**	**1,884**	**2,874**	**3,681**	**7,299**	**1,855**	**3,484**
Violence against the person	8,779	154	355	234	194	438	1,225	265	533	694	1,268	334	3,085
Rape	1,954	–	1	2	1	3	30	19	87	185	1,060	348	218
Other sexual offences	1,955	12	27	44	64	103	44	86	231	274	598	66	36
Burglary	5,958	33	169	224	265	634	2,646	574	503	493	368	38	11
Robbery	4,614	3	9	12	19	64	614	234	474	747	1,852	554	32
Theft and handling	3,185	261	485	430	241	465	888	134	108	88	82	3	–
Fraud and forgery	1,078	33	80	111	96	146	366	51	64	73	54	4	–
Drugs offences	6,098	35	120	162	202	372	1,390	358	639	831	1,572	414	3
Other offences	4,186	461	1,167	348	191	364	733	117	177	192	286	51	99
Offence not recorded	1,120	29	63	78	78	107	355	46	58	104	159	43	–
In default of payment of a fine	**114**	**109**	**5**	**–**	**–**	**–**	**–**	**–**	**–**	**–**	**–**	**–**	**–**
Adult females													
All offences	**1,815**	**96**	**182**	**147**	**81**	**148**	**409**	**65**	**116**	**127**	**269**	**47**	**128**
Offences with immediate custodial sentence	**1,813**	**94**	**182**	**147**	**81**	**148**	**409**	**65**	**116**	**127**	**269**	**47**	**128**
Violence against the person	330	4	18	10	4	19	59	10	20	21	38	10	117
Rape	2	–	–	–	–	–	–	–	–	–	2	–	–
Other sexual offences	5	–	–	–	–	1	1	–	1	–	2	–	–
Burglary	84	–	4	7	9	18	34	2	4	3	3	–	–
Robbery	93	–	1	2	4	2	38	8	19	6	12	1	–
Theft and handling	308	52	63	66	20	33	61	5	2	5	1	–	–
Fraud and forgery	119	9	22	24	13	11	30	3	5	1	1	–	–
Drugs offences	644	6	30	15	24	46	135	33	53	81	187	34	–
Other offences	170	19	30	13	5	16	40	3	8	7	16	2	11
Offence not recorded	58	4	14	10	2	2	11	1	4	3	7	–	–
In default of payment of a fine	**2**	**2**	**–**	**–**	**–**	**–**	**–**	**–**	**–**	**–**	**–**	**–**	**–**

Table 4.2 Population of adults in prison under sentence by number of previous convictions([1])

England and Wales 30 June
All adults

Year	All adults	Previous convictions not found([3])	Percentage([2])				
			Nil	1–2	3–6	7–10	11 and over
Adult males ([4])							
1993	26,545	5	17	15	22	19	23
1994	28,896	5	15	15	22	18	25
1995	31,820	5	16	15	20	17	28
1996	34,848	9	22	16	18	14	22
Adult females ([5])							
1993	975	12	39	18	16	8	7
1994	1,128	11	36	17	17	8	10
1995	1,276	15	34	17	14	10	10
1996	1,476	17	37	15	13	8	9

([1]) Excludes fine defaulters.

([2]) Rounded estimates which therefore may not add to 100

([3]) From 1996 more stringent criteria for accepting a possible match to records on the Home Office Offenders Index have been applied that will have tended to increase the number of instances where previous convictions are not found.

([4]) Based on samples of 4,605, 4,606, 6,543 and 8,601 prisoners respectively in the years 1993, 1994, 1995 and 1996.

([5]) Based on samples of 969,1,105, 1,240 and 1,536 prisoners respectively in the years 1993, 1994, 1995 and 1996.

Table 4.3   Population in prison under sentence by offence group

England and Wales 30 June
All adults   Number of persons

Offence group	1987	1988	1989	1990	1991	1992	1993	1994	1995	1996	1997
All adults											
All offences	**29,747**	**24,102**	**24,843**	**28,819**	**29,321**	**29,992**	**27,965**	**24,487**	**33,537**	**36,440**	**40,856**
Offences with immediate custodial											
sentence	**29,261**	**29,654**	**24,453**	**28,471**	**29,004**	**29,692**	**27,520**	**24,024**	**33,096**	**36,314**	**40,740**
Violence against the person	6,507	7,058	7,285	6,628	6,263	6,336	6,613	7,107	7,759	8,404	9,109
Rape	752	938	1,191	1,285	1,386	1,466	1,503	1,550	1,694	1,827	1,956
Other sexual offences	1,375	1,539	1,582	1,525	1,546	1,528	1,527	1,600	1,831	1,970	1,960
Burglary	5,525	5,245	5,020	4,272	3,779	4,029	3,500	3,770	4,477	4,737	6,042
Robbery	2,776	2,994	3,228	3,183	3,228	3,414	4,057	4,334	4,358	4,425	4,707
Theft and handling }	5,495	4,538	4,316	2,574	2,436	2,558	2,180	2,599	2,991	3,174	3,493
Fraud and forgery				821	805	833	877	934	1,150	1,196	1,197
Drugs offences	3,290	3,065	3,112	3,042	2,736	3,021	3,029	3,363	4,021	5,416	6,742
Other offences	2,839	3,318	3,387	2,839	2,722	2,960	2,829	3,330	3,624	4,093	4,356
Offence not recorded	702	959	1,332	2,302	4,103	3,547	1,405	1,437	1,191	1,072	1,178
In default of payment of a fine	**486**	**448**	**390**	**348**	**317**	**300**	**445**	**463**	**441**	**126**	**116**
All males											
All offences	**28,587**	**29,029**	**29,737**	**27,720**	**28,283**	**28,956**	**26,972**	**29,337**	**32,238**	**34,960**	**39,041**
Offences with immediate custodial											
sentence	**28,121**	**28,602**	**29,364**	**27,392**	**27,977**	**28,676**	**26,545**	**28,896**	**31,820**	**34,838**	**38,927**
Violence against the person	6,342	6,867	7,105	6,458	6,093	6,178	6,435	6,869	7,508	8,116	8,779
Rape	750	933	1,186	1,282	1,385	1,464	1,502	1,549	1,692	1,825	1,954
Other sexual offences	1,366	1,530	1,566	1,519	1,532	1,521	1,514	1,589	1,824	1,962	1,955
Burglary	5,458	5,209	4,968	4,232	3,745	3,989	3,473	3,740	4,434	4,685	5,958
Robbery	2,270	2,946	3,173	3,152	3,199	3,377	4,002	4,262	4,286	4,346	4,614
Theft and handling }	5,104	4,260	4,058	2,392	2,270	2,386	1,991	2,389	2,734	2,894	3,185
Fraud and forgery				772	765	781	816	869	1,055	1,079	1,078
Drugs offences	2,960	2,760	2,807	2,739	2,476	2,776	2,739	3,050	3,659	4,965	6,098
Other offences	2,729	3,172	3,234	2,651	2,561	2,817	2,727	3,222	3,507	3,957	4,186
Offence not recorded	692	925	1,267	2,195	3,951	3,387	1,346	1,357	1,121	1,009	1,120
In default of payment of a fine	**466**	**427**	**373**	**328**	**306**	**280**	**427**	**441**	**418**	**122**	**114**
All females											
All offences	**1,160**	**1,073**	**1,106**	**1,099**	**1,038**	**1,036**	**993**	**1,150**	**1,299**	**1,480**	**1,815**
Offences with immediate custodial											
sentence	**1,140**	**1,052**	**1,089**	**1,079**	**1,027**	**1,016**	**975**	**1,128**	**1,276**	**1,476**	**1,813**
Violence against the person	165	191	180	170	170	158	178	238	251	288	330
Rape	2	5	5	3	1	2	1	1	2	2	2
Other sexual offences	9	9	16	6	14	7	13	11	7	8	5
Burglary	67	36	52	40	34	40	27	30	43	52	84
Robbery	56	48	55	31	29	37	55	72	72	79	93
Theft and handling }	391	278	258	182	166	172	189	210	257	280	308
Fraud and forgery				49	40	52	61	65	95	117	119
Drugs offences	330	305	305	303	260	245	290	313	362	451	644
Other offences	110	146	153	188	161	143	102	108	117	136	170
Offence not recorded	10	34	65	107	152	160	59	80	70	63	58
In default of payment of a fine	**20**	**21**	**17**	**20**	**11**	**20**	**18**	**22**	**23**	**4**	**2**

Table 4.3 (continued)   Population in prison under sentence by offence group (per cent)

England and Wales 30 June
All adults   Percentage([1])

Offence group	1987	1988	1989	1990	1991	1992	1993	1994	1995	1996	1997
All Adults											
Offences with immediate custodial sentence											
Violence against the person	22.8	24.6	25.0	25.3	25.2	24.2	25.3	24.9	24.3	23.8	23.0
Rape	2.6	3.3	4.1	4.9	5.6	5.6	5.8	5.4	5.3	5.2	4.9
Other sexual offences	4.8	5.4	5.4	5.8	6.2	5.8	5.8	5.6	5.7	5.6	5.0
Burglary	19.3	18.3	17.2	16.3	15.2	15.4	13.4	13.2	14.0	13.4	15.3
Robbery	9.7	10.4	11.1	12.2	13.0	13.1	15.5	15.2	13.7	12.6	11.9
Theft and handling }	19.2	15.8	14.8	9.8	9.8	9.8	8.3	9.1	9.4	9.0	8.8
Fraud and forgery				3.1	3.2	3.2	3.4	3.3	3.6	3.4	3.0
Drugs offences	11.5	10.7	10.7	11.6	11.0	11.6	11.6	11.8	12.6	15.4	17.0
Other offences	9.9	11.6	11.6	10.8	10.9	11.3	10.8	11.6	11.4	11.6	11.0
All males											
Offences with immediate custodial sentence											
Violence against the person	23.1	24.8	25.3	25.6	25.4	24.4	25.5	24.9	24.5	24.0	23.2
Rape	2.7	3.4	4.2	5.1	5.8	5.8	6.0	5.6	5.5	5.4	5.2
Other sexual offences	5.0	5.5	5.6	6.0	6.4	6.0	6.0	5.8	5.9	5.8	5.2
Burglary	19.9	18.8	17.7	16.8	15.6	15.8	13.8	13.6	14.4	13.8	15.8
Robbery	9.9	10.6	11.3	12.5	13.3	13.4	15.9	15.5	14.0	12.8	12.2
Theft and handling }	18.6	15.4	14.4	9.5	9.4	9.4	7.9	8.7	8.9	8.6	8.4
Fraud and forgery				3.1	3.2	3.1	3.2	3.2	3.4	3.2	2.9
Drugs offences	10.8	10.0	10.0	10.9	10.3	11.0	10.9	11.1	11.9	14.7	16.1
Other offences	9.9	11.5	11.5	10.5	10.7	11.1	10.8	11.7	11.4	11.7	11.1
All females											
Offences with immediate custodial sentence											
Violence against the person	14.6	18.8	17.6	17.5	19.4	18.5	19.4	22.7	20.8	20.4	18.8
Rape	0.2	0.5	0.5	0.3	0.1	0.2	0.1	0.1	0.2	0.1	0.1
Other sexual offences	0.8	0.9	1.6	0.6	1.6	0.8	1.4	1.0	0.6	0.6	0.3
Burglary	5.9	3.5	5.1	4.1	3.9	4.7	2.9	2.9	3.6	3.7	4.8
Robbery	5.0	4.7	5.4	3.2	3.3	4.3	6.0	6.9	6.0	5.6	5.3
Theft and handling }	34.6	27.3	25.2	18.7	19.0	20.1	20.6	20.0	21.3	19.8	17.5
Fraud and forgery				5.0	4.6	6.1	6.7	6.2	7.9	8.3	6.8
Drugs offences	29.2	30.0	29.8	31.2	29.7	28.6	31.7	29.9	30.0	31.9	36.7
Other offences	9.7	14.3	14.9	19.3	18.4	16.7	11.1	10.3	9.7	9.6	9.7

([1]) Excludes offence not recorded.

84

Table 4.4 Population in prison under sentence by length of sentence

England and Wales 30 June
All adults

Length of Sentence	1987	1988	1989	1990	1991	1992	1993	1994	1995	1996	1997
All adults	**29,261**	**30,102**	**30,853**	**28,819**	**29,321**	**29,992**	**27,965**	**30,487**	**33,537**	**36,440**	**40,856**
All sentence lengths	**29,261**	**29,654**	**30,453**	**28,471**	**29,004**	**29,692**	**27,520**	**30,024**	**33,096**	**36,314**	**40,740**
Up to 3 months	1,019	742	669	623	738	821	850	828	965	1,025	1,115
Over 3 months up to 6 months	2,091	1,531	1,483	1,252	1,494	1,432	1,478	2,043	2,321	2,498	2,658
Over 6 months less than 12 months	3,954	3,056	2,818	1,162	1,365	1,400	1,322	1,387	1,554	1,733	1,792
12 months				1,232	1,205	1,312	1,234	1,284	1,426	1,458	1,432
Over 12 months up to 18 months	2,968	3,214	2,861	2,616	2,713	2,814	2,227	2,399	2,595	2,736	2,844
Over 18 months up to 3 years	7,351	7,834	7,964	6,743	6,370	6,647	5,475	6,239	6,978	7,837	9,070
Over 3 years less than 4 years	2,935	3,134	3,354	1,032	998	1,063	999	1,094	1,213	1,375	1,949
4 years				1,998	1,897	1,846	1,858	1,955	2,173	2,502	2,990
Over 4 years up to 5 years	2,189	2,308	2,477	2,381	2,398	2,403	2,344	2,483	2,914	3,261	3,808
Over 5 years up to 10 years	3,747	4,523	5,171	5,576	5,765	5,658	5,339	5,691	6,158	6,773	7,568
Over 10 years less than life	782	925	1,087	1,186	1,270	1,387	1,380	1,517	1,598	1,707	1,902
Life	2,225	2,387	2,569	2,670	2,791	2,909	3,014	3,104	3,201	3,409	3,612
In default of payment of a fine	**486**	**448**	**390**	**348**	**317**	**300**	**445**	**463**	**441**	**126**	**116**

All males

Length of Sentence	1987	1988	1989	1990	1991	1992	1993	1994	1995	1996	1997
All adult males	**28,587**	**29,029**	**29,737**	**27,720**	**28,283**	**28,956**	**26,972**	**29,337**	**32,238**	**34,960**	**39,041**
All sentence lengths	**28,121**	**28,602**	**29,364**	**27,392**	**27,977**	**28,676**	**26,545**	**28,896**	**31,820**	**34,838**	**38,927**
Up to 3 months	954	703	633	582	694	772	773	795	907	949	1,021
Over 3 months up to 6 months	1,981	1,448	1,402	1.174	1,419	1,376	1,404	1,925	2,199	2,371	2,476
Over 6 months less than 12 months	3,737	2,915	2,703	1,096	1,282	1,338	1,250	1,299	1,449	1,595	1,645
12 months				165	1,158	1,245	1,167	1,215	1,353	1,367	1,351
Over 12 months up to 18 months	2,828	3,093	2,737	2,517	2,613	2,696	2,115	2,281	2,465	2,586	2,696
Over 18 months up to 3 years	7,059	7,540	7,698	6,512	6,193	6,460	5,311	5,999	6,714	7,538	8,661
Over 3 years less than 4 years	2,831	3,020	2,238	1,008	974	1,041	981	1,064	1,178	1,337	1,884
4 years				1,922	1,825	1,786	1,812	1,888	2,103	2,419	2,874
Over 4 years up to 5 years	2,120	2,217	2,365	2,274	2,298	2,318	2,277	2,400	2,812	3,162	3,681
Over 5 years up to 10 years	3,677	4,430	5,031	5,394	5,568	5,462	5,182	5,538	5,976	6,553	7,299
Over 10 years less than life	775	915	1,068	1,165	1,253	1,365	1,360	1,494	1,571	1,671	1,855
Life	2,159	2,321	2,489	2,583	2,700	2,817	2,913	2,998	3,093	3,290	3,484
In default of payment of a fine	**466**	**427**	**373**	**328**	**306**	**280**	**427**	**441**	**418**	**122**	**114**

All females

Length of Sentence	1987	1988	1989	1990	1991	1992	1993	1994	1995	1996	1997
All adult females	**1,160**	**1,073**	**1,106**	**1,099**	**1,038**	**1,036**	**993**	**1,150**	**1,299**	**1,480**	**1,815**
All sentence lengths	**1,140**	**1,052**	**1,089**	**1,079**	**1,027**	**1,016**	**975**	**1,128**	**1,276**	**1,476**	**1,813**
Up to 3 months	65	39	36	41	44	49	77	33	58	76	94
Over 3 months up to 6 months	110	83	81	78	75	56	74	118	122	127	182
Over 6 months less than 12 months	217	141	115	66	83	62	72	88	105	138	147
12 months				67	47	67	67	69	73	91	81
Over 12 months up to 18 months	140	121	124	99	100	118	112	118	130	150	148
Over 18 months up to 3 years	292	294	266	231	177	187	164	240	264	299	409
Over 3 years less than 4 years	104	114	116	24	24	22	18	30	35	38	65
4 years				76	72	60	46	67	70	83	116
Over 4 years up to 5 years	69	91	112	107	100	85	67	83	102	99	127
Over 5 years up to 10 years	70	93	140	182	197	196	157	153	182	220	269
Over 10 years less than life	7	10	19	21	17	22	20	23	27	36	47
Life	66	66	80	87	91	92	101	106	108	119	128
In default of payment of a fine	**20**	**21**	**17**	**20**	**11**	**20**	**18**	**22**	**23**	**4**	**2**

Table 4.5 Receptions into prison by age and offence

England and Wales 1997
All adults

Number of persons

Offence	Immediate imprisonment							In default of payment of a fine
		Age						
	All ages	21–24	25–29	30–39	40–49	50–59	60 and over	
All offences	**62,089**	**16,767**	**17,251**	**18,756**	**6,415**	**2,285**	**615**	**5,781**
Violence against the person	**8,933**	**2,401**	**2,603**	**2,824**	**829**	**223**	**53**	**314**
Murder	212	46	54	77	23	11	1	–
Manslaughter	212	51	56	67	23	9	6	–
Other homicide and attempted homicide	746	151	193	268	90	34	10	–
Wounding	4,489	1,360	1,358	1,303	368	88	12	122
Assaults	2,232	576	657	742	200	44	13	158
Cruelty to children	81	19	24	22	11	3	2	–
Other offences of violence against the person	961	198	261	345	114	34	9	34
Sexual offences	**2,325**	**167**	**301**	**708**	**532**	**391**	**226**	**8**
Buggery and indecency between males	122	3	7	44	28	28	12	1
Rape	667	71	112	222	136	82	44	2
Gross indecency with children	478	14	45	119	132	93	75	1
Other sexual offences	1,058	79	137	323	236	188	95	4
Burglary	**7,734**	**3,102**	**2,443**	**1,795**	**306**	**73**	**15**	**196**
Robbery	**1,877**	**737**	**576**	**466**	**78**	**14**	**6**	**5**
Theft and handling	**12,745**	**3,745**	**3,856**	**3,665**	**1,056**	**344**	**79**	**713**
Taking and driving away	1,238	642	375	195	22	4	–	37
Other thefts	9,977	2,716	3,040	2,989	878	284	70	615
Handling stolen goods	1,530	387	441	481	156	56	9	61
Fraud and forgery	**2,688**	**373**	**577**	**944**	**490**	**244**	**60**	**136**
Frauds	2,542	346	553	898	466	223	56	128
Forgery	146	27	24	46	24	21	4	8
Drugs offences	**6,353**	**1,348**	**1,788**	**2,163**	**778**	**240**	**36**	**209**
Other offences	**18,189**	**4,565**	**4,793**	**5,813**	**2,204**	**690**	**124**	**3,674**
Arson	280	90	76	64	35	12	3	2
Criminal damage	870	240	231	250	108	32	9	371
In charge or driving under the influence of drink or drugs	2,522	269	483	997	579	174	20	138
Other motoring offences	8,144	2,124	2,349	2,620	804	217	30	2,029
Drunkenness	282	37	57	108	57	21	2	180
Blackmail	68	13	15	28	8	3	1	–
Kidnapping	144	44	40	47	11	1	1	–
Affray	934	307	266	266	68	25	2	52
Violent disorder	230	93	73	53	9	–	2	12
Perjury/libel/pervert the course of Justice	545	171	122	155	69	24	4	1
Threat/disorderly behaviour	668	175	179	225	58	21	10	116
Breach of Court Order	2,024	705	595	533	144	39	8	178
Other	1,478	297	307	467	254	121	32	595
Offence not recorded	**1,245**	**329**	**314**	**378**	**142**	**66**	**16**	**526**

86

Table 4.5 (continued)   Receptions into prison by age and offence

England and Wales 1997
Adult males   Number of persons

| Offence | Immediate imprisonment | | | | | | | In default of payment of a fine |
	All ages	21–24	25–29	30–39	40–49	50–59	60 and over	
All offences	**58,095**	**15,794**	**16,180**	**17,431**	**5,935**	**2,160**	**595**	**5,427**
Violence against the person	**8,503**	**2,275**	**2,487**	**2,688**	**786**	**217**	**50**	**297**
Murder	202	45	51	73	22	10	1	–
Manslaughter	185	45	50	58	19	7	6	–
Other homicide and attempted homicide	728	146	188	262	88	34	10	–
Wounding	4,306	1,299	1,307	1,247	355	86	12	116
Assaults	2,095	535	622	698	184	44	12	147
Cruelty to children	49	11	15	14	6	2	1	–
Other offences of violence against the person	938	194	254	336	112	34	8	34
Sexual offences	**2,311**	**166**	**296**	**701**	**532**	**390**	**226**	**8**
Buggery and indecency between males	121	3	6	44	28	28	12	1
Rape	667	71	112	22	136	82	44	2
Gross indecency with children	473	14	44	115	132	93	75	1
Other sexual offences	1,050	78	134	320	236	187	95	5
Burglary	**7,604**	**3,062**	**2,397**	**1,757**	**301**	**72**	**15**	**195**
Robbery	**1,815**	**710**	**559**	**452**	**75**	**13**	**6**	**5**
Theft and handling	**11,219**	**3,355**	**3,428**	**3,150**	**897**	**314**	**75**	**657**
Taking and driving away	1,232	640	372	194	22	4	–	37
Other thefts	8,561	2,358	2,641	2,512	728	254	68	560
Handling stolen goods	1,426	357	415	444	147	56	7	60
Fraud and forgery	**2,311**	**322**	**498**	**809**	**414**	**215**	**53**	**127**
Frauds	2,200	301	480	773	396	200	50	120
Forgery	111	21	18	36	18	15	3	7
Drugs offences	**5,692**	**1,185**	**1,614**	**1,951**	**694**	**215**	**33**	**202**
Other offences	**17,521**	**4,417**	**4,616**	**5,591**	**2,109**	**666**	**122**	**3,439**
Arson	256	84	69	57	32	11	3	2
Criminal damage	841	234	220	241	105	32	9	348
In charge or driving under the influence of drink or drugs	2,457	264	477	970	559	167	20	137
Other motoring offences	7,960	2,081	2,299	2,558	779	213	30	1,963
Drunkenness	271	37	55	102	54	21	2	173
Blackmail	61	12	14	26	6	2	1	–
Kidnapping	138	41	39	45	11	1	1	–
Affray	917	302	261	259	68	25	2	52
Violent disorder	221	90	69	52	8	–	2	12
Perjury/libel/pervert the course of Justice	509	159	114	144	64	24	4	1
Threat/disorderly behaviour	653	172	177	218	56	20	10	116
Breach of Court Order	1,879	666	549	483	134	39	8	167
Other	1,358	275	273	436	233	111	30	468
Offence not recorded	**1,119**	**302**	**285**	**332**	**127**	**58**	**15**	**497**

Table 4.5 (continued)   Receptions into prison by age and offence

England and Wales 1997
Adult females   Number of persons

Offence	Immediate imprisonment							In default of payment of a fine
		Age						
	All ages	21–24	25–29	30–39	40–49	50–59	60 and over	
All offences	**3,994**	**973**	**1,071**	**1,325**	**480**	**125**	**20**	**354**
Violence against the person	**430**	**126**	**116**	**136**	**43**	**6**	**3**	**17**
Murder	10	1	3	4	1	1	–	–
Manslaughter	27	6	6	9	4	2	–	–
Other homicide and attempted homicide	18	5	5	6	2	–	–	–
Wounding	183	61	51	56	13	2	–	6
Assaults	137	41	35	44	16	–	1	11
Cruelty to children	32	8	9	8	5	1	1	–
Other offences of violence against the person	23	4	7	9	2	–	1	–
Sexual offences	**14**	**1**	**5**	**7**	**–**	**1**	**–**	**–**
Buggery and indecency between males	1	–	1	–	–	–	–	–
Rape	–	–	–	–	–	–	–	–
Gross indecency with children	5	–	1	4	–	–	–	–
Other sexual offences	8	1	3	3	–	1	–	–
Burglary	**130**	**40**	**46**	**38**	**5**	**1**	**–**	**1**
Robbery	**62**	**27**	**17**	**14**	**3**	**1**	**–**	**–**
Theft and handling	**1,526**	**390**	**428**	**515**	**159**	**30**	**4**	**56**
Taking and driving away	6	2	3	1	–	–	–	–
Other thefts	1,416	358	399	477	150	30	2	55
Handling stolen goods	104	30	26	37	9	–	2	1
Fraud and forgery	**377**	**51**	**79**	**135**	**76**	**29**	**7**	**9**
Frauds	342	45	73	125	70	23	6	8
Forgery	35	6	6	10	6	6	1	1
Drugs offences	**661**	**163**	**174**	**212**	**84**	**25**	**3**	**7**
Other offences	**668**	**148**	**177**	**222**	**95**	**24**	**2**	**235**
Arson	24	6	7	7	3	1	–	–
Criminal damage	29	6	11	9	3	–	–	23
In charge or driving under the influence of drink or drugs	65	5	6	27	20	7	–	1
Other motoring offences	184	43	50	62	25	4	–	66
Drunkenness	11	–	2	6	3	–	–	7
Blackmail	7	1	1	2	2	1	–	–
Kidnapping	6	3	1	2	–	–	–	–
Affray	17	5	5	7	–	–	–	–
Violent disorder	9	3	4	1	1	–	–	–
Perjury/libel/pervert the course of Justice	36	12	8	11	5	–	–	–
Threat/disorderly behaviour	15	3	2	7	2	1	–	–
Breach of Court Order	145	39	46	50	10	–	–	11
Other	120	22	34	31	21	10	2	127
Offence not recorded	**126**	**27**	**29**	**46**	**15**	**8**	**1**	**29**

Table 4.6 Receptions into prison under sentence of immediate imprisonment: by age, offence group and length of sentence

England and Wales 1997
All adults

Number of persons

Age and offence group	All sentence lengths	Up to 3 months	Over 3 months up to 6 months	Over 6 months less than 12 months	12 months	Over 12 months up to 18 months	Over 18 months up to 3 years	Over 3 years less than 4 years	4 years	Over 4 years up to 5 years	Over 5 years up to 10 years	Over 10 years less than life	Life
All adults													
All ages	**62,089**	**17,546**	**15,805**	**5,351**	**3,357**	**4,668**	**8,307**	**1,214**	**1,451**	**1,545**	**2,147**	**385**	**313**
Violence against the person	8,933	2,417	1,973	727	528	774	1,202	172	274	254	315	58	239
Sexual offences	2,325	172	167	174	173	238	483	55	148	169	438	68	40
Burglary	7,734	1,071	1,193	720	551	999	2,199	308	270	233	181	8	1
Robbery	1,877	166	101	67	59	125	477	119	154	211	319	74	5
Theft and handling	12,745	4,677	3,563	1,469	671	840	1,124	118	93	93	87	9	1
Fraud and forgery	2,688	737	591	409	224	261	348	29	38	34	15	2	–
Drug offences	6,353	660	733	571	485	672	1,415	294	337	397	647	140	2
Other offences	18,189	7,344	7,217	1,048	548	614	881	105	120	133	130	26	23
Offence not recorded	1,245	302	267	166	118	145	178	14	17	21	15	–	2
Adult males													
Aged 21–29	**31,974**	**8,681**	**8,427**	**2,840**	**1,737**	**2,540**	**4,597**	**699**	**698**	**742**	**791**	**96**	**126**
Violence against the person	4,762	1,211	1,104	394	293	438	703	96	136	123	142	18	104
Sexual offences	462	43	53	38	31	45	81	9	28	27	91	11	5
Burglary	5,459	752	822	531	372	737	1,574	226	179	156	105	4	1
Robbery	1,269	118	75	44	41	80	354	82	106	146	187	31	5
Theft and handling	6,783	2,364	2,009	788	346	463	596	71	43	56	45	1	1
Fraud and forgery	820	281	205	119	50	72	77	3	7	4	2	–	–
Drugs offences	2,799	329	364	281	241	307	639	148	137	157	174	21	1
Other offences	9,033	3,430	3,681	559	306	332	489	59	53	63	42	10	6
Offence not recorded	587	153	114	86	57	66	84	5	9	10	3	–	–
Aged 30 and over	**26,121**	**7,326**	**6,477**	**2,108**	**1,420**	**1,876**	**3,330**	**468**	**682**	**728**	**1,263**	**272**	**171**
Violence against the person	3,741	1,047	791	298	218	303	447	68	129	120	164	35	121
Sexual offences	1,849	128	112	132	141	191	400	46	119	142	347	56	35
Burglary	2,145	300	351	171	164	246	595	79	88	73	74	4	–
Robbery	456	39	21	19	13	35	105	34	45	61	131	43	–
Theft and handling	4,436	1,581	1,141	509	266	310	459	42	44	35	41	8	–
Fraud and forgery	1,491	328	285	230	149	168	240	23	26	28	13	1	–
Drugs offences	2,893	245	273	243	189	301	648	121	168	197	398	109	–
Other offences	8,488	3,546	3,384	444	229	253	351	46	58	64	85	16	12
Offence not recorded	532	112	119	62	51	69	85	9	5	8	10	–	2
Adult females													
Aged 21–29	**2,044**	**818**	**471**	**212**	**85**	**126**	**196**	**20**	**33**	**37**	**34**	**5**	**7**
Violence against the person	242	92	48	22	10	19	25	4	7	3	5	1	6
Sexual offences	6	–	2	4	–	–	–	–	–	–	–	–	–
Burglary	86	9	13	14	12	11	19	1	2	4	1	–	–
Robbery	44	7	4	2	4	6	14	2	1	4	–	–	–
Theft and handling	818	416	222	88	18	33	37	1	1	2	–	–	–
Fraud and forgery	130	51	40	20	3	3	9	1	2	–	–	1	–
Drugs offences	337	48	61	26	30	32	64	11	14	20	28	3	–
Other offences	325	177	69	27	5	17	22	–	5	2	–	–	1
Offence not recorded	56	18	12	9	3	5	6	–	1	2	–	–	–
Aged 30 and over	**1,950**	**721**	**430**	**191**	**115**	**126**	**184**	**27**	**38**	**38**	**59**	**12**	**9**
Violence against the person	188	67	30	13	7	14	27	4	2	8	4	4	8
Sexual offences	8	1	–	–	1	2	2	–	1	–	–	1	–
Burglary	44	10	7	4	3	5	11	2	1	–	1	–	–
Robbery	18	2	1	2	1	4	4	1	2	–	1	–	–
Theft and handling	708	316	191	84	41	34	32	4	5	–	1	–	–
Fraud and forgery	247	77	61	40	22	18	22	2	3	2	–	–	–
Drugs offences	324	38	35	21	25	32	64	14	18	23	47	7	–
Other offences	343	191	83	18	8	12	19	–	4	4	3	–	1
Offence not recorded	70	19	22	9	7	5	3	–	2	1	2	–	–

Table 4.7   Receptions into prison under sentence of immediate imprisonment: by offence group

England and Wales
All adults   Number of persons

Offence group	1987	1988	1989	1990	1991	1992	1993	1994	1995	1996	1997
All adults											
All offences	**43,651**	**43,388**	**41,771**	**36,471**	**38,312**	**36,832**	**37,358**	**46,232**	**52,772**	**56,713**	**62,089**
Violence against the person	7,015	7,187	6,154	5,124	5,006	5,279	5,578	6,576	7,189	8,092	8,933
Sexual offences	2,094	2,083	2,055	1,880	1,806	1,687	1,744	1,815	2,211	2,321	2,325
Burglary	8,491	7,478	6,398	5,175	5,342	5,603	5,516	6,650	7,058	7,197	7,734
Robbery	1,640	1,355	1,461	1,596	1,631	1,877	1,810	1,696	1,751	1,908	1,877
Theft and handling }	12,675	11,128	10,356	{ 6,553	7,118	6,479	6,597	8,531	10,266	11,070	12,745
Fraud and forgery }				1,508	1,571	1,718	1,889	2,115	2,606	2,818	2,688
Drugs offences	3,037	2,804	2,682	2,300	2,175	2,765	2,794	3,127	4,248	5,457	6,353
Other offences	8,023	9,520	9,283	7,800	8,317	8,656	10,274	14,388	16,330	16,801	18,189
Offence not recorded(¹)	676	1,833	3,382	4,535	5,346	2,768	1,156	1,334	1,113	1,049	1,245
Adult males											
All offences	**41,268**	**41,162**	**39,611**	**34,737**	**36,464**	**35,018**	**35,429**	**43,789**	**49,875**	**53,415**	**58,095**
Violence against the person	6,794	6,921	5,947	4,965	4,856	5,114	5,363	6,308	6,850	7,717	8,503
Sexual offences	2,081	2,064	2,043	1,872	1,795	1,678	1,726	1,806	2,202	2,312	2,311
Burglary	8,354	7,379	6,293	5,102	5,279	5,536	5,447	6,558	6,976	7,080	7,604
Robbery	1,578	1,310	1,422	1,566	1,593	1,835	1,752	1,645	1,694	1,824	1,815
Theft and handling }	11,472	10,097	9,393	{ 5,974	6,505	5,872	5,915	7,550	9,140	9,910	11,219
Fraud and forgery }				1,376	1,430	1,549	1,643	1,859	2,255	2,420	2,311
Drugs offences	2,629	2,456	2,398	2,060	1,952	2,516	2,522	2,874	3,891	4,944	5,692
Other offences	7,716	9,196	8,894	7,484	8,004	8,372	10,003	13,996	15,903	16,265	17,521
Offence not recorded(¹)	644	1,739	3,221	4,338	5,050	2,546	1,058	1,193	964	943	1,119
Adult females											
All offences	**2,383**	**2,226**	**2,160**	**1,734**	**1,848**	**1,814**	**1,929**	**2,443**	**2,897**	**3,298**	**3,994**
Violence against the person	221	266	207	159	150	165	215	268	339	375	430
Sexual offences	13	19	12	8	11	9	18	9	9	9	14
Burglary	137	99	105	73	63	67	69	92	82	117	130
Robbery	62	45	39	30	38	42	58	51	57	84	62
Theft and handling }	1,203	1,031	963	{ 579	613	607	682	981	1,126	1,160	1,526
Fraud and forgery }				132	141	169	246	256	351	398	377
Drugs offences	408	348	284	240	223	249	272	253	357	513	661
Other offences	307	324	389	316	313	284	271	392	427	536	668
Offence not recorded(¹)	32	94	161	197	296	222	98	141	149	106	126

(¹) See paragraph 19 of the Notes.

Table 4.8 Receptions into prison under sentence of immediate imprisonment: by length of sentence

England and Wales
All adults   Number of persons

Length of sentence	1987	1988	1989	1990	1991	1992	1993	1994	1995	1996	1997
All adults											
All sentence lengths	**43,651**	**43,388**	**41,771**	**36,471**	**38,312**	**36,832**	**37,358**	**46,232**	**52,772**	**56,713**	**62,089**
Up to 3 months	9,693	8,905	8,630	7,086	7,455	7,370	7,982	11,299	14,320	15,224	17,546
Over 3 months up to 6 months	8,201	8,171	8,052	6,829	7,520	7,111	8,949	12,422	13,818	14,664	15,805
Over 6 months less than 12 months	8,780	8,730	8,032	4,080	4,336	4,090	4,119	4,476	4,915	4,976	5,351
12 months				2,955	3,152	2,998	2,863	3,151	3,263	3,298	3,357
Over 12 months up to 18 months	5,170	5,199	4,859	4,413	4,696	4,303	3,730	4,172	4,322	4,511	4,668
Over 18 months up to 3 years	7,381	7,857	7,395	6,696	6,590	6,292	5,415	6,182	6,981	7,784	8,307
Over 3 years less than 4 years	1,654	1,727	1,746	588	674	632	532	641	762	967	1,214
4 years				969	935	1,043	917	921	1,068	1,368	1,451
Over 4 years up to 5 years	999	906	1,037	933	1,018	885	948	968	1,192	1,339	1,545
Over 5 years up to 10 years	1,369	1,446	1,589	1,546	1,498	1,668	1,494	1,563	1,610	1,963	2,147
Over 10 years less than life	200	254	227	186	223	236	207	248	273	341	385
Life	204	193	204	190	215	204	202	189	248	278	313
Adult males											
All sentence lengths	**41,268**	**41,162**	**39,611**	**34,737**	**36,464**	**35,018**	**35,429**	**43,789**	**49,875**	**53,415**	**58,095**
Up to 3 months	9,006	8,271	8,021	6,651	6,983	6,879	7,446	10,498	13,296	14,034	16,007
Over 3 months up to 6 months	7,713	7,696	7,596	6,485	7,137	6,762	8,515	11,819	13,121	13,951	14,904
Over 6 months less than 12 months	8,302	8,306	7,643	3,844	4,093	3,880	3,886	4,191	4,607	4,639	4,948
12 months				2,824	2,996	2,835	2,700	2,986	3,064	3,101	3,157
Over 12 months up to 18 months	4,909	4,988	4,643	4,231	4,488	4,110	3,553	3,965	4,109	4,273	4,416
Over 18 months up to 3 years	7,067	7,559	7,122	6,451	6,382	6,072	5,198	5,965	6,715	7,422	7,927
Over 3 years less than 4 years	1,585	1,654	1,680	571	660	614	512	625	740	938	1,167
4 years				925	903	999	887	883	1,027	1,310	1,380
Over 4 years up to 5 years	953	869	978	897	972	840	905	931	1,151	1,284	1,470
Over 5 years up to 10 years	1,337	1,398	1,513	1,496	1,426	1,608	1,439	1,499	1,556	1,865	2,054
Over 10 years less than life	197	240	224	182	218	229	199	246	259	330	368
Life	199	181	191	180	206	190	189	181	230	268	297
Adult females											
All sentence lengths	**2,383**	**2,226**	**2,160**	**1,734**	**1,848**	**1,814**	**1,929**	**2,443**	**2,897**	**3,298**	**3,994**
Up to 3 months	687	634	609	435	472	491	536	801	1,024	1,190	1,539
Over 3 months up to 6 months	488	475	456	344	383	349	434	603	697	713	901
Over 6 months less than 12 months	478	424	389	236	243	210	233	285	308	337	403
12 months				131	156	163	163	165	199	197	200
Over 12 months up to 18 months	261	211	216	182	208	193	177	207	213	238	252
Over 18 months up to 3 years	314	298	273	245	208	220	217	217	266	362	380
Over 3 years less than 4 years	69	73	66	17	14	18	20	16	22	29	47
4 years				44	32	44	30	38	41	58	71
Over 4 years up to 5 years	46	37	59	36	46	45	43	37	41	55	75
Over 5 years up to 10 years	32	48	76	50	72	60	55	64	54	98	93
Over 10 years less than life	3	14	3	4	5	7	8	2	14	11	17
Life	5	12	13	10	9	14	13	8	18	10	16

Table 4.9 Receptions into prison under sentence of immediate imprisonment: by age

England and Wales
All adults

Number of persons

Age	1987	1988	1989	1990	1991	1992	1993	1994	1995	1996	1997
All adults											
Age on receptions											
All ages	**43,651**	**43,388**	**41,771**	**36,471**	**38,312**	**36,832**	**37,358**	**46,232**	**52,772**	**56,713**	**62,089**
21–24	15,544	15,113	13,941	12,108	12,345	11,655	12,055	14,491	15,370	16,138	16,767
25–29	11,014	11,213	11,289	9,872	10,617	10,141	10,292	12,813	14,601	15,710	17,251
30–39	10,388	10,507	10,091	8,714	9,501	9,331	9,513	12,278	14,980	16,478	18,756
40–49	4,658	4,564	4,496	3,940	4,068	3,986	3,900	4,737	5,375	5,791	6,415
50–59	1,561	1,577	1,500	1,425	1,368	1,347	1,.259	1,486	1,969	2,058	2,285
60 and over	486	414	454	412	413	372	339	427	477	538	615
Adult males											
Age on reception											
All ages	**41,268**	**41,162**	**39,611**	**34,737**	**36,464**	**35,018**	**35,429**	**43,789**	**49,875**	**53,415**	**58,095**
21–24	14,822	14,443	13,331	11,608	11,875	11,204	11,564	13,864	14,725	15,401	15,794
25–29	10,362	10,622	10,662	9,401	10,109	9,629	9,736	12,099	13,769	14,773	16,180
30–39	9,736	9,876	9,511	8,270	8,925	8,776	8,958	11,538	14,002	15,359	17,431
40–49	4,396	4,309	4,223	3,705	3,841	3,759	3,663	4,457	5,034	5,412	5,935
50–59	1,486	1,512	1,444	1,355	1,312	1,296	1,185	1,416	1,882	1,946	2,160
60 and over	466	400	440	398	402	354	323	415	463	524	595
Adult females											
Age on reception											
All ages	**2,383**	**2,226**	**2,160**	**1,734**	**1,848**	**1,814**	**1,929**	**2,443**	**2,897**	**3,298**	**3,994**
21–24	722	670	610	500	470	451	491	627	645	737	973
25–29	652	591	627	471	508	512	556	714	832	937	1,071
30–39	652	631	580	444	576	555	555	740	978	1,119	1,325
40–49	262	255	273	235	227	227	237	280	341	379	480
50–59	75	65	56	70	56	51	74	70	87	112	125
60 and over	20	14	14	14	11	18	16	12	14	14	20

Table 4.10   Average sentence length of receptions into prison under sentence of immediate imprisonment([1]): by court sentencing and date of reception

England and Wales
All adults   Number of months

	1987	1988	1989	1990([3])	1991([3])	1992([3])	1993	1994	1995	1996	1997
All adults											
Court sentencing([2])											
Crown Court	..	..	..	..	..	26.4	25.1	24.8	24.6	25.8	26.6
Magistrates' courts	..	..	..	..	..	4.4	4.7	4.5	4.1	4.0	3.9
All courts	..	..	..	..	..	19.0	17.2	15.7	15.3	16.0	15.9
Adult males											
Court sentencing([2])											
Crown Court	22.7	23.1	24.4	24.9	25.6	26.7	25.4	25.1	25.0	26.1	26.9
Magistrates' courts	3.9	4.1	4.0	4.1	4.1	4.4	4.7	4.6	4.2	4.1	4.0
All courts	17	17.6	18	18.2	18.2	19.2	17.3	15.9	15.5	16.1	16.2
Adult females											
Court sentencing([2])											
Crown Court	16.4	18.8	20.0	19.6	21.3	20.3	20.4	19.7	18.8	21.1	21.4
Magistrates' courts	3.6	3.7	3.5	3.5	3.6	3.7	4.1	3.8	3.6	3.4	3.2
All courts	13.1	14.5	15.0	14.5	15.2	15.6	14.4	12.5	11.9	13.1	12.2

([1]) Excluding those sentenced to life imprisonment.

([2]) Type of court originally imposing a sentence of imprisonment; further sentences may have been awarded at a different court.

([3]) Figures are subject to a wider margin of error than those for other years because of a particularly large number of cases with court not recorded; such cases are included in the "All courts" figures.

Table 4.11 **Average time served in prison under sentence by prisoners discharged from determinate sentences on completion of sentence or on licence: by sex and length of sentence**

England and Wales 1997
All adults

Length of sentence(1)	Number of persons discharged(2)	Months				Percentage of sentence served under sentence	
		Average length of sentence	Average time served under sentence				
			Including remand time	Excluding remand time		Including remand time	Excluding remand time
All adults							
All lengths of sentence less than life	**58,000**	**14.8**	**8.1**	**6.9**		**55**	**46**
Up to and including 3 months	17,650	2.1	1.0	0.9		48	42
Over 3 months up to 6 months	15,850	5.0	2.4	2.1		50	42
Over 6 months less than 12 months	5,100	8.8	4.4	3.7		51	43
12 months	3,350	12.0	6.1	5.2		52	43
Over 12 months up to 18 months	4,500	16.6	8.6	7.0		53	42
Over 18 months up to 3 years	7,450	28.2	14.8	12.2		53	43
Over 3 years less than 4 years	650	42.1	22.3	18.2		53	43
4 years	1,000	48.0	29.7	24.9		62	51
Over 4 years up to 5 years	950	58.3	36.1	30.5		62	52
Over 5 years up to 10 years	1,350	85.8	53.2	46.7		62	54
Over 10 years less than life	180	154.2	95.3	88.0		59	57
Adult males							
All lengths of sentence less than life	**54,250**	**15.1**	**8.4**	**7.0**		**55**	**46**
Up to and including 3 months	16,100	2.1	0.1	0.9		48	42
Over 3 months up to 6 months	14,950	5.0	2.5	2.1		50	42
Over 6 months less than 12 months	4,700	8.7	4.5	3.7		51	42
12 months	3,150	12.0	6.3	5.1		52	43
Over 12 months up to 18 months	4,250	16.6	8.8	6.9		53	42
Over 18 months up to 3 years	7,100	28.2	14.9	12.2		53	43
Over 3 years less than 4 years	650	41.9	22.2	18.1		53	43
4 years	950	48.0	29.8	24.9		62	52
Over 4 years up to 5 years	900	58.3	36.2	30.6		62	52
Over 5 years up to 10 years	1,300	85.7	53.6	46.9		63	55
Over 10 years less than life	180	154.0	93.1	88.4		59	57
Adult females							
All lengths of sentence less than life	**3,740**	**10.5**	**5.6**	**4.7**		**53**	**45**
Up to and including 3 months	1,540	1.9	0.9	0.8		48	42
Over 3 months up to 6 months	880	5.0	2.6	2.1		51	44
Over 6 months less than 12 months	390	8.7	4.5	3.9		52	45
12 months	180	12.0	6.2	5.5		52	46
Over 12 months up to 18 months	240	16.7	9.0	7.4		54	44
Over 18 months up to 3 years	360	27.8	15.0	12.1		54	44
Over 3 years less than 4 years	20	42.8	23.4	18.8		55	44
4 years	30	48.0	26.4	22.3		55	46
Over 4 years up to 5 years	40	56.6	33.4	27.7		58	49
Over 5 years up to 10 years	53	83.7	47.5	41.6		55	48
Over 10 years less than life	3	164.5	95.9	80.2		55	49

(1) On discharge: the sentence may change after reception if there are further charges or an appeal.
(2) Excludes discharges following recall after release on licence, non-criminals, persons committed to custody for non-payment of a fine and persons reclassified as adult prisoners. A further 380 adult males and 51 adult females died or were discharged for other reasons such as transfers to other establishments or successful appeals. Figures have been rounded to the nearest fifty except for the two longest sentence bands which have been rounded to the nearest 10. All female sentence bands are rounded to the nearest ten.

94

CHAPTER 5

LIFE SENTENCE PRISONERS

Key points

Population

- There were 3,721 inmates serving life sentences in Prison Service establishments on 30 June 1997. 80 per cent of these were convicted murderers.

- The vast majority, 96 per cent, of these prisoners were male.

Receptions

- There were 384 receptions in 1997. This was a record high, and continues a rapid increase from the average of 239 receptions between 1987 and 1994.

Time served

- The average time served by life sentence prisoners first released on life licence has gradually increased over the last decade from 11.2 years in 1987 to 14.3 years in 1997.

Releases

- The number of life sentence prisoners first released on life licence rose from 85 in 1996 to 98 in 1997. The number of murderers released was the highest on record, but only a small number of discretionary lifers were released.

- Less than a tenth (9 per cent) of life licensees released between 1972 and 1993 were reconvicted of a standard list offence[1] within 2 years.

---

[1] The standard list of offences covers all indictable offences, including triable either way offences, and a number of the more serious summary offence.

Population and receptions (Tables 5.1 and 5.2)

5.1 On 30 June 1997, there were 3,721 persons serving a life sentence (including detention during Her Majesty's pleasure and custody for life) in Prison Service establishments. This was an increase of 232 (7 per cent) compared with a year earlier and 59 per cent above the figure for 30 June 1987. Receptions in 1997, at 384, were 14 per cent higher than in 1996, 37 per cent higher than in 1995 and 61 per cent higher than the average of 239 for the previous eight years, 1987 to 1994.

Figure 5.1

POPULATION OF LIFE SENTENCE PRISONERS
30 JUNE, 1987–1997

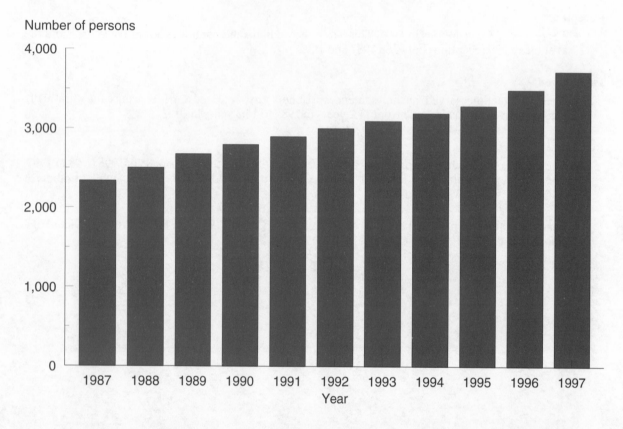

5.2 Adult males accounted for 94 per cent of the life sentence prisoner population in mid-1997, but for only 77 per cent of the 1997 receptions. Male young offenders form a higher proportion of receptions than of the population([2]), with 17 per cent of receptions compared to only 3 per cent of the population.

5.3 Some 80 per cent of lifers held by the Prison Service on 30 June 1997 were serving sentences for murder. A further 6 per cent had a principal offence of manslaughter, other homicide or attempted homicide, and 7 per cent were imprisoned for rape or other sexual offences. The female population contained no sexual offenders, but did include 10 (7 per cent) arsonists.

([2]) Young offenders are reclassified as adults before they reach the age of 22.

Figure 5.2

POPULATION OF LIFE SENTENCE PRISONERS, BY OFFENCE
30 JUNE 1997

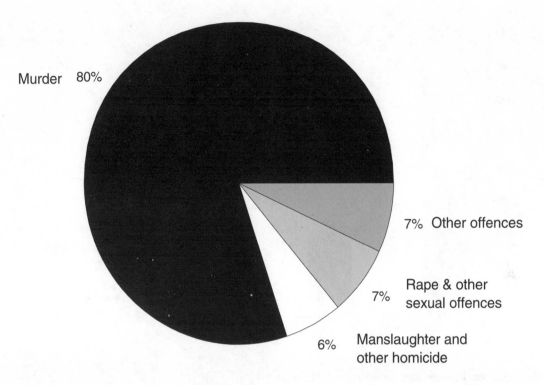

Murder 80%

7% Other offences

7% Rape & other
sexual offences

6% Manslaughter and
other homicide

Population by interval since reception (Table 5.3)

5.4   The abolition of the death penalty for murder by Acts of Parliament in 1957 and 1965 resulted in a gradual increase in the time served by those given sentences of life imprisonment, and so increased the proportion of lifers who have served long periods under sentence. On 30 June 1997, 18 per cent of those in custody serving a life sentence had been sentenced between 10 and 15 years ago, and another 18 per cent had been sentenced over 15 years ago. The comparable figures for mid-1975 were 8 per cent in the 10-15 years group and 2 per cent (including only 1 per cent of murderers) in the over 15 years group.

5.5   The life sentence prisoner population on 30 June 1997 included 187 inmates who had been recalled from release on life licence (134 murderers and 53 others). Only 5 per cent of current lifers were recalled licencees, including 13 per cent of those sentenced 15-20 years ago, 37 per cent of those sentenced 20-30 years ago and 74 per cent of those sentenced over 30 years ago.

Figure 5.3

POPULATION OF LIFE SENTENCE PRISONERS
30 JUNE 1975 AND 30 JUNE 1997
BY TIME SERVED UNDER SENTENCE

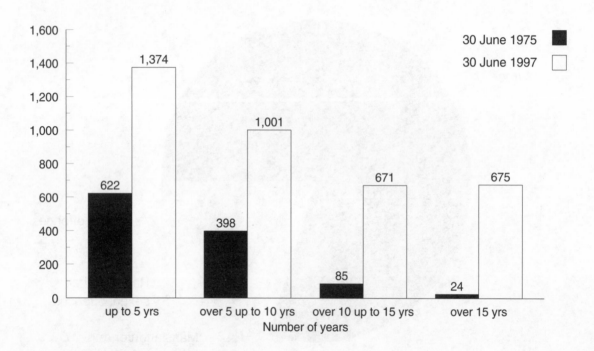

Releases on licence and time served (Tables 5.4 and 5.5)

5.6 Time served after sentence and before release on life licence by life sentence prisoners varies considerably. The few who have been released on licence within seven years are outnumbered by those discharged for other reasons, such as successful appeals, or transfers to other jurisdictions or to psychiatric hospitals. Of those received under sentence between 1965 and 1974, 50 per cent were still in custody 10 years after their reception. Those received between 1976 and 1981 tended to wait longer to be released—15 years passed before as many had been released on licence as were still in custody. Of the 1,631 people received under sentence between 1965 and 1977, 296 (18 per cent) had not been released by the end of 1997 and had therefore served at least 20 years.

5.7 Of those received between 1965 and 1984 who have since been released on licence, 8 per cent served up to 7 years before their first release, 61 per cent served from 7 to less than 13 years and 31 per cent served 13 years or more.

5.8 Table 5.5 shows the number of people first released on life licence in each year from 1987 to 1997 and the average time they served since being sentenced. The average time served has increased, rising from 11.2 years in 1987 to 14.3 years in 1997, although the small numbers involved cause a lot of fluctuation.

5.9 The introduction of Discretionary Lifer Panels (DLPs) following the 1991 Criminal Justice Act led to an increase in the numbers of discretionary life sentence prisoners who were released for the first time in 1993, as the backlog of prisoners who had served their "relevant parts" (a minimum period to be served under sentence) were reviewed by the DLP. The number of discretionary lifers released was low in both 1996 and 1997, but there were a record number (88) of mandatory lifers released in 1997.

5.10 The growth of the population does not exactly match the excess of receptions under sentence (Table 5.1) over first releases on licence (Table 5.5), as a number of other factors affect population size. The most numerous of these are recalls from licence (about 25 returning each year), second and subsequent releases on licence (about 15 leaving each year), successful appeals (again, about 15 leaving each year), transfers to and from psychiatric and other institutions (usually a few more leaving than arriving), and deaths (about 15 a year).

5.11 Life sentence prisoners are released on a life licence which can be revoked if the offender commits another offence, is at risk of doing so, or fails to comply with licence conditions or fails to co-operate with the Probation Service. Upon revocation the licensee is immediately recalled to prison to continue serving their life sentence. Between 1972 and 1993, 1,578 life sentence prisoners were released for the first time on a life licence. Of these life licensees, less than a tenth (9 per cent) were reconvicted of a standard list offence within 2 years; this group includes 1 per cent who were reconvicted for a grave offence[3]. A smaller proportion of mandatory life sentence prisoners (8 per cent) than discretionary life sentence prisoners (11 per cent) were reconvicted within 2 years. In total, 66 were reconvicted of a grave offence by the end of 1995, of whom 28 were given a further life sentence. A total of 302 were recalled to prison. Further information on reconvictions of life licensees can be found in the Home Office Statistical Bulletin 'Life licensees—reconvictions and recalls by the end of 1995: England and Wales' (issue 2/97).

---

[3] Grave offences are a subset of standard list offences, covering all indictable only offences which have a maximum sentence of life imprisonment; these are mainly offences of homicide, serious wounding, rape, buggery, robbery, aggravated burglary and arson endangering life.

Table 5.1   Population in and receptions into prison by type of prisoner and sex

England and Wales
Life sentence prisoners   Number of persons

	1987	1988	1989	1990	1991	1992	1993	1994	1995	1996	1997
Population 30 June											
Total population	**2,339**	**2,503**	**2,677**	**2,795**	**2,896**	**3,000**	**3,095**	**3,192**	**3,289**	**3,489**	**3,721**
Males:	**2,265**	**2,427**	**2,592**	**2,704**	**2,800**	**2,904**	**2,990**	**3,081**	**3,176**	**3,365**	**3,584**
Young offenders	106	106	103	121	100	87	77	83	83	75	100
Adults	2,159	2,321	2,489	2,583	2,700	2,817	2,913	2,998	3,093	3,290	3,484
Females:	**74**	**76**	**85**	**91**	**96**	**96**	**105**	**111**	**113**	**124**	**137**
Young offenders	8	10	5	4	5	4	4	5	5	5	9
Adults	66	66	80	87	91	92	101	106	108	119	128
Receptions											
Total receptions	**245**	**249**	**243**	**229**	**246**	**236**	**243**	**222**	**280**	**338**	**384**
Males:	**238**	**235**	**230**	**217**	**233**	**222**	**225**	**213**	**259**	**327**	**363**
Young offenders	39	54	40	37	27	32	36	32	29	59	66
Adults	199	181	190	180	206	190	189	181	230	268	297
Females:	**7**	**14**	**13**	**12**	**13**	**14**	**18**	**9**	**21**	**11**	**21**
Young offenders	2	2	–	2	4	–	5	1	3	1	5
Adults	5	12	13	10	9	14	13	8	18	10	16

Table 5.2   Population in prison by age and principal offence

England and Wales 30 June 1997
Life sentence prisoners   Number of persons

Offence	Males			Females			Males and females		
	Young offenders	Adults	All	Young offenders	Adults	All	Young offenders	Adults	All
All offences	**100**	**3,484**	**3,584**	**9**	**128**	**137**	**109**	**3,612**	**3,721**
Murder	69	2,803	2,872	7	105	112	76	2,908	2,984
Manslaughter	4	132	136	–	5	5	4	137	141
Other homicide and attempted homicide	1	79	80	1	5	6	2	84	86
Other violence against the person	2	71	73	–	2	2	2	73	75
Rape	4	218	222	–	–	–	4	218	222
Other sexual offences	–	36	36	–	–	–	–	36	36
Robbery	6	32	38	1	–	1	7	32	39
Arson	7	75	82	–	10	10	7	85	92
Other offences	7	38	45	–	1	1	7	39	46

Table 5.3   Population in prison by interval since date of reception under sentence

England and Wales
Life sentence prisoners   Number of persons

| Date/custody type | Offence | Interval since date of reception under sentence | | | | | | |
		Up to 5 years	Over 5 up to 10 years	Over 10 up to 15 years	Over 15 up to 20 years	Over 20 up to 30 years	Over 30 years	All intervals
30 June 1975								
Recalled from licence[1]	Murder	3	–	1	–	1	–	5
	Other	2	–	–	–	–	–	2
	All	5	–	1	–	1	–	7
Original sentence	Murder	478	294	66	11	1	1	851
	Other	139	104	18	10	–	–	271
	All	617	398	84	21	1	1	1,122
All types	Murder	481	294	67	11	2	1	856
	Other	141	104	18	10	–	–	273
	All	622	398	85	21	2	1	1,129
30 June 1980								
Recalled from licence[1]	Murder	1	–	8	9	6	1	25
	Other	–	–	5	3	3	–	11
	All	1	–	13	12	9	1	36
Original sentence	Murder	606	390	131	19	7	–	1,153
	Other	215	112	61	5	2	–	395
	All	821	502	192	24	9	–	1,548
All types	Murder	607	390	139	28	13	1	1,178
	Other	215	112	66	8	5	–	406
	All	822	502	205	36	18	1	1,584
30 June 1985								
Recalled from licence[1]	Murder	–	1	10	21	17	5	54
	Other	–	1	4	12	4	–	21
	All	–	2	14	33	21	5	75
Original sentence	Murder	743	535	191	56	11	1	1,537
	Other	175	167	68	26	3	–	439
	All	918	702	259	82	14	1	1,976
All types	Murder	743	536	201	77	28	6	1,591
	Other	175	168	72	38	7	–	460
	All	918	704	273	115	35	6	2,051
30 June 1990								
Recalled from licence[1]	Murder	4	2	8	25	39	9	87
	Other	1	2	2	7	14	–	26
	All	5	4	10	32	53	9	113
Original sentence	Murder	942	687	357	115	45	4	2,150
	Other	172	149	137	53	20	1	532
	All	1,114	836	494	168	65	5	2,682
All types	Murder	946	689	365	140	84	13	2,237
	Other	173	151	139	60	34	1	558
	All	1,119	840	504	200	118	14	2,795
30 June 1995								
Recalled from licence[1]	Murder	6	7	10	25	43	17	108
	Other	–	3	3	6	27	4	43
	All	6	10	13	31	70	21	151
Original sentence	Murder	947	844	512	214	87	10	2,614
	Other	203	129	98	59	32	3	524
	All	1,150	973	610	273	119	13	3,138
All types	Murder	953	851	522	239	130	27	2,722
	Other	203	132	101	65	59	7	567
	All	1,156	983	623	304	189	34	3,289
30 June 1997								
Recalled from licence[1]	Murder	2	0	5	36	57	34	134
	Other	0	1	6	13	27	6	53
	All	2	1	11	49	84	40	186
Original sentence	Murder	1,081	851	543	260	102	13	2,850
	Other	291	149	117	82	44	1	684
	All	1,371	1,000	660	342	146	14	3,535
All types	Murder	1,083	851	548	296	159	47	2,984
	Other	291	150	123	95	71	7	737
	All	1,374	1,001	671	391	230	54	3,721

[1] Including time spent on release under licence.

101

Table 5.4 Receptions into prison by year of reception under sentence, type of release and time spent under sentence

England and Wales
Life sentence prisoners

Number of persons

Year of reception under sentence and type of release	Total received	Number released by years under sentence[1]						Total released by end 1997	Not released by end 1997	Median[3] number of years to release on licence
		Up to 7	Over 7 up to 9	Over 9 up to 11	Over 11 up to 13	Over 13 up to 17	Over 17[4]			
1965										
On licence	76	3	19	16	15	11	5	69	4	10
Other[2]		1	2	–	–	–	–	3		
1966										
On licence	89	3	16	18	17	8	9	71	11	11
Other[2]		1	1	–	1	1	3	7		
1967										
On licence	89	6	15	22	11	12	9	75	9	10
Other[2]		1	1	–	1	–	2	5		
1968										
On licence	92	6	14	16	9	18	5	68	15	11
Other[2]		1	4	–	1	–	3	9		
1969										
On licence	103	2	25	19	15	10	12	83	12	11
Other[2]		2	–	1	2	1	2	8		
1970										
On licence	134	6	33	21	24	5	14	103	17	10
Other[2]		7	–	3	–	–	4	14		
1971										
On licence	128	11	27	19	15	8	18	98	17	10
Other[2]		5	3	–	2	1	2	13		
1972										
On licence	102	8	17	28	8	5	11	77	13	10
Other[2]		8	1	1	–	1	1	12		
1973										
On licence	139	11	16	21	12	13	6	79	37	11
Other[2]		15	1	1	1	1	4	23		
1974										
On licence	169	13	39	21	13	12	17	115	28	10
Other[2]		14	4	1	1	1	5	26		
1975										
On licence	160	7	19	24	12	20	20	102	29	13
Other[2]		14	3	–	–	12	–	29		
1976										
On licence	167	9	16	12	9	29	28	103	46	16
Other[2]		11	1	2	1	1	2	18		
1977										
On licence	185	11	16	13	17	30	13	100	58	15
Other[2]		21	2	1	–	–	3	27		
1978										
On licence	191	7	10	26	8	30	9	90	66	15
Other[2]		23	2	1	5	4	–	35		
1979										
On licence	191	8	8	21	19	27	6	89	76	15
Other[2]		15	3	1	–	4	3	26		
1980										
On licence	222	9	14	21	19	40	2	105	80	14
Other[2]		26	5	2	4	–	–	37		
1981										
On licence	185	2	9	18	26	19	–	74	87	15
Other[2]		10	2	4	3	5	–	24		
1982										
On licence	248	3	8	30	27	25	–	93	128	..
Other[2]		16	3	4	2	2	–	27		
1983										
On licence	175	3	5	8	19	9	–	44	100	..
Other[2]		23	3	2	3	–	–	31		
1984										
On licence	200	2	8	13	19	1	–	43	135	..
Other[2]		16	4	2	–	–	–	22		
1985										
On licence	213	2	1	14	16	–	–	33	152	..
Other[2]		24	1	2	1	–	–	28		
1986										
On licence	247	4	7	14	4	–	–	29	180	..
Other[2]		29	6	3	–	–	–	38		

[1] Excluding any time spent either on remand in custody or following any subsequent recall. Releases after 1997 are not included.

[2] Including successful appeals, deaths and transfers to psychiatric hospitals or to outside England and Wales.

[3] Number of complete years which 50 per cent of those received, excluding "other" releases, had been released on licence. Figures are not available for the latest years because insufficient inmates have been released to establish medians.

[4] The figures include releases only until the end of 1997 and are therefore incomplete.

Table 5.5　Persons first released from prison on life licence and average time served([1])

England and Wales
Life sentence prisoners   Number of persons/years

Year of release	Murderers		Others		Total	
	Number	Time served (years)	Number	Time served (years)	Number	Time served (years)
1987	48	11.2	2	10.3	50	11.2
1988	55	10.2	11	11.0	66	10.3
1989	71	11.5	5	15.2	76	11.7
1990	57	12.2	17	15.5	74	13.0
1991	58	11.9	14	12.7	72	12.1
1992	67	12.4	23	15.3	90	13.2
1993	66	14.4	60	14.6	126	14.5
1994	77	15.4	29	13.6	106	14.9
1995	60	14.0	32	13.5	92	13.8
1996	71	13.1	14	17.3	85	13.8
1997	88	14.4	10	13.3	98	14.3

([1])　Excluding any time spent on remand in custody or following any subsequent recall.

CHAPTER 6

ETHNIC GROUP AND NATIONALITY OF THE PRISON POPULATION

Key points

Ethnic group

- On 30 June 1997 11,200 people in Prison Service establishments in England and Wales belonged to ethnic minority groups. This was 10 per cent more than the 10,200 held in June 1996 but the rate of increase was slightly less than the 11 per cent rise between 1996 and 1997 for the prison population generally.

- Ethnic minority groups made up 18 per cent of the male and 25 per cent of the female prison populations at the end of June 1997.

- Greater proportions of male white prisoners were in prison for violent or sexual offences (31 per cent) or for burglary (19 per cent) than black prisoners (25 per cent and 11 per cent respectively). Black male sentenced prisoners were more likely than white males to be held for robbery (24 per cent compared with 12 per cent) or drug offences (21 per cent compared with 12 per cent).

- In mid-1997 61 per cent of the black sentenced adult male population were serving sentences of over 4 years. This compares with 47 per cent for white sentenced adult males, 59 per cent of sentenced adult male South Asians, and 61 per cent of sentenced adult males from Chinese and other ethnic groups.

Nationality

- In mid-1997 8 per cent (4,700) of the prison population were foreign nationals. This proportion has not changed since 1993.

- The proportion of sentenced female British nationals held for drug offences was 27 per cent. Amongst women who were foreign nationals the proportion serving sentences for drug offences was 69 per cent. The proportion of black foreign nationals serving sentences for drug offences was 80 per cent.

Ethnic group (Table 6.1)

6.1   In June 1997, 11,200 prisoners held in Prison Service establishments were known to belong to ethnic minority groups. Ethnic minority groups made up 18 per cent of the male prison population and 25 per cent of the female population where ethnic group was known. The black group, the largest ethnic minority group, accounted for 12 per cent of the male and 20 per cent of the female prison populations. South Asians accounted for 3 per cent of the male population and 1 per cent of the female population. These proportions have not changed substantially in recent years, but the proportion of male prisoners who are black has been increasing slowly, from 10 per cent in 1991 to 12 per cent in 1997.

6.2   Data on the ethnicity of prisoners are collected primarily to provide Prison Service management with information to assist in the development of race relations policy and practices. When comparing the ethnic composition of the prison population with that of the general population of England and Wales, it is important to realise the limited explanatory value of such a comparison as regards the involvement of particular ethnic groups in crime or how they are dealt with by the criminal justice system. Reception into prison is the final stage of the criminal justice process. The likelihood of a given offender being sent to prison depends on many factors, including the nature of the offence, whether the offence comes to the attention of the police, whether a prosecution is brought, the type of sentencing court, and the offender's age, history of previous convictions, and plea at court.

6.3   More information is becoming available on the various processes which take place before defendants come to court. For data on ethnic monitoring of stop/searches, arrests and cautions see 'Race and the Criminal Justice System' Home Office, December 1997. Marian FitzGerald and Rae Sibbitt discuss many of the issues in the Home Office Research Study 'Ethnic Monitoring in Police Forces: A Beginning', HORS 173. A more extensive study than is undertaken in this chapter of the information available on prisoners was published in a Home Office statistical bulletin 'The Ethnic Origin of Prisoners' (issue 21/94).

6.4   Between 1985 and 1992 the ethnic classification used in prisons was similar to that used for official surveys such as the EC Labour Force Survey. In October 1992 a new ethnic classification was introduced which is congruent with that used for the 1991 Census of Population. Although the two classifications are broadly similar, figures before and after October 1992 are not directly comparable. The footnotes on table 6.1 detail the ethnic classifications which were used pre-October 1992. See also paragraph 31 of the Notes. Further information on the method used to classify prisoners is contained in the Home Office statistical bulletin referred to above.

Nationality (Tables 6.2 and 6.3)

6.5   In mid-1997 8 per cent of the prison population were known to be foreign nationals, 7 per cent of the male population and 14 per cent of the females. The proportion of foreign nationals in the prison population has been unchanged since 1993, when Prison statistics England and Wales first began to present statistics on nationality. Over a third (36 per cent) of male foreign nationals were of European nationalities, with another 20 per cent being nationals of Asian countries, 19 per cent being African and 16 per cent West Indian. The largest group (32 per cent) of female foreign nationals were nationals of West Indian countries (see table 9.2 for the countries which are included), while 22 per cent were nationals of African countries and 24 per cent were of European nationality.

Figure 6.1

**FOREIGN NATIONALS IN THE PRISON POPULATION ON 30 JUNE 1997
BY SEX AND NATIONALITY**

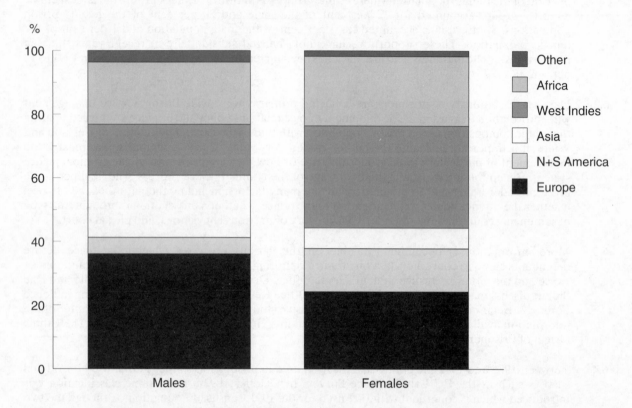

6.6 Foreign nationals account for a higher proportion of ethnic minority prisoners than of white prisoners. In 1997 foreign nationals made up 3 per cent of the white prison population but 21 per cent of black prisoners, 34 per cent of South Asians and 50 per cent of prisoners belonging to Chinese and other ethnic groups. Among black female prisoners the proportion who were foreign nationals was 44 per cent. When comparing the ethnic composition of the prison population with the ethnic composition of the general population it would be more appropriate to compare only prisoners who are usually resident in the UK with the general population. As data on prisoners' usual place of residence are lacking, nationality has been used instead. Comparisons are limited to the general population aged 15 and over as no prisoners held in Prison Service establishments in 1997 were aged less than 15. Older people (65 plus for men and 55 plus for women) have also been removed from the comparative national statistics as relatively few prisoners are included in these older age groups (see table 1.8 in chapter 1).

Figure 6.2

PRISON* AND GENERAL POPULATIONS OF ENGLAND AND WALES
ON 30 JUNE 1997 BY SEX AND ETHNIC GROUP**

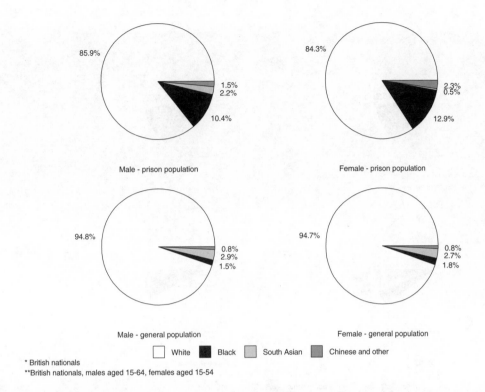

* British nationals
**British nationals, males aged 15-64, females aged 15-54

6.7 In England and Wales in 1997 94.8 per cent of the general male population with British nationality (aged 15-64) were white, 1.5 per cent were black, 2.9 per cent were South Asian and 0.8 per cent belonged to Chinese or other ethnic groups. By contrast, 86 per cent of males in the prison population who were British nationals were white, 10 per cent were black, 2 per cent were South Asian and 2 per cent belonged to Chinese or other ethnic groups. (Information on the numbers in each ethnic group during 1997 is derived from the Labour Force Survey, carried out by the Office for National Statistics, and represents an average of survey results over the year. As this is based on a sample survey the estimates can vary from year to year and comparisons with earlier years should only be made with caution, especially for smaller groups.)

6.8 For females the ethnic breakdown of the general population (aged 15-54), excluding foreign nationals, was similar to the male general population. The female prison population of British nationals was 84 per cent white, 13 per cent black, under 1 per cent were South Asian, and 2 per cent belonged to Chinese or other ethnic groups.

Type of prisoner (Table 6.3)

6.9 As figure 6.3 shows, among British nationals in prison in mid 1997, a greater proportion of fine defaulters (92.5 per cent) were white than sentenced (86.1), remand (84.7) or non-criminal (90.5) prisoners. Black prisoners formed a greater proportion of the remand population (11.3 per cent) than of the sentenced population (10.3), fine defaulters (5.3) or non-criminals (3.8). British nationals who were members of Chinese and other ethnic groups were most represented among the non-criminal or civil prisoners but still made up only 3.8 per cent of the civil prisoners.

107

Figure 6.3

**PRISON POPULATION ON 30 JUNE 1997 BY TYPE OF PRISONER AND
ETHNIC GROUP: BRITISH NATIONALS**

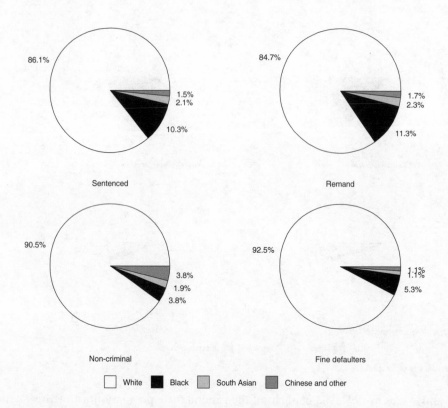

6.10   Nearly nine in ten (89 per cent) non-criminal prisoners were foreign nationals, however. The majority (over 90 per cent) were held under Immigration Act offences. If these prisoners (and a few whose nationality was not recorded) are included, the total proportion of non-criminal prisoners who belonged to ethnic minority groups was as follows: 30 per cent black, 23 per cent South Asian and 32 per cent Chinese or from other ethnic groups.

Figure 6.4

**PRISON POPULATION ON 30 JUNE 1997 BY TYPE OF PRISONER AND
ETHNIC GROUP: ALL NATIONALITIES**

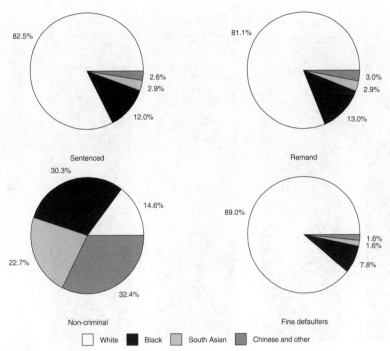

* Including a few whose nationality was not known

Offence type (Table 6.4 and 6.4a)

6.11   For adult males and females the proportions sentenced for various types of offence differed considerably between whites and members of ethnic minority groups and between foreign and British nationals.

6.12   In mid-1997 31 per cent of white sentenced males were in prison for violent or sexual offences, 19 per cent for burglary, 12 per cent for robbery and 12 per cent for drug offences. A higher proportion of black sentenced males than whites were in prison for robbery (24 per cent) or drug offences (21 per cent) and a smaller proportion for burglary (11 per cent) or violent or sexual offences (25 per cent). There were also higher proportions of drug offenders within the South Asian and the Chinese and other male sentenced populations (23 and 28 per cent respectively) than in the white sentenced male population.

Figure 6.5

**MALE POPULATION UNDER SENTENCE ON 30 JUNE 1997
BY ETHNIC GROUP AND OFFENCE TYPE: ALL NATIONALITIES**

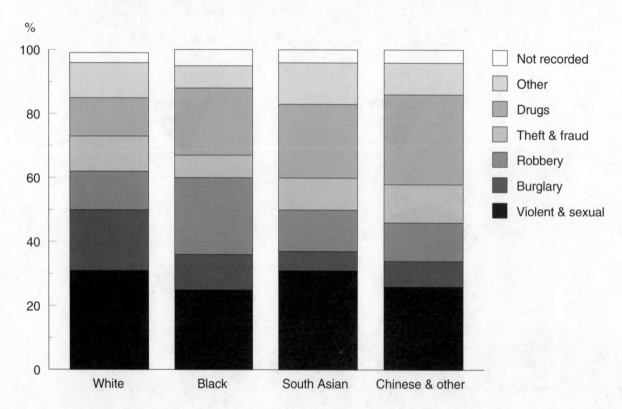

6.13 If this is compared with the composition of sentenced males of British nationality only, the main differences are in the proportions of drug offenders in the ethnic minority groups. The distribution of offence groups for the male foreign national population includes higher proportions of drug offenders in all ethnic groups. Thirty-two per cent of male foreign nationals were in prison for drug offences compared with 13 per cent of male British nationals.

Figure 6.6

**MALE POPULATION UNDER SENTENCE ON 30 JUNE 1997
BY ETHNIC GROUP AND OFFENCE TYPE: BRITISH NATIONALS ONLY**

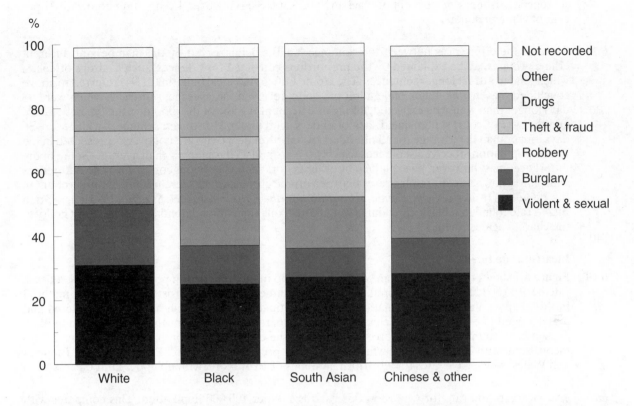

6.14 Among white sentenced females, 33 per cent were in prison for drug offences, 19 per cent for violence against the person, and 16 per cent for theft and handling offences. Among black sentenced female prisoners nearly two thirds were held for drug offences (63 per cent).

6.15 Fifteen per cent of sentenced female prisoners were foreign nationals (compared with 6 per cent of men). More than two thirds (69 per cent) of sentenced female prisoners who were foreign nationals were held for drugs offences. By contrast, the proportion of British national female prisoners sentenced for drug offences was 27 per cent. A substantial proportion of female foreign national prisoners have been arrested at ports and other locations and convicted of importing or exporting drugs. These offences carry longer sentences than average, which means that such offenders are further disproportionately represented among the prison population. Nearly three quarters of foreign national females serving sentences for drug offences were black (73 per cent) and 14 per cent belonged to other non-white ethnic groups.

6.16 Even if foreign nationals are disregarded, there are considerable differences in the types of offence for which white females and females from ethnic minority groups have been sentenced. The proportion of black British females sentenced for drug offences (49 per cent) was considerably higher than the proportion of white British national females sentenced for drug offences (24 per cent). The proportion of black British females sentenced for drug offences was also higher than the proportion of black British males sentenced for drug offences (18 per cent). The difference between the proportions of British white and black females sentenced for drug offences (25 percentage points) is more marked than the difference between the proportions of British white and black males sentenced for drug offences (6 percentage points).

Sentence length (Table 6.5)

6.17 Sixty one per cent of adult black prisoners under sentence were serving over 4 years, as well as 59 per cent of south Asians and 61 per cent of Chinese and other ethnic groups, compared with only 47 per cent of white adults. For young offenders, however, only members of black groups appear to be, on average, serving substantially longer sentences than whites. The proportion of young blacks serving over 12 months was 88 per cent. This compares with 73 per cent of white sentenced young offenders, 75 per cent of South Asians and 75 per cent of Chinese and other ethnic groups. Among adult female sentenced prisoners, 58 per cent of black prisoners were serving over 4 years compared with 31 per cent of white prisoners.

6.18 Some of the differences between the sentence lengths being served by the members of different ethnic groups may be explained by the proportions convicted for offences, such as drugs offences, which tend to attract longer sentences. The Home Office statistical bulletin (21/94) referred to above concluded that in 1990 black male adult prisoners received, on average, sentences which were 98 days longer than would be expected, taking into account the age of the offender, the type of offence and the type of court sentencing. Black offenders aged under 21 received sentences which were 36 days longer than the average for all offenders. Asian offenders (who are not over-represented in the prison population) received sentences which were around 45 days longer than average. Some of the differences may, however, be explained by other factors such as previous convictions and differences which are known to exist in plea rates between ethnic groups, which were not taken into account in the bulletin. (In her review, *Ethnic Minorities and the Criminal Justice System* (1993)([1]), Marian FitzGerald found that black defendants were more likely than other defendants to plead not guilty to the charges against them.)

Incarceration rates

6.19 Figure 6.7 shows the numbers from each ethnic group in the total prison population, expressed as a rate per 100,000 of the general population for that ethnic group. For consistency with other material in this chapter, the general population has been defined as male British nationals aged 15-64 and females aged 15-54. Note that in chapter 1, table 1.16, rates are given for the total population of all ages in each country and, therefore, the table and the chart are not comparable. The chart is also inconsistent with earlier versions which appeared in previous editions of 'Prison statistics, England and Wales' which gave rates for all British nationals of 16 or more, with no upper limit on age.

6.20 The incarceration rate for whites on this basis is 176 per 100,000 population. This compares with 1,249 for members of black groups and 150 for members of South Asian groups. There are also differences within these broad groups, for example within the South Asian group, 278 per 100,000 Pakistanis were imprisoned but only 86 per 100,000 Indians. As few as 33 in every 100,000 Chinese were in prison on 30 June 1997, but among 'Other Asian' groups 883 per 100,000 resident in England and Wales were in prison.

([1]) Research Study No 20, The Royal Commission on Criminal Justice, HMSO, 1993.

Figure 6.7

INCARCERATION RATES* BY ETHNIC GROUP, 30 JUNE 1997

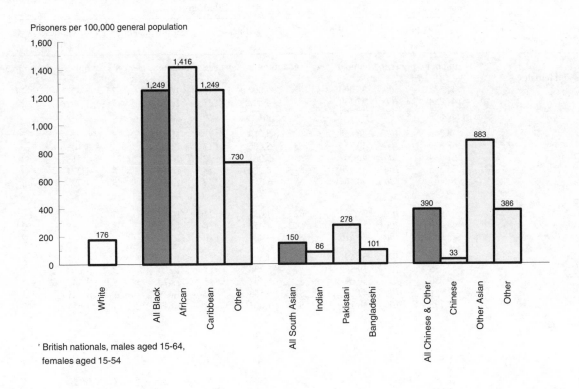

Prisoners per 100,000 general population

' British nationals, males aged 15-64,
  females aged 15-54

Table 6.1   Population in prison by sex and ethnic group(¹)

England and Wales 30 June
Males and females   Number of persons and *percentages*

Sex of prisoner	Ethnic group(¹)												
	Total		White		Black		South Asian(³)		Chinese & Other(⁴)		Unrecorded	
	number	*per cent*	number	*per cent*	number	*per cent*	number	*per cent*	number	*per cent*	number	*per cent*
Males and females												
1990	44,523	100	36,400	82	5,002	11	1,275	3	897	2	949	2
1991	44,754	100	37,130	83	4,822	11	1,323	3	952	2	527	1
1992	45,486	100	37,705	83	4,773	10	1,388	3	1,043	2	577	1
1993	44,246	100	36,855	83	5,013	11	1,356	3	926	2	96	–
1994	48,879	100	40,754	83	5,606	11	1,347	3	1,102	2	70	–
1995	51,084	100	42,207	83	5,982	12	1,497	3	1,318	3	80	–
1996	55,256	100	45,029	81	6,986	13	1,654	3	1,524	3	63	–
1997	61,467	100	50,164	82	7,585	12	1,866	3	1,795	3	57	–
Males												
1990	42,910	100	35,323	82	4,633	11	1,248	3	843	2	863	2
1991	43,210	100	36,081	84	4,470	10	1,296	3	885	2	478	1
1992	43,950	100	36,616	83	4,464	10	1,363	3	981	2	526	1
1993	42,666	100	35,691	84	4,690	11	1,335	3	854	2	96	–
1994	47,075	100	39,399	84	5,236	11	1,320	3	1,050	2	70	–
1995	49,086	100	40,697	83	5,592	11	1,470	3	1,247	3	80	–
1996	52,951	100	43,280	82	6,538	12	1,629	3	1,441	3	63	–
1997	58,795	100	48,151	82	7,062	12	1,841	3	1,684	3	57	–
Females												
1990	1,613	100	1,077	67	369	23	27	2	54	3	86	5
1991	1,544	100	1,049	68	352	23	27	2	67	4	49	3
1992	1,536	100	1,089	71	309	20	25	2	62	4	51	3
1993	1,580	100	1,164	74	323	20	21	1	72	5	–	–
1994	1,804	100	1,355	75	370	21	27	1	52	3	–	–
1995	1,998	100	1,510	76	390	20	27	1	71	4	–	–
1996	2,305	100	1,749	76	448	19	25	1	83	4	–	–
1997	2,672	100	2,013	75	523	20	25	1	111	4	–	–

(¹) Prior to 1993 coding of ethnic group was similar to that used in the EC Labour Force Survey. In 1993 a new ethnic classification system was adopted in prisons which is congruent with that used for the Census of Population. The change in coding means that figures for 1989–92 and 1993–96 are not directly comparable.

(²) Between 1988 and 1992 ethnic origin classification was 'West Indian, Guyanese, African'.

(³) Between 1988 and 1992 ethnic origin classification was 'Indian, Pakistani, Bangladeshi'.

(⁴) Between 1988 and 1992 ethnic origin classification was 'Chinese, Arab, Mixed Origin'.

Table 6.2 Population in prison on 30 June 1997 by nationality and sex

Nationality	Total	Male	Female		Nationality	Total	Male	Female
			persons					persons
All Nationalities	**61,467**	**58,795**	**2,672**		**Total Central or**			
British	**56,611**	**54,335**	**2,276**		**South America**	**158**	**131**	**27**
Foreign Nationals	**4,677**	**4,291**	**386**		Argentina	3	1	2
Total Europe	**1,646**	**1,552**	**94**		Bolivia	2	1	1
Albania	9	9	–		Brazil	15	11	4
Armenia	2	2	–		Chile	3	3	–
Austria	3	2	1		Columbia	100	83	17
Belgium	43	38	5		Honduras	2	1	1
Bosnia-Hercegovina	5	5	–		Nicaragua	3	3	–
Bulgaria	6	6	–		Peru	9	8	1
Cyprus	77	77	–		Uruguay	2	1	1
Czech Republic	4	4	–		Venezuela	15	15	–
Denmark	2	–	2		Other	4	4	–
Finland	2	2	–		**Total West Indies**	**811**	**687**	**124**
France	63	58	5		Antigua	11	11	–
Georgia	2	2	–		Barbados	28	23	5
Germany	73	61	12		Dominica	5	5	–
Gibraltar	3	3	–		Dominican Republic	2	2	–
Greece	25	25	–		Grenada	15	13	2
Hungary	7	6	1		Guyana	38	29	9
Irish Republic	734	707	27		Jamaica	651	548	103
Italy	92	90	2		Montserrat	2	2	–
Kyrgyzstan	2	2	–		Netherland Antilles	2	2	–
Lithuania	7	7	–		St. Kitts and Nevis	3	2	1
Malta	13	11	2		St Lucia	23	21	2
Netherlands	155	137	18		St Vincent &			
Poland	28	23	5		The Grenadines	5	4	1
Portugal	46	42	4		Trinidad & Tobago	22	21	1
Romania	8	8	–		Other	4	4	–
Russia	11	10	1		**Total Africa**	**920**	**836**	**84**
Slovakia	2	2	–		Algeria	78	78	–
Sweden	4	3	1		Angola	16	16	–
Spain	32	29	3		Cameroon	4	4	–
Turkey	155	152	3		Central African			
Turkmenistan	5	5	–		Republic	7	7	–
Yugoslavia	18	17	1		Congo	4	4	–
Other	5	5	–		Djibouti	2	2	–
Total Asia	**868**	**843**	**25**		Egypt	11	11	–
Bangladesh	75	73	2		Ethiopia	15	15	–
China	51	50	1		Gambia	14	14	–
Hong Kong	10	10	–		Ghana	114	96	18
India	272	266	6		Ivory Coast	7	7	–
Indonesia	2	2	–		Kenya	44	40	4
Korea (South)	2	2	–		Liberia	8	8	–
Malaysia	18	18	–		Libya	12	12	–
Nepal	3	3	–		Malawi	4	4	–
Pakistan	336	329	7		Mauritania	4	3	1
Philippines	11	5	6		Mauritius	11	11	–
Singapore	8	8	–		Morocco	38	38	–
Sri Lanka	35	35	–		Mozambique	2	2	–
Surinam	3	3	–		Nigeria	243	212	31
Thailand	6	4	2		Rwanda	3	3	–
Vietnam	32	31	1		Seychelles	3	3	–
Other	4	4	–		Sierre Leone	14	13	1
Total Middle East	**118**	**115**	**3**		Somalia	67	63	4
Afghanistan	6	6	–		South Africa	64	52	12
Iran	42	41	1		Sudan	5	5	–
Iraq	17	17	–		Tanzania	11	10	1
Israel	9	9	–		Tunisia	8	8	–
Jordan	7	7	–		Uganda	35	33	2
Kuwait	3	3	–		Zaire	35	33	2
Lebanon	15	14	1		Zambia	15	14	1
Saudi Arabia	5	5	–		Zimbabwe	16	10	6
Syrian Arab Repubic	5	4	1		Other	6	5	1
United Arab Emirates	5	5	–		**Total Oceania**	**45**	**41**	**4**
Other	4	4	–		Australia	27	26	1
Total North					Fiji	2	2	–
America	**111**	**86**	**3**		New Zealand	15	12	3
Canada	30	27	3		Other	1	1	–
USA	81	59	22		**Unrecorded**	**179**	**169**	**10**

Within each geographical area, nationalities with only one male or female have been amalgamated into 'other'.

115

Table 6.3 Population in prison by ethnic group, type of prisoner, sex and nationality([1])

England and Wales 30 June 1997
Males and females

Number of persons

Type of prisoner	Ethnic group					
	Total	White	Black	South Asian	Chinese & Other	Unrecorded
Males and females						
Total	**61,467**	**50,164**	**7,585**	**1,866**	**1,795**	**57**
British Nationals	56,611	48,526	5,946	1,223	890	26
Foreign Nationals	4,677	1,515	1,623	637	899	28
Untried	**8,563**	**6,877**	**1,156**	**252**	**272**	**6**
British Nationals	7,787	6,579	902	174	128	4
Foreign Nationals	738	268	249	77	144	–
Convicted unsentenced	**3,542**	**2,939**	**417**	**94**	**88**	**4**
British Nationals	3,367	2,866	352	84	63	2
Foreign Nationals	168	69	64	10	25	–
Sentenced	**48,674**	**40,153**	**5,834**	**1,392**	**1,253**	**42**
British Nationals	45,311	38,947	4,685	963	696	20
Foreign Nationals	3,250	1,122	1,145	427	553	3
Non-criminal	**556**	**81**	**168**	**126**	**180**	**1**
British Nationals	52	47	2	1	2	–
Foreign Nationals	495	33	164	122	176	–
Fine defaulters	**132**	**114**	**10**	**2**	**2**	**4**
British Nationals	94	87	5	1	1	–
Foreign Nationals	7	4	1	1	1	–
Males						
Total	**58,795**	**48,151**	**7,062**	**1,841**	**1,684**	**57**
British Nationals	54,335	46,607	5,653	1,211	838	26
Foreign Nationals	4,291	1,429	1,393	626	840	3
Untried	**8,134**	**6,540**	**1,089**	**248**	**251**	**6**
British Nationals	7,417	6,265	858	172	118	4
Foreign Nationals	700	266	226	75	133	–
Convicted unsentenced	**3,384**	**2,812**	**392**	**93**	**83**	**4**
British Nationals	3,220	2,742	334	83	59	2
Foreign Nationals	157	66	57	10	24	–
Sentenced	**46,611**	**38,611**	**5,415**	**1,373**	**1,170**	**42**
British Nationals	43,554	37,468	4,454	954	658	20
Foreign Nationals	2,950	1,064	957	418	508	3
Non-criminal	**537**	**77**	**156**	**125**	**178**	**1**
British Nationals	52	47	2	1	2	–
Foreign Nationals	477	29	152	122	174	–
Fine defaulters	**129**	**111**	**10**	**2**	**2**	**4**
British Nationals	92	85	5	1	1	–
Foreign Nationals	7	4	1	1	1	–
Females						
Total	**2,672**	**2,013**	**523**	**25**	**111**	**–**
British Nationals	2,276	1,919	293	12	52	–
Foreign Nationals	386	86	230	11	59	–
Untried	**429**	**337**	**67**	**4**	**21**	**–**
British Nationals	370	314	44	2	10	–
Foreign Nationals	57	21	23	2	11	–
Convicted unsentenced	**158**	**127**	**25**	**1**	**5**	**–**
British Nationals	147	124	18	1	4	–
Foreign Nationals	11	3	7	–	1	–
Sentenced	**2,063**	**1,542**	**419**	**19**	**83**	**–**
British Nationals	1,757	1,479	231	9	38	–
Foreign Nationals	300	58	188	9	45	–
Non-criminal	**19**	**4**	**12**	**1**	**2**	**–**
British Nationals	–	–	–	–	–	–
Foreign Nationals	18	4	12	–	2	–
Fine defaulters	**3**	**3**	**–**	**–**	**–**	**–**
British Nationals	2	2	–	–	–	–
Foreign Nationals	1	1	–	–	–	–

([1]) Includes persons of unknown or unrecorded nationality.

116

Table 6.4 Population in prison under sentence by ethnic group, nationality, offence and sex

England and Wales 30 June 1997
Males

Number of persons, *per cent*

Type of offence	Ethnic group										
	Total	White	Black	South Asian	Chinese & Other	Un-recorded	Total	White	Black	South Asian	Chinese & Other
	Number						per cent				
All nationalities([1])											
Total	**46,611**	**38,611**	**5,415**	**1,373**	**1,170**	**42**	*100*	*100*	*100*	*100*	*100*
Violence against the person	10,033	8,469	979	341	236	8	*22*	*22*	*18*	*25*	*20*
Rape	2,080	1,690	292	51	45	2	*4*	*4*	*5*	*4*	*4*
Other sexual offences	1,989	1,868	72	27	22	–	*4*	*5*	*1*	*2*	*2*
Burglary	7,976	7,212	579	89	89	7	*17*	*19*	*11*	*6*	*8*
Robbery	6,277	4,656	1,302	174	139	6	*13*	*12*	*24*	*13*	*12*
Theft, handling	3,929	3,519	272	70	66	2	*8*	*9*	*5*	*5*	*6*
Fraud and forgery	1,104	835	128	75	66	–	*2*	*2*	*2*	*5*	*6*
Drug offences	6,483	4,695	1,149	311	325	3	*14*	*12*	*21*	*23*	*28*
Other offences	5,046	4,374	369	181	118	4	*11*	*11*	*7*	*13*	*10*
Not recorded	1,694	1,293	272	54	64	10	*4*	*3*	*5*	*4*	*5*
British nationals											
Total	**43,554**	**37,468**	**4,454**	**954**	**658**	**20**	*100*	*100*	*100*	*100*	*100*
Violence against the person	9,435	8,242	825	212	152	4	*22*	*22*	*19*	*22*	*23*
Rape	1,910	1,628	223	32	26	1	*4*	*4*	*5*	*3*	*4*
Other sexual offences	1,909	1,829	57	16	7	–	*4*	*5*	*1*	*2*	*1*
Burglary	7,828	7,119	551	83	70	5	*18*	*19*	*12*	*9*	*11*
Robbery	5,984	4,519	1,196	150	114	5	*14*	*12*	*27*	*16*	*17*
Theft, handling	3,778	3,449	233	55	39	2	*9*	*9*	*5*	*6*	*6*
Fraud and forgery	942	790	75	43	34	–	*2*	*2*	*2*	*5*	*5*
Drug offences	5,531	4,430	788	193	120	–	*13*	*12*	*18*	*20*	*18*
Other offences	4,819	4,284	319	138	75	3	*11*	*11*	*7*	*14*	*11*
Not recorded	1,418	1,178	187	32	21	–	*3*	*3*	*4*	*3*	*3*
Foreign nationals											
Total	**2,950**	**1,064**	**957**	**418**	**508**	**3**	*100*	*100*	*100*	*100*	*100*
Violence against the person	564	199	153	129	83	–	*19*	*19*	*16*	*31*	*16*
Rape	167	60	69	19	19	–	*6*	*6*	*7*	*5*	*4*
Other sexual offences	80	39	15	11	15	–	*3*	*4*	*2*	*3*	*3*
Burglary	147	93	28	6	19	1	*5*	*9*	*3*	*1*	*4*
Robbery	292	137	106	24	25	–	*10*	*13*	*11*	*6*	*5*
Theft, handling	151	70	39	15	27	–	*5*	*7*	*4*	*4*	*5*
Fraud and forgery	162	45	53	32	32	–	*5*	*4*	*6*	*8*	*6*
Drug offences	951	265	361	118	205	2	*32*	*25*	*38*	*28*	*40*
Other offences	223	87	50	43	43	–	*8*	*8*	*5*	*10*	*8*
Not recorded	213	69	83	21	40	–	*7*	*6*	*9*	*5*	*8*

([1]) Including prisoners where nationality was unrecorded.

Table 6.4   Population in prison under sentence by ethnic group, nationality, offence and sex

England and Wales, 30 June 1997
Females   Number of persons, *per cent*

Type of offence	Ethnic group										
	Total	White	Black	South Asian	Chinese & Other	Un-recorded	Total	White	Black	South Asian	Chinese & Other
	Number						*per cent*				
All nationalities([1])											
Total	**2,063**	**1,542**	**419**	**19**	**83**	–	*100*	*100*	*100*	*100*	*100*
Violence against the person	391	340	34	5	12	–	*19*	*22*	*8*	*26*	*14*
Rape	3	2	1	–	–	–	–	–	–	–	–
Other sexual offences	5	5	–	–	–	–	–	–	–	–	–
Burglary	101	92	4	–	5	–	*5*	*6*	*1*	–	*6*
Robbery	161	127	30	1	3	–	*8*	*8*	*7*	*5*	*4*
Theft, handling	334	283	43	1	7	–	*16*	*18*	*10*	*5*	*8*
Fraud and forgery	121	91	21	3	6	–	*6*	*6*	*5*	*16*	*7*
Drug offences	691	382	264	5	40	–	*33*	*25*	*63*	*26*	*48*
Other offences	190	173	7	3	7	–	*9*	*11*	*2*	*16*	*8*
Not recorded	66	47	15	1	3	–	*3*	*3*	*4*	*5*	*4*
British nationals											
Total	**1,757**	**1,479**	**231**	**9**	**38**	–	*100*	*100*	*100*	*100*	*100*
Violence against the person	364	329	28	1	6	–	*21*	*22*	*12*	*11*	*16*
Rape	3	2	1	–	–	–	–	–	–	–	–
Other sexual offences	5	5	–	–	–	–	–	–	–	–	–
Burglary	100	92	4	–	4	–	*6*	*6*	*2*	–	*11*
Robbery	160	126	30	1	3	–	*9*	*9*	*13*	*11*	*8*
Theft, handling	313	272	35	1	5	–	*18*	*18*	*15*	*11*	*13*
Fraud and forgery	106	88	13	2	3	–	*6*	*6*	*6*	*22*	*8*
Drug offences	483	354	113	2	14	–	*27*	*24*	*49*	*22*	*37*
Other offences	176	168	4	2	2	–	*10*	*11*	*2*	*22*	*5*
Not recorded	47	43	3	–	1	–	*3*	*3*	*1*	–	*3*
Foreign nationals											
Total	**300**	**58**	**188**	**9**	**45**	–	*100*	*100*	*100*	*100*	*100*
Violence against the person	25	9	6	4	6	–	*8*	*16*	*3*	*44*	*13*
Rape	–	–	–	–	–	–	–	–	–	–	–
Other sexual offences	–	–	–	–	–	–	–	–	–	–	–
Burglary	1	–	–	–	1	–	–	–	–	–	*2*
Robbery	1	1	–	–	–	–	–	*2*	–	–	–
Theft, handling	21	11	8	–	2	–	*7*	*19*	*4*	–	*4*
Fraud and forgery	14	2	8	1	3	–	*5*	*3*	*4*	*11*	*7*
Drug offences	207	27	151	3	26	–	*69*	*47*	*80*	*33*	*58*
Other offences	14	5	3	1	5	–	*5*	*9*	*2*	*11*	*11*
Not recorded	17	3	12	–	2	–	*6*	*5*	*6*	–	*4*

([1]) Including prisoners where nationality was unrecorded.

118

Table 6.5   Population in prison by ethnic group, sex, type of prisoner and length of sentence

England and Wales 30 June 1997
Males and females   Number of persons

Type of prisoner	Ethnic group					
	Total	White	Black	South Asian	Chinese & Other	Unrecorded
Males and females						
Total	**61,467**	**50,164**	**7,585**	**1,866**	**1,795**	**57**
Remand	**12,105**	**9,816**	**1,573**	**346**	**360**	**10**
Untried	8,563	6,877	1,156	252	272	6
Convicted unsentenced	3,542	2,939	417	94	88	4
Sentenced	**48,674**	**40,153**	**5,834**	**1,392**	**1,253**	**42**
Young offenders	7,934	6,397	1,088	271	156	22
Up to 12 months	1,981	1,745	129	67	39	1
Over 12 months	5,953	4,652	959	204	117	21
Adults	40,740	33,756	4,746	1,121	1,097	20
Up to 12 months	5,564	4,901	475	144	133	1
Over 12 months up to 4 years	15,116	13,131	1,369	312	296	8
Over 4 years	19,970	15,724	2,902	665	668	11
Non-criminal	**557**	**81**	**168**	**127**	**180**	**1**
Fine defaulters	**131**	**114**	**10**	**1**	**2**	**4**
Males						
Total	**58,795**	**48,151**	**7,062**	**1,841**	**1,684**	**57**
Remand	**11,518**	**9,352**	**1,481**	**341**	**334**	**10**
Untried	8,134	6,540	1,089	248	251	6
Convicted unsentenced	3,384	2,812	392	93	83	4
Sentenced	**46,611**	**38,611**	**5,415**	**1,373**	**1,170**	**42**
Young offenders	7,684	6,196	1,050	270	146	22
Up to 12 months	1,914	1,685	125	67	36	1
Over 12 months	5,770	4,511	925	203	110	21
Adults	38,927	32,415	4,365	1,103	1,024	20
Up to 12 months	5,239	4,547	430	141	120	1
Over 12 months up to 4 years	14,408	12,559	1,254	310	277	8
Over 4 years	19,280	15,309	2,681	652	627	11
Non-criminal	**538**	**77**	**156**	**126**	**178**	**1**
Fine defaulters	**128**	**111**	**10**	**1**	**2**	**4**
Females						
Total	**2,672**	**2,013**	**523**	**25**	**111**	**–**
Remand	**587**	**464**	**92**	**5**	**26**	**–**
Untried	429	337	67	4	21	–
Convicted unsentenced	158	127	25	1	5	–
Sentenced	**2,063**	**1,542**	**419**	**19**	**83**	**–**
Young offenders	250	201	38	1	10	–
Up to 12 months	67	60	4	–	3	–
Over 12 months	183	141	34	1	7	–
Adults	1,813	1,341	381	18	73	–
Up to 12 months	415	354	45	3	13	–
Over 12 months up to 4 years	708	572	115	2	19	–
Over 4 years	690	415	221	13	41	–
Non-criminal	**19**	**4**	**12**	**1**	**2**	**–**
Fine defaulters	**3**	**3**	**–**	**–**	**–**	**–**

CHAPTER 7

PRISON REGIMES, CONDITIONS AND COSTS

Key points

Regimes

- Prisoners spent on average 11 hours out of their cells on weekdays and 9.9 hours per day on weekends in 1997.

- Average time spent on purposeful activity per prisoner was 23.1 hours per week in 1997. It was 10 per cent higher in female establishments compared with adult male establishments.

- Average time out of cell and on purposeful activities fell in recent years, due in part to population pressures.

- 2,224 completions of offending behaviour programmes counted towards exceeding the KPI target of 2,200 for 1997/98.

- Total hours of education study fell by 6 per cent between 1995 and 1997, from 9.4 million hours to 8.9 million hours.

- Numbers of prisoners employed in industrial workshops increased by 18 per cent, from 7,500 to 8,866, between 1996/7 and 1997/8.

- Releases on temporary licence rose by 53 per cent between 1993 and 1997, mainly due to increases in licences for working outside, making reparations and community service.

Conditions

- On average 11,548 prisoners were held two to a cell designed for one in 1997/98, a 22 per cent increase on the previous year.

- In 1997/98, 20.8 per cent of prisoners tested positive for drugs under Mandatory Drugs Testing, a fall on 24.4 per cent on 1996/97. Most positive tests were for cannabis.

- Escapes from establishments decreased by 88 per cent between 1993 and 1997, although escapes from magistrates courts increased by 119 per cent over the same period.

- Absconds decreased by 40 per cent between 1992 and 1997.

- Restraints were used on 2,606 male prisoners and 90 female prisoners in 1997. The most common form of restraint was confinement to a special cell. Body restraints were relatively rarely used.

- There were 70 self-inflicted deaths in prisons in 1997. The rate per 1000 prisoners has stayed more or less constant in the last three years at 1.15 to 1.16 per 1000.

Costs

- The cost per uncrowded place forecast for 1997/98 is £23,982, an expected reduction on 1996/97.

120

A new chapter

7.1   A survey of users of this publication, carried out last year as part of a review of "Prison statistics", revealed a strong demand for information on regimes and conditions to be included to provide a broader picture of prison life.

7.2   In order to meet this demand, this new chapter has been included. It draws largely on readily available statistics for this first year. It is hoped to improve the coverage and analysis of the data in future years. See notes at the end of this chapter for key points about the sources, definitions and comparability of the data presented. The authors would welcome any comments on this chapter and suggestions for future presentation of the data. Please write to the address given on page 178.

Regimes

7.3   There are currently 3 key performance indicators (KPIs) relating to regimes: time out of cell, hours spent on purposeful activity and numbers completing accredited offending behaviour programmes. Statistics for these and for education, work and temporary releases on licence are presented.

Time out of cell (Table 7.1)

7.4   In 1997, an average of 11 hours on weekdays and 9.9 hours per day on weekends were spent out of cell. Female establishments provide 32 per cent more time out of cell than adult male establishments on weekdays and 39 per cent more on weekends. Prisoners in young offender establishments were out of their cells slightly less than the average, at 10.2 hours on weekdays and 7.8 hours on weekends. Open adult male establishments, which have the lowest security requirements, have longer than average times out of cell, 17.8 hours on weekdays and 17.5 on weekends.

7.5   The KPI target for 1997/8 was for at least 60 per cent of prisoners to be held in establishments which unlock all prisoners on the standard or enhanced regime for at least 10 hours per weekday. The achievement for 1997/8 was 62 per cent. This was, however, a reduction on the 65 per cent achieved in 1996/7.

Hours spent on purposeful activity (Table 7.1)

7.6   Purposeful activity covers education and training courses, workshops, employment in farms, kitchens, gardens and laundries, induction, resettlement and rehabilitation activities, sports and P.E., religious activities and visits. In 1997 the average time spent on purposeful activities was 23.1 hours per week per prisoner. The hours spent on purposeful activities in female establishments were on average 10 per cent higher than in adult male establishments (25.4 hours compared to 23.1 hours). Young offenders establishments provided on average 23.1 hours a week of purposeful activities.

7.7   Open establishments, in keeping with their relatively low security and role in preparing prisoners for outside life, provided the most hours of purposeful activity: 41.3 hours on average in adult male open establishments and 45.4 hours in young offender open establishments.

7.8   The KPI target for 1997/98 was that prisoners across the estate should spend on average at least 22.5 hours a week in purposeful activity. This was achieved with an average of 23.3 hours. However there has been a reduction in hours over recent years:

Weekly Average Hours spent on Purposeful Activities

1992/3	23.7
1993/4	24.7
1994/5	26.2
1995/6	25.2
1996/7	23.8
1997/8	23.3

This reflects in part the population pressures facing the service and in part changes to data collection arrangements to improve the accuracy of the KPI.

121

Offending behaviour courses (Tables 7.2 and 7.3)

7.9 The Prison Service provides a range of educational and training opportunities. Of particular importance for rehabilitation are accredited courses designed to change offending behaviour. Accreditation means that in the view of an expert panel these courses would help reduce reconviction rates. There are seven accredited offending behaviour courses, all centrally administered:

> *The Sex Offender Core Treatment Programme*
> *The Sex Offender Booster Programme*
> *The Sex Offender Adapted Core Programme (accredited March 1998)*
> *The Sex Offender Extended Programme (accredited March 1998)*
> *The Reasoning and Rehabilitation Programme*
> *The Problem Solving Programme (accredited December 1997)*
> *The Enhanced Thinking Skills Programme*

7.10 Table 7.2 shows the number of completions back to 1992/93 or the year a programme started. Completions have risen from 284 in 1992/93 to 2,654 in 1997/98, although this still only covers a minority of prisoners.

7.11 In 1996/97 a KPI target for offending behaviour courses was introduced. This includes the use of an Implementation Quality Ratio (IQR) which determines the proportion of completions that an establishment can count towards the KPI target. For example an establishment that put 200 prisoners through an accredited programme but had an IQR of 80 per cent would only be able to count 160 accredited completions against the KPI. The KPI target for 1997/98 was to ensure that at least 2,200 prisoners completed programmes accredited as being effective in reducing offending, of which 670 should be completions of the Sex Offender Treatment or Booster Programme (both figures after IQR adjustment). This target was met with 2,224 IQR adjusted completions, of which 671 were for the Sex Offender Treatment or Booster programme.

7.12 Table 7.3 shows the majority of the accredited programmes in 1997/98 took place in male adult establishments, where the majority of prisoners and, in particular, the majority of sex offenders are held. Fifteen per cent of all accredited offending behaviour programmes which counted towards the 1997/98 KPI took place in Young Offender establishments and 2 per cent in female establishments.

Education provision (Tables 7.4, 7.5 and 7.6)

7.13 Education in the Prison Service is provided by contractors who are required to deliver a curriculum which is in part nationally determined and in part locally decided.

7.14 The National or "Core Curriculum" is targeted at the less able students and is accredited nationally at level 1. The core comprises Numeracy, Literacy, Information Technology, ESOL and Life and Social Skills. All establishments deliver the core curriculum and accreditation is standardised across the prison estate so that an inmate moving between prisons should be able to continue his education in his new location.

7.15 The wider curriculum is determined locally by the Governor to meet the needs of that particular population and ranges from GCSEs for the academic student to practical courses for those students wishing to gain vocational qualifications. In addition, more able students are able to study for a degree through the Open University. In 1997, 2,389 different qualifications were awarded to prisoners across the estate.

7.16 Prisoners are screened for basic skills near the beginning of their sentence. Table 7.4 gives the results of tests in 1997 and shows the lowest levels and thus greatest educational needs were in the young offender establishments, where over 40 per cent tested below level 1 in numeracy and 30 per cent below level 1 in literacy.

7.17 Average hours of education and vocational skills training per prisoner per week over the whole estate were an estimated 4.1 hours for 1997 (see table 7.5). Reflecting greater needs, average hours are highest in young offender establishments (an average of 5.8 hours per prisoner per week).

7.18   Table 7.6 shows total contracted education hours (excluding vocational skills training) have dropped over the last three years, from 9.4 million hours of student study in 1995 to 8.9 million in 1997, a drop of 6 per cent. Total teaching hours provided have fallen by 10 per cent and class sizes have increased from 7.56 to 8 over the same period. These changes reflect population and financial pressures but also increased efficiency in education provision.

Work

7.19   A range of work is provide in prisons with the aim of keeping prisoners occupied and providing skills and experience that may be useful in gaining employment on release. Areas of work include industrial workshops, farms, catering, cleaning, domestic duties and building maintenance. The numbers employed in the two main areas have increased:

Prisoners employed in:	1996/97	1997/98	% increase
Industrial workshops	7,500	8,866	18
Agriculture and Horticulture	1,395	1,725	24

Temporary release (Tables 7.7, 7.8 and 7.9)

7.20   The numbers of releases on temporary licence increased by 53 per cent between 1993 and 1997 (compared with an increase in the annual average prison population over the same period of 37 per cent). Table 7.7 shows all the increase took place in adult male establishments, where releases rose by 71 per cent, compared with a 49 per cent decrease in temporary releases from young offender establishments and a 21 per cent decrease from female establishments.

7.21   Release on temporary licence can be granted for a number of reasons, e.g. for working outside, as preparation for release, for making reparations and for compassionate reasons such as the death of a close relative. Table 7.8 illustrates that facility licences (mainly work, reparations, education and training) are now the most commonly given licences and have increased in recent years largely due to the introduction of reparations licences and the working out scheme. Licences for resettlement are the next most commonly given licence and rose between 1996 and 1997, although not to the level of 1993 and 1994. Compassionate licences have decreased by 51 per cent between 1993 and 1997. These comparisons are affected by changes in the assessment for and classification of licences in November 1994 and May 1995 and therefore trends since 1995 are the most reliable.

Conditions

7.22   Statistics are presented on six aspects of prison conditions: overcrowding, mandatory drug testing, escapes, absconds, the use of restraints and suicides.

Overcrowding (Table 7.10)

7.23   This is measured by the Prison Service as the number of prisoners held two or three to a cell designed for one. Since 1994/5 no prisoners have been held three to a cell designed for one, but the numbers held two to a cell have risen steadily in recent years as the prison population has increased. In financial year 1997/8, on average 11,548 prisoners were held two to a cell designed for one. This was a 22 per cent rise on the 9,498 held two to a cell in 1996/97. The KPI target for 1997/8 was to ensure that the percentage of the prison population above the uncrowded capacity for the estate was no more than 13 per cent. This was achieved with 12.2 per cent.

7.24   Table 7.10 shows most (88 per cent) of the prisoners held two to a cell in calendar year 1997 were in adult male establishments. Less than 1 per cent (0.7 per cent) were held in female establishments and 12 per cent in young offender establishments

Mandatory Drug Testing (Tables 7.11, 7.12 and 7.13)

7.25   Mandatory drug testing (MDT) has been operating in all establishments since the beginning of April 1996. Approximately 10 per cent of each prison's population are chosen randomly each month and tested for a range of drugs. During 1996/97, 24.4 per cent of those tested proved positive for at least one drug. This dropped to an average of 20.8 per cent for 1997/8. The KPI for 1997/8 was to ensure that the rate of positive tests was lower than in 1996/97 and was therefore met.

123

7.26 Table 7.11 and 7.12 show the rate of positive tests for each drug tested by month since the start of testing in all establishments. The highest proportion of positive tests was for cannabis followed by opiates and then benzodiazepines (rates of positive tests for March 1998: 15.3 per cent, 4.6 per cent and 1.3 per cent respectively). Since the start of testing there has been a 27 per cent fall in the rate of positive tests for cannabis, compared with a 10 per cent fall in the rate of positive tests for opiates. This may in part relate to the fact that cannabis traces remain far longer in the body compared to opiates so that the deterrent effect of MDT may be greater for cannabis.

7.27 Table 7.13 shows MDT results by type of establishment for 1997/8. The highest rate of positive tests are for local and closed training (Cat C) establishments and the lowest rates for open adult establishments, the high security dispersal establishments and young offender closed establishments.

Escapes (Table 7.14 and 7.15)

7.28 Escapes which have a minimum duration of 15 minutes or lead to further charges are measured as a Key Performance Indicator. The number of these escapes from establishments has reduced by 88 per cent between 1993 and 1997—an impressive achievement especially as the average population rose by 37 per cent over that period. In 1997 there were 23 KPI escapes from establishments. Category C establishments, which hold relatively less serious offenders, were the main location for these escapes.

7.29 KPI escapes from escorts have not reduced to the same extent between 1993 and 1997. Overall they have declined by 36 per cent between 1993 and 1997 but within this escapes from magistrates courts have increased by 119 per cent over the same period. Most of these escapes take place from the dock in magistrates courts.

Absconds (Table 7.16)

7.30 Inmates "abscond" when they unlawfully gain their liberty by an abuse of trust, without having overcome any physical security restraint and at a time when they were not in the presence of an officer specifically assigned to guard them. In 1997 there were 1,100 absconds, of which 667 were from adult male establishments, 151 were from female establishments and 282 were from young offender establishments.

7.31 The number of absconds in 1997 represent a fall of 40 per cent from a peak of 1,837 in 1992 while in the same period the average prison population rose by 33 per cent. Open adult and young offender establishments had the highest numbers of absconds as would be expected. Most types of establishment had experienced a decline in the number of absconds. This was particularly so in closed young offender establishments where the reduction between 1991 and 1997 was 95 per cent.

Use of restraints (Tables 7.17 and 7.18)

7.32 It is sometimes necessary to restrain a violent or difficult prisoner. Forms of restraint were used on 2,606 male prisoners and 90 female prisoners in 1997. Eighteen per cent of the males and 28 per cent of females were restrained on medical grounds and the remainder on non-medical grounds. The greatest use of restraints was made in local prisons, followed by closed training prisons. Between 1994 and 1997 the number of prisoners restrained in a year fell by 16 per cent.

7.33 Special cells were the most frequently used form of restraint and were used 2,715 times for male prisoners and 121 times for female prisoners in 1997, followed by protective rooms for confinement (used 565 times for males and 31 times for females). Body restraints were used relatively few times—53 applications were made to use body belts, 4 to use handcuffs and 3 to use ankle straps.

Self-inflicted deaths in custody (Table 7.19 and 7.20)

7.34 In 1997, there were 70 self-inflicted deaths of inmates in prisons (67 males and 3 females). This was the highest figure since the start of the decade, but may largely reflect the increase in the prison population as the rate per 1000 prisoners has not changed much in recent years (see table 7.20).

7.35 Of the self-inflicted deaths in 1997, 56 (80 per cent) were in adult male establishments, 1 (1 per cent) in female establishments and 11 (16 per cent) were in young offender establishments. A comparison with the population distribution across these types of establishments shows that the proportion of deaths in young offender establishments is slightly higher than would be expected (16 per cent of self-inflicted deaths compared with 14 per cent of the population in YOIs).

Costs

7.36 The cost per uncrowded place (£, cash terms) in 1997/8 is forecast at £23,982, an expected reduction on costs in 1996/7 (£24,271 per place). The KPI target for 1997/8 is to achieve at least a 1.3 per cent reduction in real terms compared to 1996/7, ensuring the average cost of an uncrowded prison place does not exceed £24,610.

Notes

1. Various parts of the Prison Service record and collate these statistics, primarily for management purposes and for measuring performance, especially the Key Performance Indicators (KPIs). The KPIs are published in the Prison Service Annual Report and Accounts (latest year April 1996—March 1997, available from the Stationery Office, price £15.90) and performance targets in the Prison Service Business Plan (latest edition 1998-99, available from Planning Group, Prison Service HQ, Cleland House, Page Street, London SW1P 4LN).

2. In line with the preferences of users as revealed in our survey, most statistics are for calendar years. Where this has not been possible, the relevant period, e.g. financial year, is indicated. In many tables establishments have been grouped by type using the Prison Service convention of putting establishments with more than one role into the category which represents the primary function of the prison. This differs from tables elsewhere in this publication where prisoners are grouped by the part of the establishment in which they reside and this also applies to a few tables in this chapter. Tables have been footnoted to indicate the classification used.

3. It has not been possible to check the accuracy and completeness of these statistics. They may also not be directly comparable to other published statistics such as the KPIs due to different time periods and definitions.

Table 7.1   Purposeful activity and time out of cell, by type of establishment([1])

England and Wales 1997
Males and females   Number of hours

Establishment type	Purposeful activity (average hours per week)	Hours out of cell	
		(average weekday hours)	(average daily weekend hours)
All establishments:	**23.1**	**11.0**	**9.9**
Adult male establishments:	**23.0**	**11.0**	**10.0**
Local Prisons	18.2	9.5	8.2
Open Training (Cat D)	41.3	17.8	17.5
Closed Training (Cat C)	27.7	12.2	11.5
Closed Training (Cat B)	22.3	10.6	9.6
Closed Training (Dispersal)	17.7	9.7	9.4
Young offender establishments([2]):	**23.1**	**10.2**	**7.8**
Open YOI	45.4	13.4	13.4
Closed YOI	23.8	10.6	7.4
Remand Centre	19.3	9.2	7.7
Female establishments:	**25.4**	**14.5**	**13.9**

([1]) Establishments have been categorised according to their main role only. Establishments that have more than one role have been placed in the category that represents the primary function of the prison. For example, the female wing at Risley has been included as part of the adult Category C estate.

([2]) Male young offenders only. Female young offenders have been included in the 'Female establishments'.

Table 7.2   Offending behaviour programme completions, by type of programme

England and Wales
Males and females   Number of completions

	Sex Offender Treatment Programme				Reasoning and Rehabilitation/ Problem solving		Thinking Skills/ Enhanced Thinking Skills		All accredited programmes	
	Core and Extended		Relapse prevention							
Financial years	Completions	KPI([1])	Completions	KPI([1])	Completions	KPI([1])	Completions	KPI([1])	Completions	KPI([1])
1992/93	284	–	–	–	–	–	–	–	284	–
1993/94	439	–	–	–	63	–	46	–	548	–
1994/95	554	–	–	–	44	–	241	–	839	–
1995/96	406	–	33	–	115	–	631	–	1,185	–
1996/97	571	559	109	108	190	175	586	530	1,456	1,372
1997/98	585	533	151	138	455	405	1,463	1,148	2,654	2,224

([1]) KPI completions—These are actual completions adjusted by the Implementation Quality Ratio to give the figure which can be counted against the KPI (see earlier text for fuller explanation.).

126

Table 7.3 Offending behaviour programme completions, by type of establishment([1]), financial year 1997/98

England and Wales
Males and females   Number of completions

Establishment type	Sex Offender Treatment Programme (Core and Booster)		Reasoning and Rehabilitation/ Problem solving		Thinking Skills/ Enhanced Thinking Skills	
	Completions	KPI([2])	Completions	KPI([2])	Completions	KPI([2])
All establishments:	736	670.70	455	405.25	1,463	1,164.00
Adult male establishments:	688	626.40	339	297.50	1,213	938.10
Local Prisons	114	107.70	57	52.05	474	320.70
Open Training (Cat D)	39	33.15	–	–	–	–
Closed Training (Cat C)	338	308.15	115	100.30	376	308.90
Closed Training (Cat B)	120	105.65	115	93.15	224	206.40
Closed Training (Dispersal)	77	71.75	52	52.00	139	102.10
Young offender establishments([3]):	48	44.30	79	72.60	250	224.30
Open YOI	–	–	–	–	116	99.40
Closed YOI	29	26.25	79	72.60	67	64.25
Remand Centre	19	18.05	–	–	67	60.65
Female establishments:	–	–	37	35.15	–	–

([1]) Establishments have been catetgorised according to their main role only. Establishments that have more than one role have been placed in the category that represents the primary function of the prison. For example, the female wing at Risley has been included as part of the adult Category C estate.

([2]) KPI completions—these are actual completions adjusted by the Implementation Quality Ratio to give the figure which can be counted against the KPI (see earlier text for fuller explanation).

([3]) Male young offenders only. Female young offenders have been included in the 'Female establishments' category.

Table 7.4 Results of the basic skills assessment screening tests

England and Wales 1997
Males and females   Number tested/results

Establishment type	Test	Number tested([2])	Standard (%)([1])		
			Below level 1	At level 1	Above level 1
All establishments:	Literacy	39,643	27.5	32.1	40.4
	Numeracy	38,695	32.4	36.4	31.2
Adult male establishments:	Literacy	27,859	27.6	29.9	42.6
	Numeracy	27,076	29.6	34.8	35.6
Young offender establishments([3]):	Literacy	8,697	30.0	38.5	31.5
	Numeracy	8,633	43.6	38.8	17.6
Female establishments:	Literacy	3,087	19.4	34.8	45.8
	Numeracy	2,986	25.8	43.5	30.7

([1]) Standard: Level 1 is about GCSE standard, above level 1 is higher while below level 1 indicates the need for remedial work.

([2]) 47,000 inmates were offered and accepted assessment tests in 1997; the results presented here are the scores received and collated at HQ. Not all inmates are assessed for both literacy and numeracy.

([3]) Male young offenders only. Female young offenders have been included in the 'Female establishment' category.

Table 7.5   Estimated([1]) average hours of education and vocational skills training in prison by type of establishment([2])

England and Wales 1997
Males and females   Number of hours

Establishment type	Average hours of education and skills training per prisoner
All establishments:	**4.11**
Adult male establishments:	**3.73**
Local Prisons	2.11
Open Training (Cat D)	5.73
Closed Training (Cat C)	5.51
Closed Training (Cat B)	3.98
Closed Training (Dispersal)	4.05
Young offender establishments([3]):	**5.84**
Open YOI	11.35
Closed YOI	6.46
Remand Centre	4.26
Female establishments:	**5.60**

([1]) Based on nine months data which has been annualised.

([2]) Establishments have been categorised according to their main role only. Establishments that have more than one role have been placed in the category that represents the primary function of the prison. For example, the female wing at Risley has been included as part of the adult Category C estate.

([3]) Male young offenders only. Female young offenders have been included in the 'Female establishments' category.

Table 7.6   Number of contracted education([1]) hours delivered in prison

England and Wales
Males and females   Number of hours/class size

Year	Total hours of student study	% reduction on previous year	Total teaching hours bought	% reduction on previous year	Average class size
1995	9,413,457	n/a	1,245,580	n/a	7.56
1996	8,947,305	4.95	1,169,717	6.09	7.65
1997	8,879,747	0.75	1,119,589	4.28	8.00

([1]) Excludes vocational training.

Table 7.7   Number of releases on temporary licence, by type of establishment(¹)

England and Wales
Males and females   Number of licences

Establishment type	1993	1994	1995	1996	1997
All establishments:	**148,484**	**177,885**	**164,521**	**181,660**	**227,078**
Adult male establishments:	**122,679**	**149,329**	**148,162**	**167,785**	**210,183**
Local Prisons	15,209	22,142	24,771	14,575	8,876
Open Training	31,613	36,272	34,664	55,466	73,725
Closed Training	75,857	90,915	88,727	97,744	127,582
Adult female establishments:	**13,422**	**15,917**	**9,204**	**8,436**	**10,540**
Young offender establishments:	**12,383**	**12,639**	**7,155**	**5,439**	**6,355**
Open YOI	3,159	2,782	1,974	1,773	2,804
Closed YOI	7,151	7,624	3,939	2,681	2,404
Juvenile YOI	984	1,196	512	241	426
Remand Centres	1,089	1,037	730	744	721

(¹) Prisoners have been categorised according to the part of the establishment in which they reside. Inmates at Bullingdon, for example, will have been included in either of the 'Local' or 'Closed Training' categories, as appropriate.

Table 7.8   Number(¹) of releases on temporary licence, by type of licence

England and Wales
Males and females   Number of licences

Licence type	1993	1994	1995	1996	1997
All licences:	**148,573**	**177,885**	**164,521**	**181,660**	**227,078**
Local visit	**39,014**	**54,012**	**32,812**	**36,095**	**44,984**
Resettlement:	**77,718**	**93,355**	**74,544**	**63,821**	**74,879**
accommodation	488	348	310	298	260
community service	28,119	39,040	33,149	31,193	38,376
employment	2,075	1,942	10,153	12,493	18,270
family ties	27,422	29,006	17,209	14,009	15,186
pre-parole release	17,797	21,543	12,687	4,919	1,995
probation service	1,817	1,476	622	377	365
in hostel etc.	–	–	414	532	427
Facility:	**16,230**	**17,180**	**49,098**	**74,585**	**99,597**
reparation	–	–	9,948	19,906	31,478
training and education	8,037	9,525	13,033	11,320	12,261
working out	–	–	22,040	41,310	54,164
other	8,193	7,655	4,077	2,049	1,694
Compassionate:	**15,611**	**13,338**	**8,067**	**7,159**	**7,618**
carer	–	–	85	177	229
deaths	968	933	467	418	389
family needs	6,812	5,101	1,655	927	649
family occasions	44	26	105	133	188
medical	7,787	7,278	5,755	5,504	6,163

(¹) In November 1994, the issue of temporary licences was subject to changes in the risk assessment and, in May 1995, the classification categories of temporary licences were revised. As a result of these changes, pre-1995 data may not be directly comparable with that for later years.

Table 7.9   Number of temporary release failures

England and Wales
Males and females   Number of reported failures

	1991	1992	1993	1994	1995	1996	1997
All establishments:	2,239	3,189	2,996	2,182	637	448	564

Table 7.10   Overcrowding in prisons, by type of establishment([1])

England and Wales 1997
Males and females   Average number and percentage

Establishment type	Average number of prisoners held two to a cell designed for one	% of population above uncrowded capacity([2])
All establishments:	**11,051**	**12.4**
Adult male establishments:	**9,706**	**13.3**
Local Prisons	8,408	21.0
Open Training (Cat D)	24([3])	−0.7
Closed Training (Cat C)	1,064	7.5
Closed Training (Cat B)	101	5.3
Closed Training (Dispersal)	110	8.7
Young offender establishments([4]):	**1,271**	8.9
Open YOI	–	−20.2
Closed YOI	409	7.0
Remand Centre	862	**15.5**
Female establishments:	**74**	**4.3**

([1]) Establishments have been categorised according to their main role only. Establishments that have more than one role have been placed in the category that represents the primary function of the prison. For example, the female wing at Risley has been included as part of the adult Category C estate.

([2]) Population surplus to planning in use certified normal accommodation as a percentage of population (calculated on annual averages).

([3]) These 24 prisoners were in the young offender section of Hollesley Bay (a mixed establishment). The Open estate proper had no prisoners held two a cell in 1997.

([4]) Male young offenders only. Female young offenders have been included in the 'Female establishments' category.

Table 7.11 **Mandatory Drug Testing: percentage testing positive by drug group**
April 1996—March 1997, all establishments

England and Wales
Males and females   Percentage testing positive

Drug group	Apr	May	Jun	Jul	Aug	Sep	Oct	Nov	Dec	Jan	Feb	Mar	Overall
Cannabis	20.9	19.7	18.5	19.3	19.6	19.7	20.2	20.4	20.5	20.8	19.6	19.2	19.9
Opiates	5.1	5.1	4.6	6.0	5.9	6.0	5.4	5.6	6.4	5.3	4.4	4.6	5.4
Cocaine	0.2	0.3	0.2	0.2	0.3	0.3	0.2	0.3	0.2	0.3	0.2	0.2	0.2
Benzodiazepines	1.5	2.1	1.9	1.3	1.3	1.4	1.2	1.2	1.1	1.5	1.2	1.4	1.4
Methadone	0.2	0.2	0.2	0.2	0.3	0.2	0.2	0.1	0.4	0.2	0.2	0.2	0.2
Amphetamines	0.2	0.2	0.2	0.1	0.2	0.2	0.2	0.1	0.2	0.2	0.4	0.4	0.2
Barbiturates	0.0	0.0	0.1	0.1	0.0	0.1	0.0	0.1	0.0	0.0	0.0	0.0	0.0
LSD	0.0	0.0	0.0	0.0	0.0	0.0	0.0	0.0	0.0	0.0	0.0	0.0	0.0

Table 7.12 **Mandatory Drug Testing: percentage testing positive by drug group**
April 1997—March 1998, all establishments

England and Wales
Males and females   Percentage testing positive

Drug group	Apr	May	Jun	Jul	Aug	Sep	Oct	Nov	Dec	Jan	Feb	Mar	Overall
Cannabis	20.3	19.8	17.8	16.6	15.4	15.9	15.8	15.3	16.7	15.9	14.1	15.3	16.5
Opiates	4.3	3.8	3.8	4.2	3.7	4.0	4.2	4.1	4.6	4.3	4.3	4.6	4.2
Cocaine	0.2	0.4	0.2	0.2	0.2	0.2	0.2	0.2	0.4	0.3	0.3	0.3	0.3
Benzodiazepines	1.2	1.1	1.4	1.3	1.3	0.8	1.0	1.6	1.5	1.4	1.5	1.3	1.3
Methadone	0.2	0.2	0.1	0.1	0.2	0.1	0.2	0.1	0.1	0.2	0.1	0.1	0.1
Amphetamines	0.3	0.4	0.3	0.3	0.2	0.1	0.2	0.2	0.1	0.2	0.3	0.4	0.3
Barbiturates	0.0	0.0	0.1	0.1	0.0	0.0	0.1	0.0	0.1	0.0	0.0	0.0	0.0
LSD	0.0	0.0	0.0	0.0	0.0	0.0	0.0	0.0	0.0	0.0	0.0	0.0	0.0

Table 7.13   Mandatory Drug Testing, by type of establishment(¹), financial year 1997/98

England and Wales
Males and females   Number of tests/percentage tested positive

Establishment type	Number sampled	Number tested	Number tested positive	Percentage tested positive
All establishments:	**63,903**	**62,681**	**13,040**	**20.8**
Adult male establishments:	**53,069**	**52,088**	**11,364**	**21.8**
Local Prisons	25,236	24,815	5,813	23.4
Open Training (Cat D)	3,229	3,166	469	14.8
Closed Training (Cat C)	16,467	16,107	3,797	23.6
Closed Training (Cat B)	5,194	5,089	855	16.8
Closed Training (Dispersal)	2,943	2,911	430	14.8
Young offender establishments(²):	**8,647**	**8,467**	**1,317**	**15.6**
Open YOI	446	427	89	20.8
Closed YOI	5,599	5,492	757	13.8
Remand Centre	2,602	2,548	471	18.5
Female establishments:	**2,187**	**2,126**	**359**	**16.9**

(¹) Establishments have been categorised according to their main role only. Establishments that have more than one role have been placed in the category that represents the primary function of the prison. For example, the female wing at Risley has been included as part of the adult Category C estate.
(²) Male young offenders only. Female young offenders have been included in the 'Female establishments' category.

Table 7.14   Number of escapes from prison establishments, by type of establishment

England and Wales
Males and females   Number of escapes

Establishment type	1993	1994	1995	1996	1997
All establishments:	**192**	**149**	**62**	**42**	**23**
Male establishments:	**126**	**101**	**47**	**35**	**18**
Local Prisons	13	8	6	2	1
Open Training (Cat D)	–	1	1	–	–
Closed Training (Cat C)	113	79	36	33	16
Closed Training (Cat B)	–	7	1	–	–
Closed Training (Dispersal)	–	6	3	–	1
Young offender institutions(²)	**53**	**29**	**11**	**5**	**4**
Remand centres	**12**	**15**	**3**	**2**	**–**
Female establishments	**1**	**4**	**1**	**–**	**1**

(¹) Establishments have been categorised according to their main role only. Establishments that have more than one role have been placed in the category that represents the primary function of the prison. For example, the female wing at Risley has been included as part of the adult Category C estate.
(²) Male young offenders only. Female young offenders have been included in the 'Female establishments' category.

Table 7.15   Number of escapes from escort

England and Wales
Males and females   Number of escapes

Type	1993	1994	1995	1996	1997
All types:	**126**	**81**	**60**	**94**	**81**
Magistrate Court	26	22	26	55	57
Other	100	59	34	39	24

Table 7.16   Number of absconds from prison establishments, by type of establishment([1])([2])

England and Wales
Males and females   Number of absconds

Establishment type	1991	1992	1993	1994	1995	1996	1997
All establishments:	**1,598**	**1,837**	**1,708**	**1,550**	**975**	**1,134**	**1,100**
Adult male establishments:	**995**	**1,134**	**1,149**	**973**	**558**	**684**	**667**
Local Prisons	49	66	54	41	14	8	3
Open Training (Cat D)	722	786	841	735	419	572	564
Closed Training (Cat C)	204	224	185	146	84	81	78
Closed Training (Cat B)	18	58	69	51	41	23	22
Closed Training (Dispersal)	2	–	–	–	–	–	–
Young offender establishments([3]):	**441**	**521**	**463**	**391**	**309**	**329**	**282**
Open YOI	251	352	309	317	293	315	270
Closed YOI	173	149	134	61	14	8	9
Remand Centre	17	20	20	13	2	6	3
Female establishments:	**162**	**182**	**96**	**186**	**108**	**121**	**151**

([1]) Establishments have been categorised according to their main role only. Establishments that have more than one role have been placed in the category that represents the primary function of the prison. For example, the female wing at Risley has been included as part of the adult Category C estate.

([2]) The breakdown provided is based on the primary function for each establishment as at the end of 1997. Due to changes in the role of individual establishments, data for preceding years may not be directly comparable.

([3]) Male young offenders only. Female young offenders have been included in the 'Female establishments' category.

Table 7.17 Persons restrained and means of restraint applied to violent or refractory prison inmates by sex and type of establishment

England and Wales 1997
Males and females   Number of persons/applications

Grounds for restraint and means of restraint used	All types of establish-ment	Type of establishment					
		Remand centres	Local prisons	Training prisons		Young offender	
				Open	Closed	Open	Closed
Males							
All males restrained	**2,606**	**348**	**1,418**	**–**	**670**	**1**	**169**
On medical grounds by direction of the medical officer([1])	472	47	406	–	14	–	5
On non-medical grounds	2,134	301	1,012	–	656	1	164
Means of restraint:							
On medical grounds							
Protective rooms for temporary confinement([3])	565	60	482	–	18	–	5
On non-medical grounds							
Body belt([2])([4])	53	9	17	–	26	–	1
Handcuffs([2])([4])	4	–	2	–	2	–	–
Ankle straps([2])([4])	3	–	2	–	1	–	–
Special cells/unfurnished cells (other than protective rooms) for temporary confinement([5])([6])	2,715	371	1,264	–	886	1	193
Females							
All females restrained	**90**	*****	**44**	**–**	**35**	**–**	**11**
On medical grounds by direction of the medical officer([1])	25	*	25	–	–	–	–
On non-medical grounds	65	*	19	–	35	–	11
Means of restraint:							
On medical grounds							
Protective rooms for temporary confinement([3])	31	*	31	–	–	–	–
On non-medical grounds							
Special cells/unfurnished cells (other than protective rooms) for temporary confinement([5])([6])	121	*	38	–	52	–	31

([1]) Under Rule 46(6), Prison Rules 1964, Rule 49(6) Young Offender Institution Rules, 1988. Period of confinement exceeded 24 hours.
([2]) Number of applications.
([3]) Number of times used where the period of confinement exceeded 24 hours.
([4]) Under Rule 46(1), Prison Rules 1964; Rule 49(1), Young Offender Institution Rules, 1988.
([5]) Under Rule 45, Prison Rules 1964; Rule 48, Young Offender Institution Rules, 1988. Number of times used.
([6]) Includes juvenile institutions.

Table 7.18 Persons restrained and means of restraint applied to violent or refractory prison inmates

England and Wales
Males and females   Number of persons

Grounds for restraint and means of restraint used	1987	1988	1989	1990	1991	1992	1993	1994	1995	1996	1997
Males											
All males restrained	**1,323**	**1,262**	**1,508**	**1,618**	**1,865**	**1,990**	**2,408**	**3,125**	**2,848**	**2,846**	**2,606**
On medical grounds(¹)	133	164	158	148	252	262	190	249	220	308	472
On non-medical grounds	1,190	1,098	1,350	1,470	1,613	1,728	2,218	2,876	2,628	2,538	2,134
Males											
Means of restraint:											
On medical grounds											
Loose canvas jacket(²)	4	4	1	1	–	–	–	–	–	–	–
Protective rooms for temporary confinement(¹)	163	195	181	193	326	319	227	290	258	375	565
On non-medical grounds											
Body belt(²)	74	83	96	107	86	57	90	91	96	87	53
Handcuffs(²)	4	8	16	22	76	123	99	32	35	88	4
Ankle straps(²)	6	11	9	13	10	1	7	7	7	3	3
Special cells/unfurnished cells (other than protective rooms) for temporary confinement(³)	1,406	1,339	1,567	1,740	1,926	2,140	2,718	3,638	3,274	3,040	2,715
Females											
All females restrained	**61**	**42**	**102**	**75**	**85**	**68**	**96**	**82**	**104**	**81**	**90**
On medical ground(¹)	8	13	10	10	43	20	35	24	49	28	25
On non-medical grounds	53	29	92	65	42	48	61	58	55	53	65

(¹) Period of confinement exceeded 24 hours.
(²) Number of applications.
(³) Number of times used.

Table 7.19 Number of self-inflicted deaths in prisons, by type of establishment([1])

England and Wales
Males and females   Number of self-inflicted deaths

Establishment type	1990	1991	1992	1993	1994	1995	1996	1997
All establishments:	**50**	**42**	**41**	**47**	**62**	**59**	**64**	**70**
Adult male establishments:	**45**	**38**	**33**	**44**	**57**	**53**	**55**	**56**
Local Prisons	35	24	22	34	40	35	41	40
Open Training (Cat D)	–	–	–	–	–	–	1	–
Closed Training (Cat C)	5	5	5	2	6	8	5	5
Closed Training (Cat B)	3	5	4	3	9	5	5	10
Closed Training (Dispersal)	2	4	2	5	2	5	3	1
Young offender establishments([2]):	**5**	**4**	**6**	**2**	**4**	**4**	**7**	**11**
Open YOI	–	–	–	–	–	–	–	–
Closed YOI	2	2	2	1	1	2	5	5
Remand Centre	3	2	4	1	3	2	2	6
Female establishments:	**–**	**–**	**2**	**1**	**1**	**2**	**1**	**1**
Prisoners under escort	**–**	**–**	**–**	**–**	**–**	**–**	**1**	**2**

([1]) Establishments have been categorised according to their main role only. Establishments that have more than one role have been placed in the category that represents the primary function of the prison. For example, the female wing at Risley has been included as part of the adult Category C estate.
([2]) Male young offenders only. Female young offenders have been included in the 'Female establishments' category.

Table 7.20 Number of self-inflicted deaths in prisons, by gender

England and Wales
Males and females   Number of selfinflicted deaths

Gender	1990	1991	1992	1993	1994	1995	1996	1997
Males and females	**50**	**42**	**41**	**47**	**62**	**59**	**64**	**70**
Males	49	42	39	46	61	57	62	67
Females	1	–	2	1	1	2	2	3
Rate per 1,000 prisoners in custody	**1.10**	**0.92**	**0.89**	**1.05**	**1.27**	**1.16**	**1.16**	**1.15**

CHAPTER 8

OFFENCES AND PUNISHMENTS

Key points

Offences

- There were 108,200 proven offences against prison discipline in 1997, 7,200 less than in 1996.

- There were 177 offences per 100 population, compared with 209 per 100 in 1996. The rate of offending was higher in young offender institutions and in female establishments. The most common offences were unauthorised drug use, possessing unauthorised articles and disobeying lawful orders.

- The rate of violent offending changed little. The number of assaults rose from 5,300 to 5,600 while the number of fighting offences rose from 7,500 to 8,400.

- Drug use and possession fell slightly to 19,500 offences, and evading drug tests was much less common than in 1996. There were big falls in other categories of offence, including other unauthorised transactions, and disobedience/disrespect.

- Black male prisoners committed around 25 per cent more proven offences than white males, while black and white females had similar adjudication rates. Both male and female prisoners of South Asian, Chinese and other ethnic groups had low adjudication rates.

Punishments

- Additional days was the most common punishment, followed by forfeiture of privileges and stoppage/reduction of earnings. Patterns of punishment varied between different establishment types. The punishment given was also affected by the type of offence committed.

- Black prisoners received more punishments per offence than white prisoners, controlling for the type of offence.

The disciplinary system

8.1 The adjudication process exists to allow prison governors to deal with breaches of prison discipline, as set out in the Prison Rules 1964 and Young Offender Institution Rules 1988 (as amended). They may also refer possible criminal offences to the police.

8.2 The tables in this chapter count only proven offences. They exclude dismissed and 'not completed' charges (about 13,400) and cases referred for prosecution (about 1,540, including 960 for drugs offences, 260 for violence and 240 for escaping or absconding); there were slightly fewer of each of these in 1997 than 1996.

Offences

8.3 There were 177 proven offences against prison discipline for every 100 prisoners in 1997, making a total of 108,200 offences. This offending rate tends to be lower in prisons and remand centres than in young offender institutions, and lower in male establishments. Offending rates were lowest in open prisons.

8.4 The rate of offending was lower in 1997 than 1996 in almost every type of establishment. The greatest falls came in male local prisons, closed training prisons and open young offender institutions. The overall offence rate was the lowest since 1989, and was down by almost a quarter from the peak years of 1993 and 1994. The rate of violent offending only fell by about 10 per cent from this peak, while the rate of escape/abscond and 'other' offences has halved. Unauthorised transactions/possession is higher than in any year apart from 1996, but the introduction of Mandatory Drug Testing (MDT) in late 1995 and early 1996 allowed the detection of many offences which would previously have gone unpunished.

Figure 8.1

TYPES OF OFFENCES COMMITTED IN 1994 AND 1997

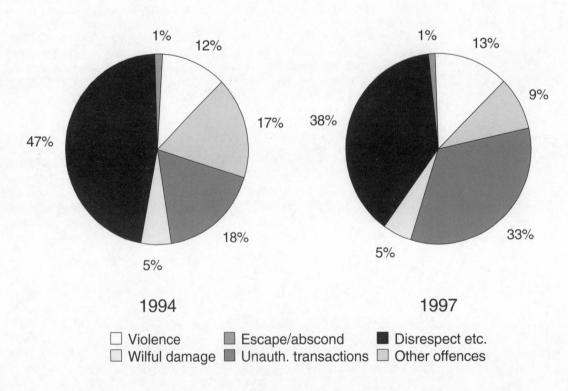

1994

1997

☐ Violence   ◼ Escape/abscond   ◼ Disrespect etc.
☐ Wilful damage   ◼ Unauth. transactions   ◼ Other offences

Figure 8.2

OFFENCES PUNISHED PER 100 AVERAGE POPULATION
BY TYPE OF ESTABLISHMENT, 1987–1997

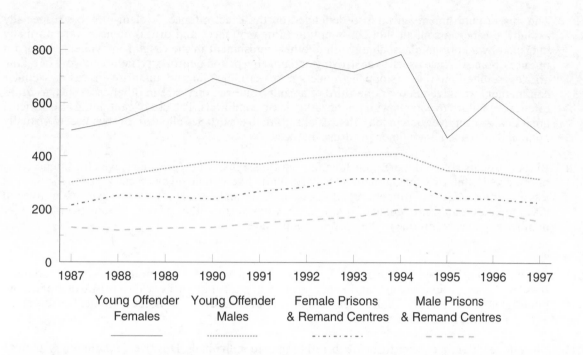

8.5 The types of offence committed varied greatly. Violence and wilful damage were most common in remand centres and closed and juvenile young offender institutions. There was a high level of abscondment from open young offender institutions. Disobedience and disrespect rates were low in open prisons, moderate in male local and closed training prisons, and high elsewhere. 'Other' offences, many of which are associated with freedom of movement, were most common in open establishments. The most common offences overall were unauthorised drug use, possessing unauthorised articles and disobeying lawful orders.

8.6 Male black prisoners had an adjudication rate about 25 per cent higher than male white prisoners. The difference was particularly marked in violent offences, where there were more than twice as many proven offences per head for blacks, whereas black males had fewer adjudications for wilful damage or escape. South Asian, Chinese and other male prisoners had fewer adjudications than either group, especially for disobedience or disrespect. In the female estate, there was little overall difference between the black and white populations, but blacks had higher violence and disobedience rates while whites had higher rates for the other offences, especially escape and wilful damage. The female Chinese and other ethnic origin population had slightly fewer adjudications per head and the tiny female South Asian population experienced no adjudications.

Punishments

8.7 Additional days was the most often awarded punishment, with 121 such punishments per 100 average population. Forfeiture of privileges and stoppage or reduction of earnings were each used 68 times per 100 inmates, while all other punishments were in far less frequent use. It is estimated that additional days increased the average prison population by about 1,320.

8.8   The use of punishments varied by establishment. Remand centres tended to give several punishments for each offence, used forfeiture of privileges as much as additional days (partly because remand prisoners' additional days only take effect if they are convicted and given a custodial sentence). Male young offender institutions also gave a high number of punishments per offence. Open prisons barely used forfeiture of privileges or cellular confinement at all, presumably because of the difficulty of applying these punishments in the open environment. Cautions were given more often in female establishments.

8.9   The mix of punishments given also depended on the exact offence. Violent offences (especially assault), escapes, arson, alcohol consumption (a new offence) and drugs offences were normally punished by additional days, along with another punishment in the case of the violent and arson offences. Some offences, such as destroying or damaging prison or property, failure to work or taking articles resulted in fines (stoppage/reduction of earnings) in the majority of cases. Cellular confinement was given in over one-third of assaults, but was very rare in other cases such as drugs offences or failure to comply with temporary release conditions. The use of cautioning also varied a great deal—from over one in ten offences of sells/delivers articles allowed for own use, to virtually none of the escape/abscondment or drugs offences.

8.10   Black prisoners received more punishments per offence than white prisoners, even for similar types of offence. Cellular/room confinement is particularly likely to be given to black prisoners; there is less of a difference in punishments of additional days for males, and they are less likely to be given to black females than white females. South Asian, Chinese and other prisoners were given a smaller number of punishments due to their low offending rate.

Notes

8.11   A number of other tables concerning the prison discipline system are produced, corresponding to those in the discontinued Command Paper series 'Statistics of offences against prison discipline and punishments, England and Wales'. These tables are available free of charge from the address given at the end of the general Notes section.

8.12   The ethnic differences refer to incidents rather than to individuals. However, a preliminary analysis of prison discipline and population data from 1996 suggests that a higher proportion of black males than white males have at least one disciplinary offence to their name, and that the difference between the two groups is confined to British citizens (in fact, black foreign nationals have lower offending rates than white foreign nationals). The difference does not seem to be explained by age or criminal offence, both of which are connected with behaviour in custody.

8.13   The calculation of the population effect of additional days includes allowances for prospective and suspended punishments (prospective additional days are given to remand prisoners and are activated if they are given a custodial sentence), and for the remission of punishments.

Table 8.1 Offences(^{1}) punished per 100 populations by sex and type of prison

England and Wales
Males and females

Number of offences punished

Type of establishment	1987	1988(^{2})	1989	1990	1991	1992	1993	1994	1995	1996	1997
All establishments	**153**	**163**	**167**	**182**	**191**	**200**	**226**	**225**	**207**	**209**	**177**
Males											
All establishments	**150**	**159**	**163**	**179**	**188**	**196**	**222**	**220**	**204**	**206**	**174**
Prison and remand centres	**121**	**129**	**132**	**149**	**162**	**171**	**201**	**200**	**188**	**190**	**157**
Remand centres	256	261	310	333	385	321	370	359	312	277	264
Local prisons	96	100	105	122	133	142	186	194	184	195	151
Open prisons	66	84	87	89	83	116	140	119	90	93	96
Closed training prisons	124	133	138	159	172	183	195	191	189	189	153
Young offender establishments	**302**	**324**	**353**	**378**	**371**	**393**	**405**	**410**	**348**	**339**	**316**
Open young offender institutions	*	360(^{4})	368	461	383	407	396	414	383	403	318
Closed young offender institutions(^{3})	*	330(^{4})	321	346	353	387	388	375	308	310	281
Juvenile young offender institutions	*	718(^{4})	622	737	689	550	566	579	484	422	426
Short sentence young offender institutions	*	384(^{4})	434	247	236	303	*	*	*	*	*
Open youth custody centres	347	368(^{4})	*	*	*	*	*	*	*	*	*
Closed youth custody centres	290	309(^{4})	*	*	*	*	*	*	*	*	*
Senior detention centres	296	244(^{4})	*	*	*	*	*	*	*	*	*
Junior detention centres	336	363(^{4})	*	*	*	*	*	*	*	*	*
Females											
All establishments	**240**	**274**	**271**	**268**	**291**	**311**	**340**	**343**	**262**	**268**	**244**
Prisons and remand centres	**214**	**252**	**246**	**238**	**268**	**284**	**316**	**316**	**245**	**240**	**226**
Remand centres	311	389	374	424	*	*	*	*	*	*	*
Local prisons	195	229	218	229	286	317	383	368	299	288	277
Open prisons	164	160	179	154	196	218	159	211	128	122	128
Closed training prisons	225	290	278	259	295	278	307	307	225	236	213
Young offender establishments	**497**	**532**	**602**	**692**	**643**	**752**	**719**	**785**	**471**	**624**	**489**
Open young offender institutions	*	869(^{4})	472	287	419	396	431	642	275	316	271
Closed young offender institutions	*	534(^{4})	629	855	741	891	831	832	518	695	533
Open youth custody centres	349	417(^{4})	*	*	*	*	*	*	*	*	3
Closed youth custody centres	554	502(^{4})	*	*	*	*	*	*	*	*	*

(^{1}) Including attempts.

(^{2}) Establishments which became young offender institutions on 1 October 1988 were included as youth custody centres and detention centres before that date.

(^{3}) Includes Wetherby short sentence young offender institution (until 1992).

(^{4}) Part year only.

Table 8.2   Offences punished per 100 population: by sex, type of prison and offence([1])

England and Wales 1997
Males and females   Number of offences punished per 100 population

Type of establishment	All Offences	Violence	Escapes or absconds	Disobedience or disrespect	Wilful Damage	Unauthorised transactions([2])	Other Offences
All establishments	**177**	**23**	**2**	**68**	**9**	**59**	**16**
Males							
All establishments	**174**	**23**	**2**	**66**	**10**	**59**	**15**
Prisons and remand centres	**157**	**16**	**2**	**58**	**8**	**59**	**14**
Remand Centres	264	77	2	91	29	54	11
Local prisons	151	15	3	55	8	61	9
Open prisons	96	1	2	16	–	44	33
Closed training prisons	153	8	–	64	5	60	15
Young offender institutions	**316**	**78**	**3**	**127**	**23**	**62**	**23**
Open young offender institutions	318	24	26	98	12	72	87
Closed young offender institutions	281	66	1	118	19	62	15
Juvenile young offender institutions	426	131	4	165	40	56	30
Females							
All establishments	**244**	**27**	**5**	**110**	**8**	**44**	**49**
Prisons	**226**	**26**	**5**	**101**	**8**	**43**	**43**
Local prisons	277	41	8	130	13	57	28
Open prisons	128	3	9	25	1	34	56
Closed training prisons	213	19	1	103	6	30	54
Young offender institutions	**489**	**45**	**5**	**240**	**14**	**55**	**129**
Open young offender institutions	271	6	19	68	–	68	110
Closed young offender institutions	533	3	3	275	16	53	133

([1]) Including attempts.
([2]) Includes possession and/or unauthorised use of controlled drugs.

Table 8.3 Offences punished per 100 population for all establishments: by type of offence(¹)

England and Wales
Males and females   Number of offences per 100 populations

Type of establishment and offence type	1987	1988	1989(²)	1990	1991	1992	1993	1994	1995	1996	1997
All establishments	**153**	**163**	**167**	**182**	**191**	**200**	**226**	**225**	**207**	**209**	**177**
Violence	7	7	17	22	22	23	26	26	24	23	23
Escapes or absconds	4	3	3	4	4	4	4	3	2	2	2
Disobedience or disrespect	64	73	83	93	96	97	105	105	96	83	68
Wilful damage	9	9	10	10	10	10	12	12	10	11	9
Unauthorised transactions/ possessions	21	23	22	24	25	27	36	40	48	69	59
Other offences	45	48	32	29	34	39	44	39	26	21	16
Male prisons and remand centres	**121**	**129**	**132**	**149**	**162**	**171**	**201**	**200**	**188**	**190**	**157**
Violence	5	5	12	16	17	18	21	20	18	16	16
Escapes or absconds	2	2	1	3	3	3	3	3	2	2	2
Disobedience or disrespect	54	58	65	76	82	82	93	94	88	75	58
Wilful damage	7	7	8	8	8	8	10	10	9	9	8
Unauthorised transactions/ possessions	17	20	19	20	22	24	33	37	46	70	59
Other offences	36	36	27	26	30	36	41	36	25	19	14
Male young offender establishments(³)	**302**	**324**	**353**	**378**	**371**	**393**	**405**	**410**	**348**	**343**	**316**
Violence	17	15	43	55	55	62	71	73	68	75	78
Escapes or absconds	11	14	11	14	13	10	10	7	4	4	3
Disobedience or disrespect	117	136	171	191	181	197	190	190	154	136	127
Wilful damage	18	16	24	25	22	23	23	29	25	25	23
Unauthorised transactions/ possessions	35	38	41	45	47	48	59	64	67	75	62
Other offences	104	106	62	48	53	53	53	46	31	29	23
Female prisons and remand centres	**214**	**252**	**246**	**238**	**268**	**284**	**316**	**316**	**245**	**240**	**226**
Violence	10	15	22	32	30	32	39	40	35	30	26
Escapes or absconds	6	4	5	4	10	12	5	10	5	5	5
Disobedience or disrespect	106	130	140	128	126	120	135	133	115	104	101
Wilful damage	15	14	13	12	12	17	21	14	11	12	8
Unauthorised transactions/ possessions	22	26	21	23	28	33	41	37	39	46	43
Other offences	55	63	46	39	63	70	75	82	39	42	43
Female young offender establishments	**497**	**532**	**602**	**692**	**643**	**752**	**719**	**785**	**471**	**624**	**489**
Violence	17	10	26	61	47	78	54	59	65	73	45
Escapes or absconds	8	6	15	6	13	18	1	16	7	11	5
Disobedience or disrespect	293	316	402	424	360	387	363	333	227	297	240
Wilful Damage	27	10	20	36	13	26	25	18	14	21	14
Unauthorised transactions/ possessions	27	41	41	54	37	36	23	35	41	48	55
Other offences	125	148	99	110	172	208	245	324	118	173	129

(¹) Including attempts.
(²) A new set of offences came into effect on 1 April 1989.
(³) Includes figures for youth custody centres and detention centres until 1988.

143

Table 8.4   Punishments per 100 population: by sex, type of prison and type of punishment

England and Wales 1997
Males and females   Number of punishments per 100 population

Type of establishments	All punish-ments	Cellular confine-ment(^{1})	Removal from activities	Forfeiture of privileges	Stoppage or reduction of earnings	Caution	Removal from wing or living unit	Extra work	Exclusion from associated work	Additional days
All establishments	**298**	**24**	**1**	**68**	**68**	**8**	**2**	**2**	**4**	**121**
Males										
All establishments	**295**	**23**	**1**	**66**	**67**	**8**	**2**	**2**	**4**	**121**
Prisons and remand centres	**254**	**22**	*	**57**	**57**	**7**	*	*	**5**	**106**
Remand centres	553	52	*	176	128	10	*	*	14	173
Local prisons	251	23	*	65	48	7	*	*	4	105
Open prisons	119	1	*	7	32	9	*	*	–	70
Closed training prisons	227	19	*	37	56	7	*	*	5	102
Young offender institutions	**623**	**37**	**6**	**138**	**156**	**12**	**15**	**19**	*	**239**
Open young offender institutions	494	3	–	23	126	19	22	90	*	211
Closed young offender institutions	551	33	5	133	138	10	13	9	*	209
Juvenile young offender institutions	887	59	11	189	222	15	21	28	*	343
Females										
All establishments	**361**	**30**	–	**97**	**87**	**17**	–	**1**	**3**	**127**
Prisons	**336**	**29**	–	**92**	**79**	**16**	*	*	**3**	**116**
Local prisons	440	46	–	160	89	14	*	*	3	128
Open prisons	143	1	–	–	25	8	*	*	–	109
Closed training prisons	306	23	–	56	95	22	*	*	4	105
Young offender institutions	**704**	**39**	–	**155**	**184**	**34**	**4**	**17**	*	**272**
Open young offender institutions	326	3	–	3	55	13	–	–	*	252
Closed young offender institutions	781	46	–	186	210	39	5	20	*	276

(^{1}) Includes confinement to room.
* Not applicable.

144

Table 8.5 Offences punished and punishments given in prison

England and Wales 1997
Males and females

Prison Rule 47 or YOI Rule 50 Offence(1)(2) Paragraph	Confinement to cell or room	Forfeiture of privileges	Stoppage or reduction of earnings	Caution	Other(4)	Additional days	All punishments(5)	All offences(5)	Average number of punishments per offence
All offences	**14,524**	**41,350**	**41,731**	**5,103**	**5,137**	**74,062**	**181,907**	**108,234**	**1.7**
Violence	**3,416**	**8,057**	**5,377**	**417**	**1,205**	**11,331**	**29,803**	**13,997**	**2.1**
1 Assault	2,100	3,440	1,776	101	519	4,884	12,820	5,608	2.3
on staff	*1,018*	*1,471*	*722*	*35*	*181*	*2,010*	*5,437*	*2,404*	*2.3*
on an inmate	*994*	*1,828*	*968*	*63*	*307*	*2,603*	*6,763*	*2,902*	*2.3*
on any other person	*88*	*141*	*86*	*3*	*31*	*271*	*620*	*302*	*2.1*
2 Detains any person	8	7	5	0	1	14	35	17	2.1
4 Fights with any person	1,308	4,610	3,596	316	685	6,433	16,948	8,372	2.0
Escape/abscond	**101**	**171**	**139**	**5**	**88**	**1,205**	**1,709**	**1,232**	**1.4**
7 Escapes from prison or legal custody	69	131	109	4	78	1,112	1,503	1,133	1.3
22 Attempted escape	32	40	30	1	10	93	206	99	2.1
Disobedience/disrespect	**7,158**	**17,259**	**17,337**	**2,486**	**2,196**	**23,976**	**70,412**	**41,476**	**1.7**
16 Is disrespectful	76	191	234	29	28	269	827	481	1.7
17 Threats/abusive words or behaviour	2,284	5,281	4,745	384	708	6,815	20,217	10,965	1.8
18 Fails/refuses to work	79	463	881	114	80	812	2,429	1,510	1.6
19 Disobeys any lawful order:	2,440	5,015	4,682	840	695	8,076	21,748	13,114	1.7
refusal to provide drug test sample	*40*	*131*	*148*	*9*	*5*	*730*	*1,063*	*801*	*1.3*
falsifying drug test sample	*9*	*36*	*12*	*1*	*4*	*123*	*185*	*134*	*1.4*
any other lawful disorder	*2,391*	*4,848*	*4,522*	*830*	*686*	*7,223*	*20,500*	*12,179*	*1.7*
20 Disobeys any rules or regulation	1,442	4,014	4,507	770	442	5,019	16,194	10,192	1.6
21 Good order and discipline offences	837	2,295	2,288	349	243	2,985	8,997	5,214	1.7
Wilful damage	**905**	**2,817**	**3,880**	**175**	**364**	**2,823**	**10,964**	**5,797**	**1.9**
13 Sets fire to prison or property	93	257	244	11	19	402	1,026	523	2.0
14 Destroys/damages prison or property	812	2,560	3,636	164	345	2,421	9,938	5,274	1.9
Unauthorised transactions	**2,100**	**10,140**	**10,713**	**1,178**	**753**	**29,109**	**53,993**	**35,876**	**1.5**
8A Drugs offences:	798	4,534	4,132	109	277	18,525	28,375	19,527	1.5
unauthorised use if controlled drug	*597*	*3,529*	*3,264*	*86*	*185*	*14,470*	*22,131*	*15,327*	*1.4*
possession of an unauthorised drug	*200*	*979*	*839*	*23*	*90*	*3,997*	*6,128*	*4,137*	*1.5*
sells/delivers drugs to any person	*1*	*26*	*29*	*0*	*2*	*58*	*116*	*63*	*1.8*
9 Has in his possession:	1,251	5,369	6,253	992	444	10,219	24,528	15,617	1.6
(a) an unauthorised article,	*1,212*	*5,150*	*6,005*	*939*	*406*	*9,795*	*23,507*	*14,926*	*1.6*
(b) greater quantity than authorised	*39*	*219*	*248*	*53*	*38*	*424*	*1,021*	*691*	*1.5*
10 Sells/delivers unauthorised article	18	66	72	11	10	118	295	181	1.6
11 Sells/delivers articles allowed only for own use	25	164	230	61	19	185	684	471	1.5
8A Knowingly consumes alcohol	8	6	25	5	3	62	109	79	1.4
Other offences	**844**	**2,906**	**4,285**	**842**	**531**	**5,618**	**15,026**	**9,856**	**1.5**
3 Denies access to any part of the prison to an officer	71	127	75	8	24	232	537	287	1.9
5 Endangers the health or personal safety of others	219	579	590	64	76	888	2,416	1,287	1.9
6 Intentionally obstructs an officer in executing his duty	81	179	166	22	20	294	762	458	1.7
8 Fails to comply with any temporary release condition	39	198	382	204	54	1,086	1,963	1,472	1.3
12 Takes any article belonging to another person or to a prison	70	315	435	43	30	377	1,270	731	1.7
15 Absent from where required to be or present at unauthorised place	364	1,508	2,637	501	327	2,741	8,078	5,621	1.4

(1) Includes offences committed at one establishment and punished at another.
(2) Includes attempting, inciting and assisting under Rule 47(22) and 50(22), except for attempted escapes, which are shown separately.
(3) Including suspended and prospective punishments.
(4) Includes exclusion from associated work (prisons and remand centres only), and removal from activities, removal from wing or living area, and extra work or fatigues (all young offender institutions only).
(5) The number of offences punished and punishments given are not equal because in many cases two or more punishments are given for a single offence.

Table 8.6 Punishments per 100 population(1) given by ethnicity and offence

England and Wales 1997
Males

Number of punishments per 100 population

Offence(2) / Ethnicity	Type of punishment(3)								All punishments(4)	All offences(4)	Average number of punishments per offence
	Confinement to room	Removal from activities	Forfeiture of privileges	Stoppage or reduction in earnings	Caution	Removal from wing	Work: extra or excluded from	Additional days			
Male establishments											
Total(5)											
All offences	**23**	**1**	**66**	**67**	**8**	**2**	**6**	**120**	**293**	**173**	**1.7**
Violence	5	–	13	9	1	1	1	18	49	23	2.2
Escapes or absconds	–	–	–	–	–	–	–	2	3	2	1.4
Disobedience or disrespect	11	–	27	27	4	1	3	39	112	66	1.7
Wilful damage	1	–	5	6	–	–	–	5	18	9	1.9
Unauthorised transactions	3	–	17	18	2	–	1	48	89	59	1.5
Other offences	1	–	4	6	1	–	1	8	23	15	1.6
White											
All offences	**22**	**1**	**63**	**65**	**8**	**2**	**6**	**120**	**286**	**171**	**1.7**
Violence	4	–	11	8	1	1	1	17	42	20	2.1
Escapes or absconds	–	–	–	–	–	–	–	2	3	2	1.4
Disobedience or disrespect	11	–	26	27	4	1	3	39	111	65	1.7
Wilful damage	1	–	5	7	–	–	–	5	19	10	1.9
Unauthorised transactions	3	–	16	17	2	–	1	49	89	59	1.5
Other offences	1	–	4	6	1	–	1	9	22	14	1.6
Black											
All offences	**36**	**1**	**97**	**93**	**10**	**2**	**6**	**142**	**387**	**214**	**1.8**
Violence	13	–	27	18	1	1	2	32	95	41	2.3
Escapes or absconds	–	–	–	–	–	–	–	–	1	–	1.9
Disobedience or disrespect	15	–	37	38	4	1	2	46	145	82	1.8
Wilful damage	2	–	5	5	–	–	–	4	16	8	2.0
Unauthorised transactions	5	–	21	22	2	–	1	52	103	65	1.6
Other offences	2	–	7	9	2	–	–	8	28	17	1.6
South Asian											
All offences	**13**	**1**	**44**	**45**	**6**	**1**	**3**	**79**	**193**	**114**	**1.7**
Violence	3	–	10	7	1	1	1	14	37	17	2.2
Escapes or absconds	–	–	–	–	–	–	–	1	1	1	1.3
Disobedience or disrespect	5	–	15	16	3	1	1	20	62	37	1.7
Wilful damage	1	–	2	3	–	–	–	1	7	4	1.7
Unauthorised transactions	3	–	14	14	1	–	1	35	68	42	1.6
Other offences	1	–	3	5	1	–	–	8	18	13	1.4
Chinese & other(6)											
All offences	**19**	**1**	**51**	**47**	**8**	**2**	**4**	**81**	**213**	**127**	**1.7**
Violence	7	1	12	7	1	1	2	13	43	19	2.2
Escapes or absconds	–	–	–	–	–	–	–	1	1	1	1.9
Disobedience or disrespect	8	–	19	18	3	1	2	23	74	44	1.7
Wilful damage	1	–	3	4	–	–	–	3	11	6	1.8
Unauthorised transactions	2	–	13	13	3	–	–	35	67	45	1.5
Other offences	1	–	3	5	1	–	–	6	17	11	1.5

(1) Based on population of 30 June 1997.
(2) Includes offences committed at one establishment and punished at another.
(3) Includes suspended and prospective punishments.
(4) The number of offences punished and punishments given do not agree because in many cases two or more punishments are given for a single offence.
(5) Includes a small number of cases with no ethnic classification recorded.
(6) Includes Other Asian.

Table 8.6 Punishments per 100 population([1]) given by ethnicity and offence

England and Wales 1997
Females

Offence([2]) / Ethnicity	Confinement to room	Removal from activities	Forfeiture of privileges	Stoppage or reduction in earnings	Caution	Removal from wing	Work: extra or excluded from	Additional days	All punishments([4])	All offences([4])	Average number of punishments per offence
Female establishments											
Total([5])											
All offences	30	–	97	87	17	–	4	127	361	244	1.5
Violence	7	–	14	7	1	–	1	20	49	27	1.8
Escapes or absconds	–	–	–	–	–	–	–	6	6	6	1.0
Disobedience or disrespect	15	–	52	46	9	–	1	44	168	110	1.5
Wilful damage	2	–	4	4	–	–	–	3	13	8	1.5
Unauthorised transactions	2	–	14	11	3	–	1	30	61	44	1.4
Other offences	3	–	13	18	5	–	1	25	65	49	1.3
White											
All offences	28	–	96	87	17	–	4	131	363	250	1.5
Violence	6	–	12	6	1	–	1	18	45	25	1.8
Escapes or absconds	–	–	–	–	–	–	–	7	7	7	1.0
Disobedience or disrespect	14	–	52	45	8	–	2	44	165	109	1.5
Wilful damage	2	–	4	4	–	–	–	3	14	10	1.5
Unauthorised transactions	3	–	16	12	3	–	1	32	65	47	1.4
Other offences	3	–	12	19	4	–	1	27	67	51	1.3
Black											
All offences	37	–	101	90	21	–	4	118	372	239	1.6
Violence	10	–	17	8	1	–	1	26	65	36	1.8
Escapes or absconds	–	–	–	–	–	–	–	1	1	1	1.9
Disobedience or disrespect	19	–	56	51	11	–	1	47	186	120	1.5
Wilful damage	2	–	2	2	–	–	–	2	8	4	1.7
Unauthorised transactions	2	–	11	11	2	–	–	24	50	34	1.4
Other offences	4	–	14	18	7	–	1	18	63	43	1.5
South Asian											
All offences	–	–	–	–	–	–	–	–	–	–	*
Violence	–	–	–	–	–	–	–	–	–	–	*
Escapes or absconds	–	–	–	–	–	–	–	–	–	–	*
Disobedience or disrespect	–	–	–	–	–	–	–	–	–	–	*
Wilful damage	–	–	–	–	–	–	–	–	–	–	*
Unauthorised transactions	–	–	–	–	–	–	–	–	–	–	*
Other offences	–	–	–	–	–	–	–	–	–	–	*
Chinese & other([6])											
All offences	33	–	93	72	14	–	2	109	322	207	1.6
Violence	9	–	25	11	–	–	–	28	74	39	1.9
Escapes or absconds	–	–	–	–	–	–	–	1	1	1	1.0
Disobedience or disrespect	20	–	50	40	7	–	2	41	159	103	1.5
Wilful damage	–	–	3	5	–	–	–	2	9	7	1.4
Unauthorised transactions	2	–	7	7	4	–	–	14	35	24	1.4
Other offences	2	–	7	8	4	–	–	23	45	33	1.4

([1]) Based on population of 30 June 1997.
([2]) Includes offences committed at one establishment and punished at another.
([3]) Includes suspended and prospective punishments.
([4]) The number of offences punished and punishments given do not agree because in many cases two or more punishments are given for a single offence.
([5]) Includes a small number of cases with no ethnic classification recorded.
([6]) Includes other Asian.

CHAPTER 9

RECONVICTIONS OF PRISONERS DISCHARGED FROM PRISON IN 1994

Key points

- The proportion of prisoners reconvicted within two years of discharge is strongly associated with a number of factors—the number and rate of previous convictions, age at sentence, type of offence for which imprisoned, and sex.

- 56 per cent of all prisoners discharged in 1994 were reconvicted for a standard list offence within two years of their discharge. The rates for the main groups were:—

    - 50 per cent for adult males

    - 75 per cent for male young offenders

    - 46 per cent for females.

- Between 1987 and 1990 the reconviction rate within two years of discharge decreased from 57 to 52 per cent and remained around this level until rising to 56 per cent in 1994. About one percentage point of the increase in the rate between 1993 and 1994 (from 53 to 56 per cent) can be accounted for by widening in the range of offences held on the Home Office Offenders Index.

- Among prisoners discharged in 1994 who were reconvicted within two years, 32 per cent were sentenced to imprisonment on first reconviction; 26 per cent were fined, 14 per cent given probation, 8 per cent community service and 5 per cent a combination order.

- 48 per cent of male young offenders discharged from prison in 1994 received a new custodial sentence within two years, compared with 26 per cent for adult males, and 17 per cent for adult females. These rates all increased between 1992 and 1994, reflecting changes in sentencing practice.

- Reconviction rates varied with the type of original offence; from a two year rate for those discharged in 1994 of 74 per cent for burglary and 68 per cent for theft and handling offences to 28 per cent for fraud and forgery and 16 per cent for sexual offences.

- For most categories of offence for which the prisoner was originally convicted, a theft or handling offence was the most common at first reconviction. However, for those originally convicted of burglary, fraud and forgery and drugs offences a first reconviction for the same offence was more common.

Introduction

9.1 The tables in this chapter give estimated reconviction rates for offenders, excluding fine defaulters and non-criminal prisoners, discharged in 1994 from custodial sentences and also for earlier years back to 1987. Provisional figures are also included for 1995, based on a sample of prisoners discharged in the first quarter of that year. Previously published data, for reconvictions of those discharged in 1993, were contained in the statistical bulletin 5/97. Previously published information on reconviction rates for those starting community penalties in 1993 was contained in statistical bulletin 6/97.

9.2 Reconviction rates are limited to reconvictions for "standard list" offences. Further details and a description of the sampling methods are given in paragraph 23 of the Notes.

9.3 It is important to recognise that an offender's propensity to re-offend is affected by many factors other than the experience of custody, such as age and previous criminal history. The results of a comprehensive study of the factors affecting reconviction rates has been published in "Explaining reconviction rates: a critical analysis" Home Office Research Study, 136. Care must also be used when interpreting the basic reconviction rates, as they only give a limited picture of the pattern of convictions. The reconviction rate does not indicate the number or seriousness of the offences concerned and does not, of course, include any reoffending that is undetected or does not result in conviction for a "standard list" offence.

Changes in reconviction rates over time

9.4 Changes in reconviction rates over time should be viewed with caution because they may be due to many factors other than the effect of the custodial sentence. The characteristics of the prisoners discharged change over time. In particular, an analysis reported in Prison Statistics, England and Wales, 1993 (Cm. 2893) attributed much of the fall in reconviction rates since 1987 to the decline between 1987 and 1990 in the proportion of those discharged from prison who were young offenders (see Table 9.1). The likelihood of reconviction for a particular ex-prisoner will also be affected by changes in the extent to which offending is detected and results in a conviction.

9.5 A separate analysis, performed in connection with the calculation of the Probation Service's Key Performance Indicator 1 (KPI 1), compared rates for different years by fitting a statistical model to the data, similar to that used in Home Office Research Study No. 136. This model made allowance for number of previous convictions, offence type, sex, age at sentence, age at first offence, numbers of previous imprisonments and the rate at which the offender had acquired convictions before entering prison. Results of fitting this model indicated that between 1989 and 1993 the two year reconviction rates for those discharged from prison had hardly changed once one had made adjustment for changes in the characteristics of prisoners discharged. KPI 1 results for 1994 indicate that the two year reconviction rate for 1994 was 1.4 percentage points higher than the 1993 rate after making similar adjustments and taking account of changes in the coverage of standard list offences.

Reconviction rates by year of discharge and sex (Table 9.1)

9.6 The rate of reconviction within a two year period for all offenders discharged from custody in 1994 was 56 per cent. This represents a change of some three percentage points over the previous year (53 per cent reconvicted). However, several offences were added to the "standard list" on 1 July 1995 and 1 January 1996 (see paragraph 25 of the Notes). If these offences had not been included in the calculation of reconviction rates for 1994, the rate would have been around 1 percentage point lower. The reconviction rate for discharges in 1987 was 57 per cent. By 1990 it had decreased to 52 per cent and it remained close to this figure until the latest rise.

9.7 For males the reconviction rate was 56 per cent for discharges in 1994 and for females 46 per cent (some six percentage points up on the previous year). Results of the model fitting described in paragraph 9.26 indicated that more than half of the increase in the reconviction rate for females can be accounted for by changes in the characteristics of the females discharged. The higher reconviction rate for males relative to females was partly due to differences in age composition and the number of previous convictions (eg. 16 per cent of females discharged in 1994 were young offenders as opposed to 24 per cent for males). For male young offenders the reconviction rate was 75 per cent in 1994 and for adult males 50 per cent. Comparable rates for females were lower (63 and 43 per cent respectively).

Figure 9.1

PRISONERS RECONVICTED WITHIN TWO YEARS

Percentage

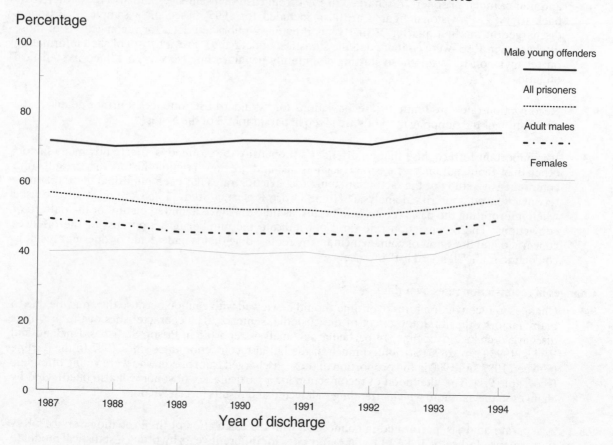

Reconviction rates by time since discharge (Table 9.2)

9.8   Among prisoners discharged in 1994 the proportion reconvicted after three months was 9 per cent, after one year 39 per cent and after two years 56 per cent. Information on a longer follow-up period is available for those discharged in 1987 and 1988. For those discharged in 1988, the proportion reconvicted after four years was 64 per cent. For those discharged in 1987 the proportions reconvicted after five and seven years were 70 and 73 per cent respectively. This rapid levelling-off in the proportion reconvicted as the follow-up period lengthened indicates that the longer these ex-prisoners remained without a reconviction the lower the likelihood became of a reconviction in each subsequent period.

150

Figure 9.2

PRISONERS RECONVICTED BY TIME TO RECONVICTION
BASED ON 1994 DISCHARGES

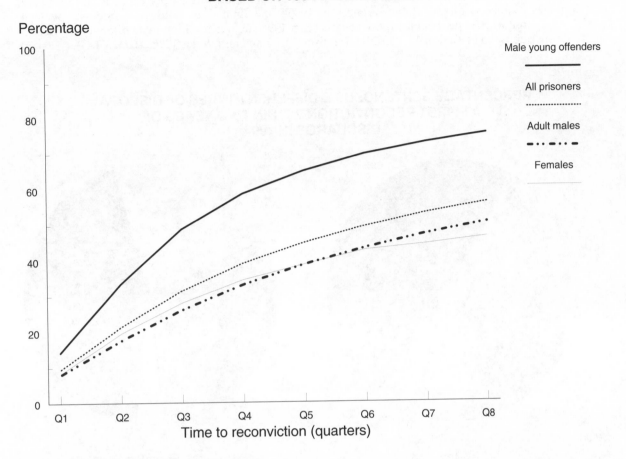

Percentage

Number of reconvictions (Table 9.2)

9.9 After two years 34 per cent of those discharged in 1994 had two or more reconvictions (only one reconviction per court appearance is counted in these calculations), 20 per cent 3 or more and 11 per cent four or more. After two years an average of 1.4 reconvictions were recorded per ex-prisoner in the 1994 discharge sample. The longer term follow-up reveals that although the proportion reconvicted did not increase to any great extent beyond the four year point, the number of convictions per ex-prisoner continued to rise.

Sentence length (Tables 9.3 and 9.4)

9.10 Reconviction rates were generally lower for offenders given longer sentences. In part this is known to reflect differences in the characteristics of prisoners (from information available on the Offenders Index). It is also likely to be affected by factors which influenced sentencing, but are not available from the Offenders Index, and by the greater proportion of the follow-up period that those with longer sentences spend on post-release supervision (as well as differences in the intensity of supervision). A similar pattern occurred for both sexes and for offenders in different age groups.

Sentence on first reconviction (Tables 9.3 and 9.4)

9.11 The patterns of sentencing on first reconviction for males and females differed. For example, of the males who were discharged in 1994 and reconvicted within two years, 32 per cent were sentenced to immediate custody on first reconviction and 27 per cent to the main community penalties (probation, community service and combination orders) as compared to 20 per cent and 33 per cent respectively for females. There were also differences among males. Adult males were more likely to be fined on first reconviction than young male offenders (28 per cent and 21 per cent respectively). The proportion of young males sentenced to immediate custody was higher at 34 per cent. In Figure 9.3 and associated tables 'Other' disposals refer mainly (but not solely) to conditional discharges.

151

9.12   As in previous years, the types of sentence given to adult males discharged in 1994 on a first reconviction were rather different to those for all adult male offenders sentenced for indictable offences around the same time. Immediate custody was used proportionately more often for reconvicted ex-prisoners—32 per cent of sentences compared with 24 per cent for all those adult males sentenced for indictable offences in 1995—and fining was used less often—28 per cent compared with 34 per cent for those sentenced in 1995 (figures for adult male offenders sentenced were published in Table 7.11, "Criminal statistics, England and Wales 1996" (Cm. 3764)).

Figure 9.3

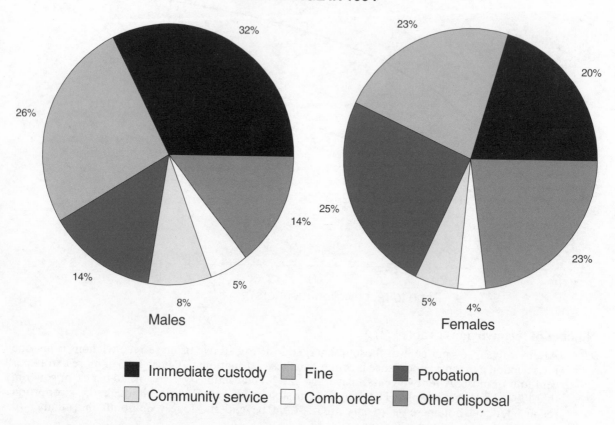

PERCENTAGE SENTENCED TO DIFFERENT TYPES OF DISPOSAL AT FIRST RECONVICTION WITHIN TWO YEARS OF DISCHARGE IN 1994

Males

Females

Immediate custody   Fine   Probation

Community service   Comb order   Other disposal

Reconviction rates and percentage recommitted to prison (Tables 9.5, 9.6 and 9.7)

9.13   Among adult male offenders discharged in 1994, 26 per cent were recommitted to custody within two years of discharge with over half of these receiving a custodial sentence on first reconviction (16 per cent). This represents an increase on the 1993 figures of 23 and 15 per cent respectively and a substantial increase on the 1992 figures (19 and 10 per cent respectively), and is almost identical to those recorded in 1987 of 26 and 15 per cent respectively.

9.14   Young male offenders were more likely to be recommitted to prison within two years (48 per cent of those discharged from custody in 1994) and more likely to be sentenced to custody on first reconviction (26 per cent of those discharged). These figures are slightly higher than those for 1993 when the comparable rates were 46 and 24 per cent respectively. However, they represent a substantial increase on figures recorded for 1992 when the rates were 38 and 18 per cent respectively. In 1987 they were 40 and 25 per cent respectively.

9.15   Both reconviction and recommittal rates for those discharged in 1994 varied according to the age of the young offender. The rate of reconviction within two years declined from 88 per cent for those aged 14-16, to 86 per cent for those aged 17 and 71 per cent for those aged 18-20. The corresponding figures for recommittal to prison were 64, 63 and 42 per cent respectively.

152

9.16   The recommittal rate for adult females discharged in 1994 was 17 per cent, having previously increased from 11 per cent to 16 per cent between 1992 and 1993.

9.17   The increases in the recommittal rate for 1994 discharges reflect a greater use of custodial sentencing generally in the period of follow-up. *For all* offenders sentenced for indictable offences in 1996, 22 per cent were sentenced to immediate custody compared to 17 per cent in 1994. The trend to increasing use of custody was further reflected in the rise in prison receptions following immediate custodial sentence, from around 61,000 in 1994 to over 74,000 in 1996.

Figure 9.4

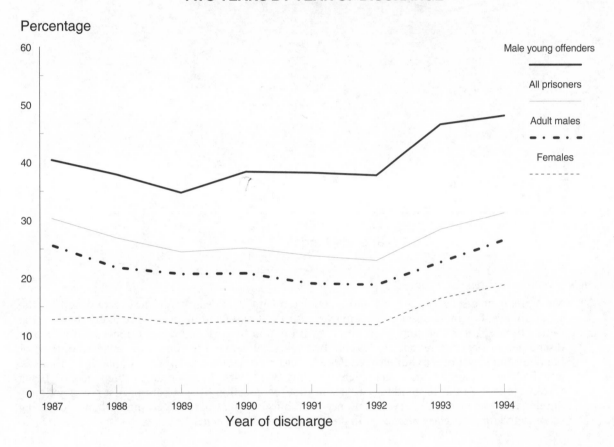

PRISONERS RECOMMITTED TO PRISON WITHIN TWO YEARS BY YEAR OF DISCHARGE

Types of offence

Offences for which originally convicted (Table 9.8)

9.18   Male prisoners discharged in 1994 from sentences for burglary or for theft and handling were the most likely to be reconvicted within two years (74 and 69 per cent respectively). Rates of reconviction within two years were generally lowest for those who had served sentences for sexual offences, fraud and forgery or drug offences (16, 28 and 33 per cent, respectively).

9.19   For all offence groups the reconviction rate for male young offenders was higher than for adult males. In particular, the respective rates for theft and handling were 85 and 62 per cent, while for offences of violence they were 61 and 40 per cent. The higher overall reconviction rate for male young offenders (75 per cent) compared with adult males (50 per cent), was partly a reflection of these differences and partly of the fact that a larger proportion of discharged young offenders were originally convicted for burglary offences (29 per cent of discharged young male offenders as opposed to 16 per cent of adult males), for which reconviction rates were high for both age groups (82 and 70 per cent respectively).

153

Figure 9.5

Percentage

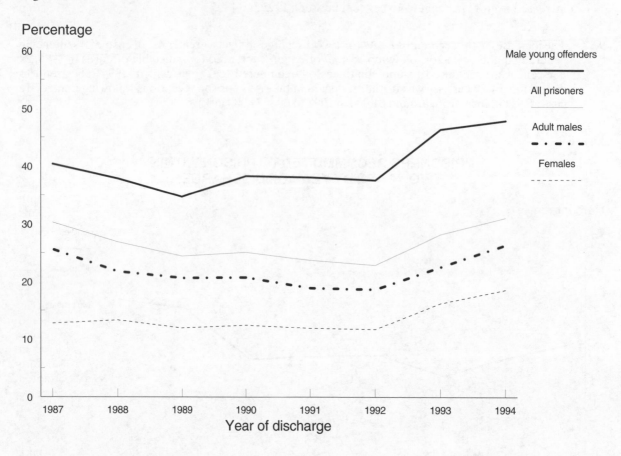

Year of discharge

Offences on first reconviction (Table 9.8)

9.20 Most prisoners discharged in 1994 and reconvicted within two years were not reconvicted for the same offence. For most offences, reconviction for theft and handling was more likely than for the same offence. The exceptions were burglary, fraud and forgery and drugs offences. Of all males discharged in 1994 and reconvicted within two years, 29 per cent were first reconvicted of theft or handling and 17 per cent of burglary. Males who had served sentences for theft or handling offences, and had subsequently been reconvicted within two years, had the highest chance of being reconvicted for a theft or handling offence at first reconviction (41 per cent of first reconvictions). Similarly, those who had served sentences for burglary had a relatively high chance of being reconvicted for a burglary offence at first reconviction (30 per cent).

9.21 Of males discharged after custodial sentences for sexual offences 16 per cent were reconvicted within two years. Among those reconvicted, 14 per cent were reconvicted for a sexual offence on first reconviction (ie. less than 3 per cent of those discharged for sexual offences were both reconvicted within two years *and* recorded a sexual offence at first reconviction). Those whose original offence was not sexual had a very much smaller chance of being reconvicted for a sexual offence on first reconviction (less than one per cent).

Ethnic group (Table 9.9)

9.22 Overall reconviction rates differed by ethnic group. The sample size permitted analysis of four broad ethnic group categories (white, black, south Asian and other). For those discharged from custody in 1994 the proportion of white prisoners reconvicted within two years of release was 57 per cent. For the black group, 'South Asian' and the 'other' group the proportions were 50, 36 and 38 per cent respectively. These differences are, in part, a result of foreign nationals leaving the country after release. Among offenders who were British nationals the percentages were 58, 53, 41 and 44, respectively. It is, however, important to note that nationality is an imprecise surrogate measure for country of usual residence.

154

9.23 For 1994 discharges, those in the black group were more likely than those in the white group to have been discharged after serving sentences for drug offences, which had a relatively low reconviction rate, and less likely to have served sentences for burglary which had a relatively high reconviction rate. The numbers in the 'south Asian' groups were relatively small and so must be interpreted with care, but they are also substantially less likely to have served a sentence for burglary than white prisoners.

9.24 An analysis was performed similar to that used for KPI 1 calculations (see paragraph 9.5) to examine the extent to which differences in reconviction rates between ethnic groups can be accounted for by differences in the characteristics of prisoners (the prediction model was based solely on prisoners discharged in 1994 but in other respects used the same factors as the analysis described in paragraph 9.5). The results indicated that, after making allowance for these factors, the rate for black prisoners was around 1 percentage point below predicted (irrespective of nationality) and for the 'south Asian' group around 4 percentage points below the level expected for all offenders and 5 points below for British nationals. A similar pattern applies (ie. reconviction rates are lower than expected for 'south Asians') across individual age groups and sexes (although the number of females from ethnic minority groups was too small to draw firm conclusions). These results are similar to those for previous years.

Comparison with reconviction rates for community penalties (Table 9.10)

9.25 For those given probation, community service or combination orders in 1994 the respective two year reconviction rates were 59, 48 and 60 per cent (with an average rate for these orders of 54 per cent) as compared with a rate for those discharged from prison of 56 per cent. It should, however, be noted that an offender discharged from prison was less likely to be convicted after discharge for offences committed before the discharge date (such offences could be dealt with while an offender is in prison) than an offender on a community penalty would be in respect of offences committed before the date his or her order started. These were termed "pseudo-reconvictions" in the research quoted in paragraph 9.3, which showed that removing such offences from consideration is likely to decrease reconviction rates for community penalties by about four percentage points relative to those for immediate custody.

9.26 In making comparisons between custody and community penalties, it is also necessary to take account of differences in the characteristics of offenders commencing community penalties and those discharged from prison (e.g. age, sex and number of previous convictions). An analysis of the 1994 samples indicated that an upward adjustment in the reconviction rate for community penalties of about six per cent relative to custody should be made on account of these factors. After making both types of adjustment the difference between the overall reconviction rates for immediate custody and community penalties was 0.1 percentage point in favour of custody. **This suggests that there is currently no discernible difference between reconviction rates for custody and all community penalties.** A similar analysis based on data for the first quarter of 1995 indicated a similar picture with a difference in favour of custody of one percentage point after all these adjustments had been made.

9.27 In these comparisons breach proceedings, where a further penalty is imposed, are treated as reconvictions. If one excludes breach proceedings from these analyses the results are more favourable for community penalties, with around a 3 and 2 percentage point advantage in favour of community penalties in 1994 and 1995 respectively. Further details of reconviction rates for offenders starting community penalties in 1993 are contained in statistical bulletin 6/97.

Table 9.1   Prisoners reconvicted(¹) by year of discharge and sex, within two years of discharge from prison

England and Wales
All males and females   Number of persons/Percentage reconvicted

Sex Year of Discharge	Young offenders(³)		Adults		Total	
	Number	Per cent	Number	Per cent	Number	Per cent
Males						
All discharges(²) within 2 years						
1987	23,298	72	39,459	49	62,757	57
1988	20,750	70	37,973	48	58,723	56
1989	15,980	71	36,518	46	52,498	53
1990	12,389	72	33,208	45	45,597	53
1991	12,744	72	34,122	46	46,866	53
1992	10,554	72	33,151	45	43,705	52
1993	11,681	75	33,700	47	45,381	54
1994	12,635	75	40,296	50	52,931	56
1995(⁴)	3,085	76	10,644	49	13,729	55
Females						
All discharges within 2 years						
1987	692	52	2,175	36	2,867	40
1988	513	55	2,087	37	2,600	40
1989	431	57	1,858	37	2,289	41
1990	302	59	1,574	36	1,876	40
1991	321	52	1,673	38	1,994	40
1992	265	51	1,587	36	1,852	38
1993	334	51	1,737	38	2,071	40
1994	388	63	2,059	43	2,447	46
1995(⁴)	126	61	549	49	675	51
All prisoners						
All discharges within 2 years						
1987	23,990	71	41,634	49	65,624	57
1988	21,263	70	40,060	47	61,323	55
1989	16,411	71	38,376	45	54,787	53
1990	12,691	72	34,782	45	47,473	52
1991	13,065	72	35,795	45	48,860	53
1992	10,819	71	34,738	45	45,557	51
1993	12,015	74	35,437	46	47,452	53
1994	13,023	75	42,355	50	55,378	56
1995(⁴)	3,211	75	11,193	49	14,404	55

(¹) Estimates based on sample of discharges. The number reconvicted includes only those reconvicted for standard list offences.

(²) Numbers are based on scaling-up figures from the sample file. This involves some rounding.

(³) Figures for young offenders are based on age at sentence.

(⁴) Figures for 1995 are based on a sample of discharges in the first quarter of the year. These will be updated with a full year sample when the data becomes available. The 'number discharged' figure for 1995 are those for the first quarter of 1995.

Table 9.2 Reconviction rates(¹), by time between discharge from prison and first reconviction, number of reconvictions and type of offender within two years of discharge from prison during 1994, within three and four years for those discharged in 1988 and five, six and seven years for those discharged in 1987

England and Wales
All males and females   Number of persons/Percentage reconvicted

Year of discharge Time since discharge Number of reconvictions	Male young offenders	Adult males	All males	All females	All prisoners
Result of follow up:					
Number discharged in 1994	**12,635**	**40,296**	**52,931**	**2,447**	**55,378**
3 months after discharge					
% with 1 or more	14	8	10	8	9
2 or more	1	1	1	1	1
3 or more	–	–	–	–	–
4 or more	–	–	–	–	–
Average number of reconvictions(²)	0.16	0.09	11	0.10	0.11
1 year after discharge					
% with 1 or more	59	33	39	34	39
2 or more	29	12	16	16	16
3 or more	11	5	6	6	6
4 or more	4	2	2	3	2
Average number of reconvictions(²)	1.03	0.55	0.67	0.62	0.66
2 years after discharge					
% with 1 or more	75	50	56	46	56
2 or more	55	28	35	30	34
3 or more	36	16	21	19	20
4 or more	21	8	11	11	11
Average number of reconvictions(²)	2.08	1.16	1.38	1.24	1.38
Number discharged in 1988	**20,750**	**37,973**	**58,723**	**2,600**	**61,323**
3 years after discharge					
% with 1 or more	77	55	63	46	62
2 or more	57	32	41	28	40
3 or more	39	19	26	17	25
4 or more	24	10	15	10	14
Average number of reconvictions(²)	2.22	1.45	1.72	1.17	1.70
4 years after discharge					
% with 1 or more	79	58	65	47	64
2 or more	60	36	45	30	44
3 or more	44	21	30	19	29
4 or more	29	12	18	12	18
Average number of reconvictions(²)	2.52	1.63	1.94	1.32	1.92
Number discharged in 1987	**23,298**	**39,459**	**62,757**	**2,867**	**65,624**
5 years after discharge					
% with 1 or more	84	64	71	52	70
2 or more	69	44	53	34	53
3 or more	53	30	38	23	38
4 or more	41	20	28	16	27
Average number of reconvictions(²)	3.29	2.11	2.54	1.59	2.50
6 years after discharge					
% with 1 or more	85	66	73	53	72
2 or more	71	48	56	36	55
3 or more	58	34	43	25	42
4 or more	46	24	32	18	32
Average number of reconvictions(²)	3.80	2.44	2.93	1.82	2.89
7 years after discharge					
% with 1 or more	86	67	74	54	73
2 or more	73	50	58	38	57
3 or more	61	37	45	27	45
4 or more	50	27	36	20	35
Average number of reconvictions(²)	4.27	2.73	3.29	2.05	3.24

(¹) Estimates based on sample of discharges. The number reconvicted includes only those reconvicted for standard list offences.

(²) The number of reconvictions(this includes fifth and subsequent reconvictions) divided by the numbers discharged. Only on reconviction per court appearance is counted.

Table 9.3   Prisoners reconvicted([1]), by length of sentence and sentence for the principal offence on first reconviction, within two years of discharge from prison during 1994

England and Wales
All males and females   Number of persons/Percentage reconvicted

Sex Sentence on first reconviction	All dis- charges	Total unsus- pended	Up to 12 months	Over 12 months up to 4 years	Over 4 years up to 10 years	Over 10 years not in- cluding life	Life	Partly sus- pended sen- tence
Adult males								
Result of follow up:								
Number discharged	**40,296**	**39,772**	**25,967**	**11,488**	**2,054**	**190**	**74**	**2**
% reconvicted within 2 years of discharge	50	50	53	48	33	26	3	100
Sentence on first reconviction:								
All sentences (=100%)	**20,297**	**20,003**	**13,794**	**5,492**	**673**	**49**	**2**	**2**
Immediate custody	32	32	30	35	31	42	50	–
Fully suspended sentence	1	1	1	1	1	2	–	–
Fine	28	28	28	28	28	16	–	–
Probation	14	14	14	13	11	20	–	100
Community service order	8	8	8	7	7	5	–	–
Combination order	4	4	5	3	6	2	–	–
Other	13	13	13	12	16	12	50	–
All males								
Number discharged	**52,931**	**52,287**	**35,675**	**14,149**	**2,165**	**203**	**95**	**2**
% reconvicted within 2 years of discharge	56	56	60	51	34	27	5	100
Sentence on first reconviction:								
All sentences (=100%)	**29,880**	**29,487**	**21,417**	**7,286**	**730**	**55**	**4**	**2**
Immediate custody	32	32	31	36	31	43	25	–
Fully suspended sentence	–	–	–	1	1	2	–	–
Fine	26	26	26	27	29	16	25	–
Probation	14	14	14	13	11	20	–	100
Community service order	8	8	8	7	7	4	–	–
Combination order	5	5	5	4	5	4	–	–
Other	14	14	15	12	16	10	50	–
All females								
Result of follow up:								
Number discharged	**2,447**	**2,415**	**1,878**	**479**	**52**	**3**	**3**	**–**
% reconvicted within 2 years of discharge	46	46	51	33	15	–	–	–
Sentence on first reconviction:								
All sentences (=100%)	**1,132**	**1,117**	**949**	**158**	**8**	**–**	**–**	**–**
Immediate custody imprisonment	20	20	19	26	20	–	–	–
Fully suspended sentence	2	2	2	1	–	–	–	–
Fine	22	22	21	29	40	–	–	–
Probation	25	25	26	15	–	–	–	–
Community service order	5	5	6	4	–	–	–	–
Combination order	4	4	4	1	–	–	–	–
Other	23	22	22	22	40	–	–	–
All prisoners								
Result of follow up:								
Number discharged	**55,378**	**54,702**	**37,553**	**14,628**	**2,217**	**206**	**98**	**2**
% reconvicted within 2 years of discharge	56	56	60	51	33	27	5	100
Sentence on first reconviction:								
All sentences (=100%)	**31,027**	**30,619**	**22,376**	**7,448**	**740**	**55**	**4**	**2**
Immediate custody	32	32	31	35	31	43	25	–
Fully suspended sentence	1	1	1	1	1	2	–	–
Fine	26	26	25	27	29	16	25	–
Probation	14	14	15	13	11	20	–	100
Community service order	8	8	8	7	7	4	–	–
Combination order	5	5	5	4	5	4	–	–
Other	14	14	15	13	17	10	50	–

([1]) Estimates based on sample of discharges. The number reconvicted includes only those reconvicted for standard list offences.

Table 9.4   Young males reconvicted([1]), by length of sentence and sentence for the principal offence on first reconviction, within two years of discharge from prison during 1994

England and Wales
All males and females   Number of persons/Percentage reconvicted

Age at sentence Sentence on first reconviction	All dis- charges	Total unsus- pended	Up to 12 months	Over 12 months up to 4 years	Over 4 years up to 10 years	Over 10 years not in- cluding life	Life	Partly sus- pended sen- tence
Young male offenders								
Age 14–16								
Result of follow up:								
Number discharged	**1,650**	**1,633**	**1,535**	**86**	**7**	**1**	**4**	–
% reconvicted within 2 years of discharge	*88*	*88*	*88*	*79*	*57*	*100*	*25*	–
Sentence on first reconviction:								
All sentences (=100%)	**1,446**	**1,430**	**1,356**	**68**	**4**	**1**	**1**	–
Immediate custody	36	36	36	38	50	–	–	–
Fully suspended sentence	–	–	–	–	–	–	–	–
Fine	10	10	10	24	25	–	100	–
Probation	8	8	8	14	25	–	–	–
Community service order	9	9	9	2	–	–	–	–
Combination order	4	4	4	10	–	100	–	–
Other	32	32	33	12	–	–	–	–
Age 17–20								
Result of follow up:								
Number discharged	**10,985**	**10,882**	**8,174**	**2,575**	**104**	**12**	**17**	–
% reconvicted within 2 years of discharge	*74*	*74*	*76*	*67*	*51*	*46*	*7*	–
Sentence on first reconviction:								
All sentences (=100%)	**8,084**	**8,004**	**6,220**	**1,723**	**53**	**5**	**1**	–
Immediate custody	34	34	32	38	31	60	–	–
Fully suspended sentence	–	–	–	–	–	–	–	–
Fine	23	23	23	25	33	20	–	–
Probation	14	14	15	12	8	20	–	–
Community service order	9	9	9	8	10	–	–	–
Combination order	6	6	7	5	–	–	–	–
Other	13	13	13	13	17	–	100	–
All ages								
Result of follow up:								
Number discharged	**12,635**	**12,515**	**9,709**	**2,661**	**111**	**13**	**21**	–
% reconvicted within 2 years of discharge	*75*	*75*	*78*	*67*	*51*	*51*	*11*	–
Sentence on first reconviction:								
All sentences (=100%)	**9,530**	**9,434**	**7,576**	**1,791**	**57**	**7**	**2**	–
Immediate custody	34	34	33	38	33	50	–	–
Fully suspended sentence	–	–	–	–	–	–	–	–
Fine	21	21	21	25	33	17	50	–
Probation	13	13	14	12	10	17	–	–
Community service order	9	9	9	8	10	–	–	–
Combination order	6	6	6	5	–	17	–	–
Other	16	16	17	13	15	–	50	–

([1]) Estimates based on sample of discharges. The number reconvicted includes only those reconvicted for standard list offences.

Table 9.5 Adult prisoners by type of custody, percentage reconvicted(¹) and recommitted to prison within two years of discharge from prison

England and Wales
Adult males and females   Number of persons/percentage reconvicted

| | Number discharged | | Reconvicted | | | |
| | | | All | | Recommitted to prison under sentence during period of follow up | |
Type of custody Year of discharge	Adult males Number	Adult females Number	Adult males Per cent	Adult females Per cent	Adult males Per cent	Adult females Per cent
All discharges						
1987	39,459	2,175	49	36	26	12
1988	37,973	2,087	48	37	22	12
1989	36,518	1,858	46	37	21	11
1990	33,208	1,574	45	36	21	11
1991	34,122	1,673	46	38	19	11
1992	33,151	1,587	45	36	19	11
1993	33,700	1,737	47	38	23	16
1994	40,296	2,059	50	43	26	17
1995(²)	10,644	549	49	49	27	22
Unsuspended imprisonment						
Up to 18 months						
1987	27,844	1,533	53	43	27	14
1988	26,163	1,463	52	43	23	14
1989	24,214	1,251	50	45	23	14
1990	21,608	1,086	50	43	23	15
1991	22,764	1,180	50	45	20	14
1992	22,524	1,135	49	44	20	13
1993	23,879	1,375	50	42	24	18
1994	29,950	1,740	53	45	28	17
1995(²)	7,917	463	50	50	28	24
Over 18 months up to 4 years						
1987	7,810	294	46	25	25	6
1988	8,429	329	43	23	21	6
1989	8,575	343	42	21	18	4
1990	8,344	293	42	24	20	6
1991	7,510	277	42	21	18	4
1992	7,444	254	42	22	18	8
1993	6,905	215	45	32	23	11
1994	7,505	240	46	31	25	17
1995(²)	1,939	66	50	39	28	11
Over 4 years						
1987	1,277	13	31	–	15	–
1988	1,414	34	28	16	14	3
1989	1,789	48	27	5	13	2
1990	2,054	59	28	12	11	–
1991	2,523	89	25	19	11	8
1992	1,297	107	26	6	11	2
1993	2,813	133	24	4	10	–
1994	2,318	53	31	11	15	3
1995(²)	493	9	33	–	17	–
All unsuspended imprisonment						
1987	36,981	1,841	51	40	26	13
1988	36,006	1,827	49	39	22	13
1989	34,578	1,642	47	39	21	11
1990	32,006	1,438	46	38	21	12
1991	32,797	1,546	46	39	19	12
1992	32,266	1,496	46	38	19	11
1993	33,597	1,722	47	38	22	16
1994	39,772	2,033	50	43	26	17
1995(²)	10,350	538	49	48	27	22
Partly suspended sentences						
1987	2,528	334	29	17	13	6
1988	1,967	260	29	20	13	5
1989	1,934	215	26	19	11	4
1990	1,163	133	24	14	10	2
1991	858	104	24	13	8	1
1992	540	84	22	10	8	1
1993	24	3	52	–	43	–
1994	2	–	100	..	100	..
1995(²)	–	–	..	..	..	..

(¹) Estimates based on sample of discharges. The number reconvicted includes only those reconvicted for standard list offences.
(²) Figures for 1995 are based on a sample of discharges in the first quarter of the year. These will be updated with a full year sample when the data becomes available.

Table 9.6   Young males by type of custody, percentage reconvicted([1]) and recommitted to prison within two years of discharge from prison

England and Wales
Young male offenders

Year of discharge	Number of persons/Percentage reconvicted/recommitted to prison			
	Aged 14–16([2])	Aged 17([2])	Aged 18–20([2])	Aged 14–20([2])
Number discharged				
1987	3,660	4,230	15,054	22,943
1988	3,135	3,731	13,884	20,750
1989	2,014	2,897	11,068	15,980
1990	1,302	2,125	8,962	12,389
1991	1,339	1,896	9,509	12,744
1992	1,184	1,527	7,843	10,554
1993	1,333	1,864	8,485	11,681
1994	1,650	1,904	9,081	12,635
1995([3])	447	413	2,226	3,085
Per cent reconvicted				
1987	83	77	67	72
1988	83	78	65	70
1989	86	78	66	71
1990	89	80	68	72
1991	88	78	69	72
1992	89	77	68	72
1993	89	81	72	75
1994	88	86	71	75
1995([3])	88	82	72	76
Per cent recommitted to prison				
1987	54	47	35	40
1988	53	44	33	38
1989	54	42	29	35
1990	57	49	33	38
1991	62	44	33	38
1992	62	44	33	38
1993	65	56	41	46
1994	64	63	42	48
1995([3])	63	61	46	50

([1]) Estimates based on sample of discharges. The number reconvicted includes only those reconvicted for standard list offences.

([2]) Figures are based on age at sentence.

([3]) Figures for 1995 are based on a sample of discharges in the first quarter of the year. These will be updated with a full year sample when the data becomes available.

Table 9.7 Prisoners reconvicted(¹), by sentence for the principal offence on first reconviction, within two years of discharge from prison

England and Wales
All males and females

Number of persons/percentage reconvicted

				Sentence on first reconviction						
Year of discharge	Number reconvicted	Un-suspended imprison-ment	Partly suspended sentence	Youth custody/ detention centre/ detention in a YOI	Fully suspended sentence	Fine	Probation	Community service order	Com-bination order(²)	Other

Sentence on first reconviction
Within 2 years of discharge

Male young offenders

1987	16,610	7	–	27	3	24	14	15	–	11
1988	14,541	7	–	24	3	24	17	13	–	13
1989	11,336	5	–	21	3	24	18	14	–	14
1990	8,951	6	–	21	3	23	19	14	–	15
1991	9,215	7	–	21	2	22	17	14	1	17
1992	7,558	7	–	17	–	25	15	12	3	21
1993	8,759	8	–	23	–	22	15	10	5	17
1994	9,530	8	–	26	–	21	13	9	6	16
1995(³)	2,340	8	–	27	–	23	13	9	7	14

Adult males

1987	19,623	31	1	–	15	24	11	7	–	10
1988	18,113	29	1	–	15	27	12	6	–	10
1989	16,678	27	–	–	14	26	13	6	–	13
1990	15,105	27	1	–	12	25	13	7	–	15
1991	15,623	26	–	–	9	28	12	9	–	16
1992	15,034	21	–	1	3	31	13	8	2	20
1993	15,707	28	–	–	1	30	14	9	4	14
1994	20,297	31	–	–	1	28	14	8	4	13
1995(³)	5,255	31	–	–	1	28	15	6	4	14

All males

1987	36,033	20	1	12	10	24	13	10	–	10
1988	32,683	19	–	11	10	26	14	9	–	11
1989	28,062	18	–	8	9	26	15	9	–	13
1990	24,113	19	–	8	9	24	15	9	–	15
1991	24,891	19	–	8	6	26	14	11	–	16
1992	22,635	17	–	6	2	29	14	9	3	21
1993	24,503	21	–	8	1	27	14	9	5	15
1994	29,880	24	–	9	–	26	14	8	5	14
1995(³)	7,610	24	–	9	1	27	14	7	5	14

(¹) Estimates based on sample of discharges. The number reconvicted includes only those reconvicted for standard list offences.

(²) Combination orders first became available as a sentencing option from 1 October 1993. In consequence no prisoners discharged from prison before 1 October 1990 could have been sentenced to such a order within the two year follow-up period.

(³) Figures for 1995 are based on a sample of discharges in the first quarter of the year. These will be updated with a full year sample when the data becomes available.

Table 9.7 (Continued) Prisoners reconvicted([1]), by sentence for the principal offence on first reconviction, within two years of discharge from prison

England and Wales
All males and females   Number of persons/percentage reconvicted

Year of discharge	Number reconvicted	Un-suspended imprison-ment	Partly suspended sentence	Youth custody/ detention centre/ detention in a YOI	Fully suspended sentence	Fine	Probation	Community service order	Com-bination order([2])	Other
					Sentence on first reconviction					

Sentence on first reconviction
Within 2 years of discharge

All females

Year of discharge	Number reconvicted	Un-suspended imprison-ment	Partly suspended sentence	Youth custody/ detention centre/ detention in a YOI	Fully suspended sentence	Fine	Probation	Community service order	Com-bination order([2])	Other
1987	1,136	15	1	3	12	14	29	7	–	19
1988	1,047	15	–	4	14	16	28	6	–	17
1989	932	12	–	4	11	18	28	6	–	20
1990	743	13	–	2	11	18	28	5	–	23
1991	806	15	–	3	7	24	24	4	–	22
1992	711	10	–	2	3	27	26	4	3	24
1993	837	15	–	3	1	25	29	4	4	19
1994	1,132	16	–	4	2	22	25	5	4	23
1995([3])	344	21	–	5	1	21	25	3	3	21

All prisoners

Year of discharge	Number reconvicted	Un-suspended imprison-ment	Partly suspended sentence	Youth custody/ detention centre/ detention in a YOI	Fully suspended sentence	Fine	Probation	Community service order	Com-bination order([2])	Other
1987	37,233	20	1	12	10	24	13	10	–	10
1988	33,739	19	–	10	10	25	14	9	–	12
1989	29,008	18	–	8	9	25	16	9	–	14
1990	24,864	19	–	8	9	24	15	9	–	15
1991	25,707	19	–	8	6	26	14	11	–	16
1992	23,358	16	–	6	2	29	14	9	3	21
1993	25,358	20	–	8	1	27	15	9	5	15
1994	31,027	23	–	8	1	26	14	8	5	14
1995([3])	7,956	24	–	8	1	26	14	7	5	15

([1]) Estimates based on sample of discharges. The number reconvicted includes only those reconvicted for standard list offences.

([2]) Combination orders first became available as a sentencing option from 1 October 1993. In consequence no prisoners discharged from prison before 1 October 1990 could have been sentenced to such a order within the two year follow-up period.

([3]) Figures for 1995 are based on a sample of discharges in the first quarter of the year. These will be updated with a full year sample when the data becomes available.

Table 9.8 Prisoners reconvicted(^{1}), by offence for which originally convicted and offence on first reconviction, within two years of discharge from prison during 1994

England and Wales
All males and females   Number of persons/percentage reconvicted

Offence on first conviction	All offences	Violence against the person	Sexual offences	Burglary	Robbery	Theft and handling	Fraud and forgery	Drugs offences	Other offences	Offence not recorded
						Offence for which originally convicted				
Male young offenders										
All discharges	**12,635**	**1,568**	**114**	**3,686**	**841**	**2,756**	**46**	**224**	**2,394**	**1,006**
% reconvicted within 2 years	*75*	*61*	*38*	*82*	*65*	*85*	*57*	*43*	*76*	*67*
All reconviction offences(=100%)	9,530	962	43	3,014	548	2,343	26	96	1,811	677
Violence against the person	*5*	*10*	*5*	*4*	*8*	*4*	*16*	*5*	*4*	*5*
Sexual offences	*–*	*1*	*8*	*–*	*–*	*–*	*–*	*–*	*–*	*–*
Burglary	*21*	*14*	*21*	*32*	*16*	*16*	*4*	*11*	*15*	*22*
Robbery	*2*	*1*	*10*	*2*	*6*	*1*	*–*	*1*	*1*	*2*
Theft and handling	*30*	*29*	*18*	*27*	*29*	*35*	*24*	*20*	*30*	*29*
Fraud and forgery	*1*	*1*	*–*	*1*	*1*	*1*	*12*	*2*	*1*	*1*
Drugs offences	*4*	*7*	*3*	*3*	*6*	*2*	*–*	*27*	*3*	*5*
Other offences	*37*	*37*	*36*	*31*	*34*	*40*	*44*	*33*	*46*	*36*
Adult males										
All discharges	**40,296**	**5,691**	**1,674**	**6,315**	**1,809**	**6,637**	**1,489**	**2,400**	**11,991**	**2,290**
% reconvicted within 2 years	*50*	*40*	*15*	*70*	*46*	*62*	*27*	*32*	*51*	*46*
All reconviction offences(=100%)	20,297	2,291	249	4,423	825	4,110	402	779	6,112	1,061
Violence against the person	*6*	*15*	*8*	*4*	*7*	*4*	*2*	*4*	*8*	*5*
Sexual offences	*1*	*1*	*15*	*–*	*1*	*–*	*–*	*–*	*1*	*1*
Burglary	*15*	*8*	*6*	*29*	*12*	*10*	*6*	*6*	*12*	*12*
Robbery	*1*	*1*	*1*	*2*	*6*	*1*	*–*	*1*	*1*	*2*
Theft and handling	*29*	*22*	*19*	*28*	*26*	*44*	*21*	*20*	*24*	*30*
Fraud and forgery	*4*	*4*	*2*	*3*	*3*	*4*	*32*	*2*	*3*	*5*
Drugs offences	*6*	*8*	*5*	*4*	*8*	*4*	*2*	*37*	*5*	*9*
Other offences	*38*	*43*	*43*	*30*	*36*	*33*	*36*	*30*	*47*	*36*
All males										
All discharges	**52,931**	**7,259**	**1,788**	**10,001**	**2,650**	**9,393**	**1,536**	**2,624**	**14,385**	**3,296**
% reconvicted within 2 years	*56*	*45*	*16*	*74*	*52*	*69*	*28*	*33*	*55*	*53*
All reconviction offences(=100%)	29,880	3,248	292	7,432	1,371	6,464	429	875	7,955	1,742
Violence against the person	*6*	*14*	*8*	*4*	*7*	*4*	*3*	*4*	*7*	*5*
Sexual offences	*1*	*1*	*14*	*–*	*1*	*–*	*–*	*–*	*1*	*1*
Burglary	*17*	*10*	*8*	*30*	*14*	*12*	*6*	*7*	*13*	*16*
Robbery	*1*	*1*	*3*	*2*	*6*	*1*	*–*	*1*	*1*	*2*
Theft and handling	*29*	*24*	*19*	*28*	*27*	*41*	*21*	*20*	*26*	*30*
Fraud and forgery	*3*	*3*	*2*	*2*	*2*	*3*	*31*	*2*	*2*	*3*
Drugs offences	*6*	*7*	*5*	*4*	*7*	*3*	*2*	*36*	*5*	*7*
Other offences	*38*	*41*	*42*	*30*	*35*	*36*	*36*	*30*	*47*	*36*

(^{1}) Estimates based on sample of discharges. The number reconvicted includes those reconvicted for standard list offences.

Table 9.8 (Continued)   **Prisoners reconvicted(¹), by offence for which originally convicted and offence on first reconviction, within two years of discharge from prison during 1994**

England and Wales
All males and females

Number of persons/percentage reconvicted

Offence on first conviction	All offences	Violence against the person	Sexual offences	Burglary	Robbery	Theft and handling	Fraud and forgery	Drugs offences	Other offences	Offence not recorded
All females										
All discharges	**2,447**	**309**	**9**	**108**	**89**	**887**	**177**	**244**	**401**	**223**
% reconvicted within 2 years	46	40	11	60	51	56	28	18	55	37
All reconviction offences(=100%)	1,132	122	1	65	46	497	50	43	219	83
Violence against the person	4	12	–	–	5	2	3	–	10	1
Sexual offences	–	–	–	–	–	–	–	–	–	–
Burglary	3	2	–	10	3	3	3	–	2	–
Robbery	1	1	–	3	5	–	–	–	1	–
Theft and handling	54	35	–	42	38	67	41	26	45	66
Fraud and forgery	8	6	–	7	8	8	21	17	6	7
Drugs offences	5	3	–	5	3	3	3	37	4	8
Other offences	25	42	100	32	40	17	31	20	33	18
All prisoners										
All discharges	**55,378**	**7,567**	**1,797**	**10,109**	**2,739**	**10,280**	**1,713**	**2,868**	**14,786**	**3,519**
% reconvicted within 2 years	56	45	16	74	52	68	28	32	55	52
All reconviction offences(=100%)	31,027	3,371	293	7,498	1,417	6,964	479	921	8,175	1,826
Violence against the person	6	14	8	4	7	4	3	4	7	5
Sexual offences	1	1	14	–	1	–	–	–	1	1
Burglary	16	9	8	30	13	12	6	6	13	15
Robbery	1	1	3	2	6	1	–	1	1	2
Theft and handling	30	24	19	28	28	43	23	20	26	31
Fraud and forgery	3	3	2	2	3	3	30	3	3	3
Drugs offences	5	7	5	4	7	3	2	36	5	8
Other offences	37	41	42	30	35	35	36	30	46	35

(¹) Estimates based on sample of discharges. The number reconvicted includes those reconvicted for standard list offences.

Table 9.9 Prisoners reconvicted([1]), by ethnic group, nationality and offence, within two years of discharge from prison during 1994

England and Wales
All males and females   Number of persons/percentage reconvicted

Ethnic origin([2]) and nationality	All offences	Violence against the person	Sexual offences	Burglary	Robbery	Theft and handling	Fraud and forgery	Drugs offences	Other offences	Offence not recorded
England and Wales										
All ethnic groups										
Number discharged	**55,378**	**7,567**	**1,797**	**10,109**	**2,739**	**10,280**	**1,713**	**2,868**	**14,786**	**3,519**
% reconvicted										
British	57	45	17	74	52	68	29	34	56	53
All offenders	56	45	16	74	52	68	28	32	55	52
White										
Number discharged	**49,111**	**6,664**	**1,641**	**9,357**	**2,159**	**9,354**	**1,395**	**2,277**	**13,282**	**2,982**
% reconvicted										
British	58	46	16	75	53	69	30	34	57	54
All offenders	57	46	16	74	52	68	30	33	56	53
Black										
Number discharged	**4,209**	**624**	**91**	**570**	**429**	**631**	**170**	**436**	**859**	**399**
% reconvicted										
British	53	42	33	71	50	70	23	33	52	50
All offenders	50	40	28	71	50	69	20	28	48	47
South Asian										
Number discharged	**1,592**	**210**	**47**	**121**	**122**	**214**	**125**	**101**	**553**	**99**
% reconvicted										
British	41	29	21	67	49	43	12	37	47	24
All offenders	36	25	13	65	45	40	13	31	40	23
Other										
Number discharged	**2,058**	**279**	**65**	**182**	**151**	**295**	**148**	**155**	**645**	**138**
% reconvicted										
British	44	32	25	69	51	48	12	36	48	33
All offenders	38	28	16	67	48	44	14	29	42	27

([1]) Estimates based on sample of discharges. The number reconvicted includes only those reconvicted for standard list offences. Although the sampling intensities are high for offenders in ethnic minority groups the small numbers on which some reconviction rates are based mean that the year on year chance variation in rates will be relatively high.

Table 9.10 All offenders reconvicted([1]), by age at discharge from prison or commencement of a probation, community service or combination order and number of previous court appearances, within two years of discharge or commencement during 1994 and also by sex and number of previous convictions

England and Wales
All males and females   Percentage reconvicted

	Number of previous convictions([2])					
	None	1 or 2	3–6	7–10	11 or more	Total
All prisoners						
Aged under 21						
Probation	49	64	80	92	94	71
Community service	43	73	83	88	100	66
Combination	55	78	83	92	96	76
All community penalties	46	70	82	91	96	69
Immediate custody	40	69	84	91	95	76
Aged 21 to 24						
Probation	24	53	67	77	86	64
Community service	30	46	62	77	89	55
Combination	35	53	67	79	90	65
All community penalties	28	50	65	77	88	60
Immediate custody	19	43	64	76	86	64
Aged 25 to 29						
Probation	14	43	54	69	86	60
Community service	20	27	38	59	80	43
Combination	15	31	48	64	82	52
All community penalties	17	34	47	65	84	52
Immediate custody	16	28	43	60	79	54
Aged 30 and over						
Probation	14	27	40	52	69	45
Community service	12	15	35	41	65	31
Combination	10	22	37	56	66	41
All community penalties	12	21	37	49	68	39
Immediate custody	6	13	30	44	62	37
All males						
Probation	29	50	63	70	78	61
Community service	29	44	55	63	75	49
Combination	36	55	63	71	78	61
All community penalties	30	48	60	67	77	55
Immediate custody	18	41	59	68	74	57
All females						
Probation	23	44	54	76	75	46
Community service	16	46	57	67	95	40
Combination	25	45	60	83	63	47
All community penalties	21	45	55	75	79	45
Immediate custody	11	33	61	74	82	46
All ages						
Probation	28	49	62	70	78	59
Community service	28	44	55	63	76	48
Combination	34	54	63	72	77	60
All community penalties	28	47	59	68	77	54
Immediate custody	18	40	59	68	74	56

([1]) The number reconvicted includes only those reconvicted for standard list offence.

([2]) Appearances at court that led to a conviction for standard list offences before the commencement or discharge date, excluding the last conviction before commencement or discharge if no conviction is recorded on the day of commencement or discharge date – this would normally be the number of previous convictions prior to the sentencing date.

CHAPTER 10

HOME OFFICE RESEARCH ON PRISON-RELATED TOPICS

The following are brief summaries of Home Office research on prison-related issues which have been published in the last two years.

Mandatory drug testing in prisons—an evaluation Research Findings No. 75, 1998. Home Office Research Study forthcoming

This research assessed the impact of the Prison Service's Mandatory Drug Testing programme on the extent and nature of prisoners' drug misuse. Both staff and prisoners were interviewed in five establishments serving different functions and located in different parts of the country.

Review of comparative costs and performance of privately and publicly operated prisons 1996–97 Prison Service Research Report, No. 3, 1997

The review compared the cost and performance of four privately managed prisons—Wolds, Doncaster, Blakenhurst and Buckley Hall—relative to similar prisons operated within the public sector. Costs were adjusted to ensure comparability and then compared to ensure factors such as overcrowding and refurbishment are taken into account.

Changing offenders' attitudes and behaviour: what works? Home Office Research Study 171, Research Findings No. 61, 1997

Programmes designed to rehabilitate offenders may draw on a range of different theories and methods. Those based on cognitive-behavioural approaches, i.e. tackling deficiencies in offenders' ways of thinking, reasoning and associated behaviour are increasingly favoured. This research assessed the effectiveness of cognitive-behaviourial methods in changing offenders' attitudes and behaviour.

Control in Category C establishments Research Findings No. 54, 1997

A survey of just over half the Category C prisons in England and Wales examined interactions between a prison's regime, population and physical environment and the way they influence the maintenance of control. The research highlights the difficulties of managing the diverse population within a wide range of building types and suggests possible solutions.

A reconviction study of HMP Grendon therapeutic community Research Findings No. 53, 1997

This study examines the reconviction rates (within four years) of a number of prisoners who went to HMP Grendon for therapy in the years 1984 to 1989. The findings show that prisoners treated have lower reconviction rates than might have been expected had they not gone to Grendon.

Imprisoned women and mothers Home Office Research Study 162 and Research Findings No. 38, 1997

This study was designed to provide systematic information on all imprisoned mothers, ranging from their own childhood experiences, to their children and arrangements for their care before and during custody as well as those anticipated after release.

Victimisation in prisons Research Findings No. 37, 1996

The Prison Service launched its anti-bullying strategy in 1993. The need to obtain accurate information on the extent of bullying in prison was an important part of the strategy. This research studied both the extent of victimisation in prisons and the ways in which it might best be tackled.

Wolds remand prison—an evaluation Research Findings No. 32, 1996. Occasional Paper, 1997.

This study evaluated key aspects of the design and operation of the regime at HMP Wolds, the first contracted out remand prison in the UK. The main findings were compared with concurrent developments in new public sector prisons.

Mental disorder in remand prisoners Occasional Paper, 1996

This project aimed to determine the nature and extent of mental disorder in remanded prisoners in England and Wales. It also sought to determine their treatment needs.

Home Office Research Studies and Research Findings are available from Information and Publications Group, Research and Statistics Directorate, Room 201, Home Office, 50 Queen Anne's Gate, London SW1H 9AT. Telephone: 0171 273 2084.

Occasional Papers can be purchased from the Home Office Publications Unit, Room 1024, 50 Queen Anne's Gate, London SW1H 9AT. Telephone: 0171 273 2302.

Copies of Prison Service Research Report No. 3 are available from Planning Group, Prison Service, Abell House, John Islip Street, London SW1P 4LH

Imprisonment—adults

1.   Imprisonment is the most severe penalty ordinarily available to the courts who have the power to impose a sentence up to a maximum term given by the Act of Parliament which created the particular offence. Where an offender is sentenced to imprisonment for more than one offence, the sentences may be ordered by the court to run either consecutively or concurrently. There are a number of factors which a court will take into account when deciding whether sentences should be consecutive or concurrent. Consecutive sentences will generally be appropriate, for example, where different types of offending behaviour are involved. The maximum penalty reflects the gravity of the worst possible case and is thus high for the most serious offences, eg: life imprisonment for rape, robbery or manslaughter; 14 years for burglary of a dwelling. A magistrates' court may not sentence to longer than six months or less than five days for any one offence nor to longer than 12 months in total, where sentences are being imposed for two or more triable either way offences and are to run consecutively.

Custodial penalties for young offenders

2.   The Criminal Justice Act 1991 made a number of changes in the custodial sentencing arrangements for young offenders. It set a common minimum age of 15 for both boys and girls for the imposition of a sentence of detention in a young offender institution (previously the minimum age was 14 for boys and 15 for girls). The Act also set two months as a minimum period for which young offenders of either sex aged 15 to 17, may be sentenced to detention in a young offender institution (the previous minima for those under 17 were 21 days for males and 4 months for females). The maximum determinate sentence for 15 to 17 year olds was set at 12 months, but this was increased to 2 years with effect from 3 February 1995 under the Criminal Justice and Public Order Act 1994. For young offenders aged 18-20, the minimum is 21 days and the maximum is the same as the adult maximum for the offence.

3.   An important part of the activities of a Young Offender Institution is to prepare the offender for return to the outside community. A flexible but coherent programme of activities is provided, aimed at assisting the offender to develop personal responsibility, self-discipline, physical fitness and to obtain suitable employment after release. Youths of compulsory school age must receive a minimum of 15 hours education a week. Vocational training and work form an important part of the regime for older inmates. Links with families and the community are maintained as far as possible.

4.   Under section 53 of the Children and Young Persons Act 1933, youths aged 14-17 convicted at the Crown Court may be sentenced to be detained for up to the adult maximum, including life for offences carrying maximum sentences of 14 years or more imprisonment in the case of an adult or for the offences of causing death by dangerous driving, causing death by careless driving while under the influence of alcohol or drugs and, for those aged 16 and 17, indecent assault on a woman. This also applies to offenders aged 10-13 convicted of murder or manslaughter. The Criminal Justice and Public Order Act 1994 extended these provisions for 10-13 year olds. As of January 1995 10-13 year olds convicted at the Crown Court of offences carrying maximum sentences of 14 years or more imprisonment in the case of an adult etc. may also be detained for up to the adult maximum. Detainees may be held either in Prison Service establishments, local authority secure or open community homes, or Department of Health Youth Treatment Centres. The youngest detainees are held outside Prison Service establishments. The statistics in this publication relate only to those held in Prison Service establishments.

Life imprisonment

5.   Life imprisonment, or its equivalent, **must** be imposed on all persons convicted of murder. These are known as mandatory life sentences. Life imprisonment is also the maximum penalty which a court may pass for a number of the most serious crimes, including manslaughter, robbery, rape, wounding with intent to do grievous bodily harm, aggravated burglary and certain firearms offences. These are known as discretionary life sentences. For such offences, the court may choose instead to impose a determinate prison sentence of any length or a non-custodial penalty. Under section 2 of the Crime (Sentences) Act 1997 offenders who are convicted for a second time of a serious sexual or violent offence and who were 18 or over at the time of that second offence must be sentenced to life imprisonment unless the court is of the opinion that there are exceptional circumstances. These sentences are known as automatic life sentences.

6. Anyone found guilty of murder committed when under the age of 18 must be sentenced to 'detention during Her Majesty's pleasure'. A person aged under 18 convicted of an offence other than murder for which a life sentence may be passed on an adult, may be sentenced to 'detention for life'. A person convicted of murder who is aged 18 or over at the time of the offence but under 21 on conviction must be sentenced to 'custody for life'. This is also the maximum penalty when an offender aged 18 but under 21 is convicted of any other offence for which an offender aged over 21 would be liable to life imprisonment.

7. A life sentence is wholly indeterminate. There is no entitlement to release at any stage but offenders may be considered for release on licence. For those serving a mandatory life sentence, release may only be authorised by the Home Secretary on the recommendation of the Parole Board and after consulting the Lord Chief Justice and, if available, the trial judge. For discretionary lifers (that is offenders who receive life sentences as a maximum, rather than mandatory sentence), the procedures changed with the implementation of section 34 of the Criminal Justice Act 1991 in October 1992. A court sentencing a person to life imprisonment for an offence other than murder, must specify a term called the relevant part. On the expiry of this term they become eligible for the new release procedures which are now contained in section 28 of the Crime (Sentences) Act 1997. A discretionary life sentence prisoner is entitled to require the Home Secretary to refer his or her case to a Discretionary Lifer Panel (DLP) under the remit of the Parole Board, if the Home Secretary has not already done so when the relevant part has been served. The Board has the power to direct the release of the prisoner on licence if satisfied that it is no longer necessary for the protection of the public that the prisoner should be confined. The Home Secretary has no residual power as in the case of mandatory life sentences, to reject a recommendation by the Parole Board. Under the Crime (Sentences) Act 1997, these arrangements also apply to those sentenced to an automatic life sentence under section 2 of that Act and to prisoners sentenced to 'detention during Her Majesty's pleasure'. If released, life sentence prisoners are on licence for the rest of their lives and liable to recall at any time if their conduct so demands.

Summary of relevant legislation

8. The following legislation is of relevance to the consideration of trends in the series of data for 1987-1997 presented in the tables of this volume:

9. *The Prison (Amendment) Rules 1987, Youth Custody Centre (Amendment) Rules 1987 and Detention Centre (Amendment) Rules 1987*

These rules came into force on 13 August 1987 and increased from one third to one half of sentence the term for which remission could be granted for sentences of 12 months or less.

10. *Criminal Justice Act 1988*

Section 123 of this Act, which came into effect on 1 October 1988, made changes in the custodial sentences available for offenders aged under 21 by tightening the restrictions on the use of custody, which were contained in Section 1 of the Criminal Justice Act 1982. At the same time, youth custody and detention centre orders were unified into a single custodial sentence -detention in a young offender institution. Under Ministerial requirements for this sentence, juveniles should be held in separate institutions or in discrete accommodation in mixed institutions. Short sentenced (taken to be up to and including 4 months) young adult offenders should similarly be held separately from the longer sentenced groups.

The following changes were also made:

(i) With effect from 29 September 1988, the maximum penalty was increased from 14 years to life for two offences under the Firearms Act 1968: carrying, or possessing, firearms in furtherance of crime. In addition the maximum penalty for uncertified possession of a shotgun was increased.

(ii) With effect from 29 September 1988, the maximum term of imprisonment for the offence of cruelty to children was increased from 2 to 10 years.

(iii) With effect from 12 October 1988, driving while disqualified, taking a motor vehicle without authority, common assault and criminal damage involving amounts not exceeding £2,000 became triable only as summary offences.

(iv) With effect from 5 January 1989, the maximum term of imprisonment for most levels of fine was reduced by a half.

11.   *Aggravated Vehicle-Taking Act 1992*

With effect from 1 April 1992, this created an aggravated form of the offence of taking a motor vehicle without the owner's consent or driving or being carried in a conveyance, knowing that it has been taken without consent. The aggravated offence is triable-either-way. The maximum penalty is from six months where only minor damage is caused to five years where an accident causing death occurs.

12.   *Road Traffic Act 1991*

With effect from 1 July 1992, the offence of reckless driving was amended to dangerous driving and new offences were introduced including causing death by careless driving when under the influence of drink or drugs.

13.   *Criminal Justice Act 1991*

The main principles of the sentencing framework introduced in October 1992 by the Criminal Justice Act 1991 were:

   (i) The severity of the sentence should reflect primarily the seriousness of the offence, in particular, that previous convictions should only be considered relevant where the circumstances of the previous offence disclosed aggravating factors of the current offence. (However, the 1993 Criminal Justice Act, implemented on 16 August 1993, see (15) below, allows courts to take into account any previous convictions of the offender).

  (ii) Custody should generally be reserved for the most serious offences: however, custodial sentences may also be passed to protect the public from serious harm from violent or sexual offenders and longer sentences than otherwise justified by the seriousness of the offence may be passed on the same grounds.

 (iii) Community sentences should play a full role in sentencing and not simply be an alternative to custody.

  (iv) The way young people are dealt with should closely reflect their age and development, including bringing 17 year olds within the jurisdiction of the juvenile court and renaming it as the youth court.

This led to changes in the sentences available to the courts, including:

   (v) The introduction of combination orders, whereby elements of probation supervision and community service work are combined in a single order given for one offence.

  (vi) Making probation orders, supervision orders and combination orders available for 16 and 17 year olds.

 (vii) Abolishing the sentence of detention in a young offender institution for 14 year old boys and changing the minimum and maximum sentence lengths for 15 to 17 year olds to two and twelve months respectively.

(viii) Abolishing partly suspended sentences of imprisonment and restricting the use of a fully suspended sentence of imprisonment to only those circumstances where a court decides the offence is so serious to justify an immediate custodial sentence of not more than two years imprisonment, but there are exceptional circumstances which merit its suspension.

  (ix) Reducing the maximum term of imprisonment for non-domestic burglary from 14 to 10 years and for theft from 10 to 7 years.

Part II of this Act deals with the early release of prisoners and introduced provisions to replace the previously existing systems of parole and remission. The relevant parts of the Act were implemented on 1 October 1992 and apply to those sentenced on or after that date. There are three schemes based on sentence length.

   (x) Automatic unconditional release

        Those sentenced to less than 12 months are released automatically half way through their sentence (unless "additional days" have been imposed for breaches of prison discipline). Adults are not subject to supervision following release, but young offenders are subject to a minimum of three months supervision (or until their 22nd birthday if that is sooner). All will be 'at risk' until the very end of their sentence; that is, if they commit a further imprisonable offence before the end of their original sentence, the court dealing with the new offence may add all or part of the outstanding sentence to any new sentence it imposes.

(xi) Automatic conditional release

Those sentenced to 12 months or more but less than four years are released automatically half way through their sentence (subject to "additional days"). They are released on licence and subject to supervision up to three quarters (or to the end in the case of some sex offenders) and are 'at risk' to the end of the original sentence.

(xii) Discretionary release

Those sentenced to four years or more are eligible for parole half way through their sentence, if parole is not granted then release occurs at the two-thirds point of the sentence (or at a subsequent parole review). Release, when it occurs, is on licence and subject to supervision up to three quarters (or to the end in the case of some sex offenders) and all are 'at risk' until the end of the original sentence.

Part III of the Act made further changes to the custodial sentences available for young offenders under the 1982 and 1988 Acts. The minimum age at which juveniles could be sentenced to detention in a young offender institution was unified for boys and girls at 15. Previously, boys aged 14 could be so sentenced. The special provisions for offenders under 17 (juveniles) were extended to cover those aged 17.

14. *Criminal Justice Act 1993*

The Criminal Justice Act 1993 made the following change to the provisions in the Criminal Justice Act 1991:

From 16 August 1993, the provisions described in note 13(i) were repealed. Thus, in considering the seriousness of any offence, account may be taken of any previous convictions or of failure to respond to previous sentences and in considering whether custody or a community sentence is justified, the court may look at all the offences currently before it.

15. *Criminal Justice and Public Order Act 1994*

Several new offences, mainly in the area of Public Order were created with effect from 3 November 1994. However, the remaining provisions of this Act were mainly implemented in 1995, including:

(i) Extension of the provisions of section 53 of the Children and Young Persons Act 1933 for 10 to 13 year olds, with effect from 9 January 1995.

(ii) Increasing the maximum sentence length for 15 to 17 year olds to 2 years, with effect from 3 February 1995 (see note 13(vii)).

(iii) No bail for those defendants charged or convicted of homicide or rape after previous convictions for such offences and no right to bail for persons accused or convicted of committing an offence while on bail, with effect from 10 April 1995.

(iv) The introduction of provisions for the reduction of sentences for early guilty pleas, with effect from 3 February 1995.

(v) Increasing the maximum sentence length for certain firearm offences, with effect from 3 February 1995.

(vi) Relaxation of the requirements for pre sentence reports (PSRs), with effect from 3 February 1995.

16. *Crime (Sentences) Act 1997*

Arrangements for plea before venue, as made possible by the implementation of parts of the Criminal Procedures and Investigations Act 1996, were implemented in October 1997. The Act also requires that automatic life sentences should be given to offenders convicted for a second time of serious sexual or violent offences. Similarly courts are required to impose minimum prison sentences of 7 years on offenders convicted of trafficking in class A drugs if he or she has two or more previous convictions for similar offences.

17. Also of relevance to the consideration of trends in the series of data shown in this volume were:

(i) A restricted parole policy, announced on 30 November 1983, which meant that prisoners sentenced to more than 5 years for a single offence of violence, sex, arson and drug trafficking would be granted parole only when release under supervision for a few months before the end of a sentence was likely to reduce the long term risk to the public or in circumstances which were genuinely exceptional. This restricted parole policy was lifted in June 1992.

173

(ii) Guidelines on sentencing of rape offenders set out by the Lord Chief Justice in February 1986, recommended a starting point of 5 years for contested cases of substantive rape where there were no aggravating or mitigating factors and a starting point of 15 years for a campaign of rape.

(iii) In November 1995 a Queens Bench Judgement in Cawley and Others (R v Oldham Justices and another, ex parte Cawley and other applications. Queen's Bench Division. 30, 31 October, 28 November 1995) clarified the legislative position whereby all fine enforcement measures have to be actively considered or tried before imprisonment can be imposed by the courts. Following this judgement a number of fine defaulter cases have been subject to judicial review in which it was found that it was not clear that the magistrates had considered all the possible enforcement measures and so the prisoner was immediately released. In the light of this the Magistrates' Association and the Justices' Clerks' Society produced a model pronouncement which takes each enforcement measure in turn and invites magistrates to detail why they believe that the measure is not appropriate. A number of initiatives under the Government's Working Group on the Enforcement of Financial Penalties were taken forward in 1996 and will also have contributed to the fall in the use of imprisonment for fine defaulters. These included issuing good practice guidance for the courts in July 1996 and the extension of the power to impose an attachment of earnings order in the Criminal Procedure and Investigations Act 1996.

Data sources and accuracy

18.   Prison Service establishments routinely provide records of the numbers of persons held in custody at the end of each month, broadly subdivided according to age, sex, custody type and sentence length. The records are collated and processed centrally, to produce the main estimates of average and mid-year population presented in this report. Establishments also record electronically details for individual inmates such as date of birth, sex, custody type and reception and discharge dates and, for sentenced prisoners, offence and sentence length. These data are collected on a central computer data base and are used to produce the various analyses of receptions, discharges and time served in custody. They also form the basis of detailed population breakdowns, supplementing the aggregates derived from establishments' monthly population returns to which they are scaled for consistency.

19.   Efforts are made to ensure the completeness and accuracy of the data, as far as is practicable. Establishments are not, however, always in receipt of the necessary details, notably regarding offences. Where the offence data are incomplete we use the category "offence not recorded". Similarly "committal type not recorded" is used in the tables for non-criminal prisoners in Chapter 1.

20.   In general, the information given in this publication remains subject to the inaccuracies inherent in any large-scale, centralised recording system. While the figures shown have been checked as far as practicable, they must be regarded as approximate and not necessarily accurate to the last digit shown.

21.   Where figures in the tables have been rounded to the nearest final digit, for instance when annual averages or percentages have been calculated, the rounded components do not always add to the totals which are calculated and rounded independently.

22.   The term "previous conviction" used in the tables refers to a court appearance at which there was a finding of guilt in respect of one or more offences. Estimates of the number of prisoners with previous convictions have been derived from the large Home Office criminal database known as the Offenders Index. The latest available data are for 1996.

Reconviction data

23.   The reconviction rate is defined as the proportion reconvicted at least once for a "standard list" offence within a given period (see paragraph 25 below). The results are based on a sample of those discharged from Prison Service establishments and so are subject to sampling error. The 1994 discharge sample consisted of 43 per cent of the total number discharged. The sample was stratified by age, sex, type of custody, type of offence, ethnic group and length of sentence. Provisional figures are also included for 1995, based on a sample of prisoners discharged in the first quarter of that year. All results relate to age at sentence (except for table 9.10, for which age at discharge is used).

24.   Under the sampling scheme different percentages of white male offenders aged 18 to 20 and over 21 were selected depending on age and sentence length, but including all those imprisoned for robbery, sexual and drugs offences. All available records were included in the sample for other groups (ie female prisoners and males aged under 18 years at sentence). The sample of discharged prisoners is matched against the Home Office Offenders Index, a computerised database containing details of all convictions for "standard list" offences since 1963, thus producing criminal histories of offenders. In practice it was not always possible to match offender details of those discharged with details held on the Offenders Index (this occurred in 11 per cent of cases). Figures for numbers discharged and numbers reconvicted given in Chapter 9 have been scaled up to reflect the fact that some offenders could not be found on the Offenders Index.

25.   For those discharged in 1994, rates of reconviction within two years were obtained by identifying offenders in the sample whose criminal histories included any convictions in the two years following discharge. Appendices 4 and 5 of "Criminal Statistics, England and Wales 1996" (Cm. 3764) give the list of offences included in the "standard list" and indicate the offence groups used in tables. These offences include all indictable and some of the more serious summary offences (eg. indecent exposure, assault on a constable and cruelty to or neglect of children) but exclude most summary motoring offences and other less serious summary offences such as drunkenness and prostitution. Several offences were added to the "standard list" on 1 July 1995 and 1 January 1996. All categories of common assault became standard list offences from July 1995 onwards. From January 1996 the following became standard list offences: driving whilst disqualified from holding a licence; driving or attempting to drive a motor vehicle while having breath, urine or blood alcohol concentration in excess of a prescribed limit; and dangerous driving when tried summarily. If these offences had not been included in the calculation of reconviction rates for 1994 and 1995, the rates would have been around 1 percentage point lower for both years. The addition of these extra offences to the standard list should improve the extent to which discharged prisoners are matched to Offenders Index records.

Recording practice

Police cells

26.   With the exception of Tables 1.2 to 1.4 and 2.1, prisoners held in police cells fall outside the scope of this publication.

Counting of receptions

27.   There are four main categories of receptions—untried (ie awaiting commencement or continuation of trial prior to verdict), convicted unsentenced (ie awaiting sentence), sentenced and non-criminal. In the tables on remand receptions, a person is generally counted separately once if received as untried and once if received as convicted unsentenced for each fresh set of charges. If subsequently received under sentence, he is counted in that category also. An individual may thus appear in the tables more than once in different categories or on separate occasions in one year. However, Table 1.1 also shows the remand figures with those received as untried and subsequently as convicted unsentenced counted only once.

28.   When a person is received under sentence and at the same time is dealt with for a non-criminal matter, or is already in custody under sentence for a criminal offence and is given a further criminal sentence or is dealt with for a non-criminal matter, only the initial reception for the criminal sentence is counted. Recalls to custody after release on licence or parole are excluded from the sentenced reception figures, but those whose original sentence had been re-activated because of a new offence committed during the 'at risk' period (see 13(x) above) are included. Persons transferred in from other countries, special hospitals or other non-Prison Service establishments are included in the appropriate category of reception.

Recording of offences

29.   When a person is received on sentence for several offences, or if a person is received on sentence and at the same time is committed for a non-criminal matter, only the principal criminal offence is recorded in the tables. The basis of selection of the principal criminal offence is as follows:

   (i)   where a person is received on sentence for two or more criminal offences, the offence selected is the one for which the heaviest sentence is imposed;

   (ii)   where the same sentences are imposed for two or more criminal offences the offence selected is the one for which the statutory maximum penalty is the most severe.

The offence groups shown in this volume are broadly similar to, but not the same as, those shown in Criminal statistics.

Recording of length of sentence

30.   When a person is received on sentence for two or more sentences which have been passed at the same time and ordered to run consecutively they are treated as one sentence equal in length to the sentences added together. In the case of concurrent sentences, the longest sentence is recorded. When a person is received to serve a period of imprisonment composed of a sentence for a criminal offence and a consecutive period of imprisonment in connection with a non-criminal matter, the total period of imprisonment is recorded against the criminal offence.

Recording of ethnic group

31.   The current classification of ethnic group of a prisoner was introduced in October 1992 and is congruent with that used for the Census of Population. It consists of 10 codes which can be grouped into four broader categories as follows:

White	White
Black—African Black—Caribbean Black—Other	} Black
Asian—Bangladeshi Asian—Indian Asian—Pakistani	} South Asian
Asian—Other Chinese Other	} Chinese and Other

Prisoners are asked to choose the ethnic code that they feel is most appropriate; only if they refuse will the officer assign a code, informing them which code has been chosen and giving them further opportunity to express their own preference. The information is then passed to the central computer system of inmate records from which the statistics are compiled.

When comparing the ethnic composition of the prison population with the national population, it is important to realise the limited explanatory value either as regards the involvement of particular ethnic groups in crime or in relation to the practices of the courts. More detailed analysis of the ethnic group of prisoners is available in the Home Office Statistical Bulletin 21/94 'The Ethnic Origins of Prisoners' (see paragraph 37).

Remand prisoners

32.   In Chapter 2 the term "remand prisoners" includes both untried and convicted unsentenced prisoners committed to custody on criminal charges by any court so empowered. A person first enters the remand population when remanded in custody on or after his first appearance in court on a charge or summons.

Adults and young offenders

33.   In the statistics of receptions, adults are those aged 21 and over at the date of sentence and young offenders are those aged under 21; juveniles are young offenders aged between 14 and 16 for the years up to and including 1992 whilst youths are those aged 15-17 for 1993 and later. In population tables, for instance Table 1.3, "adults" include those aged 21 and over at the date of sentence and those sentenced to detention in a young offender institution who have had their sentence converted to imprisonment. The term "young offender" refers to those given a custodial sentence when aged under 21 who have not subsequently been reclassified as adults, it therefore encompasses inmates under 21 and those who have reached 21 but have not been reclassified.

Acknowledgements

34.   This publication has been prepared by the Offenders and Corrections Unit of the Home Office Research and Statistics Directorate. This unit, under Chris Lewis, handles the collection and publication of research and statistical information on prisons, probation and parole. Acknowledgement is made of the contributions made by Mike Lock (editor), Maureen Colledge, Roger Stevens, Philip White, Jo Woodbridge, Philip Howard, Penny Butler, Nick Hooper, Michael Poole, Michael Auld, Hassan Hassan, Ramona Hoyte, and the staff of the Data Collection Unit. A review of the publication was conducted last year by a group chaired by Maureen Colledge and comprising the five individuals listed after her name, above, plus Rose Atkinson and Julian Blackwell of the Information and Publication Group of the Research and Statistics Directorate. Thanks are made to them and to the users who participated in that review.

Mission Statement

35. The Research and Statistics Directorate is an integral part of the Home Office, serving Ministers and the department, its services, Parliament and the public through research, development and statistics. Information and knowledge from these sources informs policy development and the management of programmes; their dissemination improves wider public understanding of matters of Home Office concern.

Symbols

36. The following symbols are used in the tables:

   .. = not available
   – = nil or negligible
   * = not applicable

Related publications

37. Readers may also be interested in the following Statistical Bulletins, published by the Home Office:

Issue	Date	Title
2/94	10.01.94	Parole recommendations and ethnic origin, England and Wales 1990
21/94	11.08.94	The ethnic origins of prisoners
2/97	29.01.97	Life Licensees—Reconvictions and Recalls by the end of 1995: England and Wales
5/97	24.03.97	Reconvictions of Prisoners Discharged from Prison in 1993, England and Wales
6/97	24.03.97	Reconvictions of those commencing community penalties in 1993, England and Wales
2/98	29.01.98	Revised projections of long term trends in the prison population to 2005
12/98	20.05.98	Summary probation statistics, England and Wales 1997
05/98	26.03.98	The prison population in 1997

Other reports which may be of interest include:

Date	Title
July 1994	The Offenders Index. A short guide
March 1995	The Criminal Justice System in England and Wales 1995 by Gordon C Barclay
December 1995	Digest 3 of information on the Criminal Justice System in England and Wales

Copies of all the publications above are available from Information and Publications Group, Research and Statistics Directorate, Room 201, Home Office, 50 Queen Anne's Gate, London SW1H 9AT.

Other publications, which may be of interest and are available from HMSO include:

Date	Title	Price
1992	The National Prison Survey 1991 main findings Home Office Research Study No. 128	£7.60
October 1997	Report of the Parole Board for and 1996/97	£9.85
November 1997	Criminal statistics, England and Wales 1996, Cm 3764	£22.70
November 1997	Prison Service Annual Report and Accounts April 96 to March 97	£15.90

Available from the Department of Health:

October 1996   Children Accommodated in Secure Units During
                                          the Year Ending 31 March 1996 England

Enquiries

If you have any enquiries about figures in this publication you should contact: Penny Butler. The address is:

Offenders and Corrections Unit
Home Office Research and Statistics Directorate
Room 818
Abell House
John Islip Street
London SW1P 4LH   Telephone 0171-217-5654

or by internet email via: ocu.ho.abell@gtnet.gov.uk

Printed in the UK for The Stationery Office Limited on behalf of the
Controller of Her Majesty's Stationery Office
Dd 5068214   7/98   65536   Job No. J0054227   29/43411